MW00977408

This book and compilation of thoughts is dedicated to:

my husband Luke, who is strong when I am not

my wonderful and gracious son Jackson

and to my strong and fierce daughter Alaina

Thank you for being avenues to help me see Jesus daily

And to all of you who encouraged me, uplifted me,

and motivated me to write.

I am continually grateful and humbled by you.

A Note From Jackson:

Hi every one! Its Jackson here, sayin hello. I get to be the brother of an amazing little lady. I have to admit, I'm a little jealous of Alaina's scars. But, anyhow I get to teach her a lot of things. For example, Minecraft, (which is a popular video game) tattoos, (which I'm very good at, mind you) and so on. If any of you big brothers are reading this, I've got two things for you...

#1. I encourage you to read this book because it is pretty awesome and it talks about what happened in the Minneapolis hospital while dad and I watched America's Funniest Home Videos and ate pizza every night.

#2. Keep loving that little sibling. I know that it might be hard, but hang in there.

Santi, (who is one of my good friends) thank you for keeping me company and playing air soft while Lanie was in the hospital. But, most of all, thank you Alaina for just being my little sis. That's right Alaina! Enjoy it while it lasts!

Introduction

"I will praise you, Lord, with all my heart; I will tell of all of the marvelous things you have done. I will be filled with joy because of You. I will sing praises to your name O Most High." – King David Psalm 9: 1-2

I've been sitting in a local coffee shop this morning trying to figure out for the life of me how to write the beginning of a story. I mean, I know how to write what's happening in my life right now and what lessons I'm learning or the struggles I'm feeling in the moment, but to write about the beginning of something seems daunting. I've even read the beginnings of some of my favorite books over again, because hey, why not. For real. Where does a person even begin? I mean, do I start with my life? Or my husband, Luke's? Or that time I discovered who God was and told Him He could be in charge of my life not knowing what that meant or how to live? I'm not sure. But all of those things seem distant. And boring. And not necessarily even relevant.

So maybe, we should start by talking about what made this story worth telling...

Like the majority of stories that we love today, this story is about a journey. It's about love and misunderstanding and about being a mama while trying to first follow Jesus. And it's about what life looks like when God wrecks plans and wreaks havoc on my ideals and desires.

Chapter 1: Every story has a beginning

I don't think that I was a normal girl growing up. I never dreamed of what my wedding day would look like or who my husband would be (okay, that's not completely true. The game MASH was fantastic, and I was pretty sure for a while there that Mark Wahlberg would come to my small town and meet me and fall completely and madly in love with my charming self and he would whisk me away to his Hollywood mansion). I never really even thought about how many kids I would have or what their names would be. I knew for sure I wouldn't have three...or even five because then you have a middle child and that child may or may not have extremely dramatic feelings about how they should be treated and what rules should be bent just for them because they are much more responsible than their sister was at that same age. Not that I, of course, can speak from experience.

I never even really thought about the idea of wanting to be a mom. Until my sister was becoming a mom, that is. To be honest, I hadn't spent much time around anyone pregnant and when my sister started showing that adorable little baby bump, I just about died from excitement. And then my niece was born. And she was beautiful. And my sister got to choose a name from all of the names in the world (or from all of the letters in the world mashed together in general to become something that might or might not make sense...names these days, am I right?) and buy dresses and snuggle her at night. And all of that sounded like a good time. I moved in with my sister and her new little family the day after I graduated high school and soon learned that having a baby was maybe a tad bit harder than I had envisioned. I loved my niece more than ever, but the glow around motherhood had faded some. Mostly because...you guys...diapers. And crying. I had no idea.

That summer of sisterhood ended the day my big sister dropped me off at college and drove her truck away, probably breathing a sigh of relief. I'm told that I was a bit of a struggle. I personally find that very hard to believe. The first few weeks of college were...rough. My partying lifestyle and lack of caring about anything (including taking care of my financial aid) quickly landed me in the Dean's office. I played the "I know nothing of what you're talking about" card when confronted, but still left the office with the "pay a third of your bill right now or leave" kick in the pants response. Do y'all know how much a Texas university is? Let's just say I drank and smoked the majority of the money I had made during the summer that I was supposed to be saving for school and was at this point eating toast with spray butter for every single meal. My only viable option was to leave. Through a series of ridiculous events, a bible college in Iowa said I could come there even though I would be starting off the year a little behind (I actually told everyone I was moving to Idaho because Texas people don't understand the Midwest or geography in general). When you have one option, that option is the VERY BEST NEWS you've ever heard. Off to Idaho it was. Or Iowa. Whatever. Did I mention I did not love anything bible? Or conservative? Or anything that wasn't the University of Texas? Hook 'em!

Once I got over the initial culture shock of moving from Texas to wherever it is that I was AND finally decided to leave my new dorm room and start attending actual class, I met a boy. Oh man. I can't even. I was smitten from the very first moment I saw him. Do people still use that word? Smitten? I guess that's neither here nor there. Anyway, I could literally go on forever about this. For your benefit, I won't. But I will tell you that his name was Luke and he was downright gorgeous. *insert starry teenage eyes*

Long story short, I found a community of people who understood me and didn't judge me, met Jesus, and started dating this incredibly handsome and amazing guy my first year of this new adventure. In Iowa. Who knew. Long story even shorter, this guy asked me to marry him two years into our relationship and I, of course, said yes. I'm not a romantic for the most part. I don't even know if I fully understand the word. Maybe that's why I never dreamed of weddings and babies and white picket fences. But something happened after I got married. My friends were all getting married. And we all know what married people do...they have babies. Everyone in the whole wide world was having babies. So naturally, I wanted to do the trendy thing and have one too. *And yes...I actually would consider jumping off a bridge if my friends were doing it. Why do you ask?*

It turns out you can't just decide you want a baby and have one right away. And right away as in nine months. C'mon...I know that much. We made the decision to be pregnant in June. I honestly think a part of me was super confused when we weren't pregnant that next day. Or next week. I married young, okay. I was maybe a bit naive. When we did get pregnant at the end of November that year, you would've thought I had waited a lifetime. It's all perspective I guess. I was told to wait to go to the doctor for at least a month, so I did, and only when I started feeling kind of weird and having some minor, cramp-like stomach pain. It turns out I had miscarried. And I was super angry. At myself for being excited in the first place. At life for playing with my emotions. At all my adorable pregnant friends. And at God, because of course it was somewhat his fault.

Time went on. The few people left on the planet who weren't pregnant all of the sudden got pregnant and I was even more angry and annoyed. And I showed it by crying and being super grumpy ALL OF THE TIME. *Oh Luke. You were amazing even back in those days. How in the world did you deal with me? I can't even.* After a few short months, I got pregnant again. Luke and I decided not to tell people just in case the same thing happened again and that night over dinner he told every single person we saw. Bless. Thankfully I didn't kill him then and there, and we had an easy and awesome pregnancy. I loved every second of being pregnant. I never once felt sick or tired and my biggest craving was for raspberry sorbet. I'm pretty sure I was the easiest pregnant woman in the world. Also, I have no idea if Luke has the same story here so let's just all agree right now to never ask him, mmmkay?

So it goes, eight and a half months later in November, I gave birth to the easiest child that was ever born on planet earth. I'm not exaggerating here people. My son Jackson started sleeping through the night at 8 weeks. Motherhood was a breeze. I honestly thought on numerous occasions how I'm pretty sure we could have 20 babies and hardly break a sweat. It was time for me to start writing a parenting book. This was cake.

When Jackson was 5 and a half months old, we were sure we had this parenting thing completely under control and decided, why not try again and see what happened. You guys. A month later I found out I was pregnant. The same day actually that we had packed up our small little house to move to a small town in Iowa that interestingly enough wanted us to pastor their church. Also, we were 24. I have no idea what that church was thinking, but we decided to take them up on it before they changed their minds. Because packing and moving and transition wasn't enough for the day, I also decided to tell Luke, as we were exhausted from the day and laying on the hard wood floor because everything else was packed, that we were going to have another baby. Once again we decided to wait to tell people and once again Luke told every single person we saw as soon as he woke up the next morning. For the love. This guy is not a secret keeper by any means.

This pregnancy started the same as the last; easy and fun. I loved being pregnant. At about the four month mark (or roughly 16 weeks for those of you who are pregnant and still count according to the days and hours) I started having trouble with my body. Weird right? My joints would start to lock up and then I literally wouldn't be able to move that joint all day without terrible amounts of pain. The next day I would be fine and then the day after that it would be a different joint. Again and again this would happen. Around the six month mark I somehow developed a new annoying pregnancy ailment...on top of the joint pain. PUPS. Have you heard of it? It's sort of like chicken pox for pregnant people. Oh, you guys. I've never had chicken pox. When I was little my mom put both my brother and I into a bath with my sore spotted sister so that we would all get it at the same time and be done with it. My brother and I to this day have never had them still...but I think PUPS counts. It's the worst. I didn't love pregnancy as much anymore.

Because Jackson had been a c-section, the doctors thought it best to do the same with baby number two. Almost 15 months after Jackson was born, Luke, his parents, Jackson, and I headed to Waterloo, Iowa to stay the night in a hotel because February is cold and who knows what kind of terrible snow thing Iowa can come up with in the middle of the night that would have made us late for our scheduled little baby. Iowa doesn't disappoint, folks. The next day, February 17, was one of the coldest days in Iowa history at that time. Look it up. I'm not kidding. Why do people live here?!?

The c-section went great. Everything was awesome. And also...I didn't have to go outside for at least a couple days so, there's that. Alaina was a breeze (but aren't all newborn babies?!). When she was one day old a heart doctor came and talked to us. Apparently she had a murmur. At first, like any mother of a perfect baby, I was shocked and worried, but felt fairly relieved when the doctor told us that lots of babies have murmurs and usually nothing happens with them. That was exactly what I needed to hear. When we left the hospital with Lanie, she was put on a biliblanket to bring her jaundice down. We weren't worried at all. Jackson had to come home with one as well and was able to come off of it in less than a week. Plus, it's kinda fun pretending you gave birth to a baby glow worm.

After a week Lanie's biliruben levels continued to stay elevated. Darn blanket. It didn't even work. Eight days after Lanie was born, I got a phone call from her hospital. It appeared that there was something wrong with her liver and they wanted us to go to Iowa City to see a specialist. I don't know why, but I felt some serious grief. I've never been more thankful for my Luke's mom and sister being around when I got that news. I don't know if it was after-baby hormones or exhaustion (or maybe because I still didn't really understand God's sovereignty at that time) but I immediately felt like it was my fault. *What if all of those things that were happening to my body during pregnancy had caused this? What if I did something while I was pregnant with her to cause this? I mean...I HADN'T EVEN TAKEN ALL OF MY PRENATAL VITAMINS DURING PREGNANCY AND WE ALL KNOW THAT CAN*

SCREW UP EVERYTHING ALWAYS! Yeah...maybe it was hormones. So incredibly thankful for sweet words of wisdom and truth provided over those days. I was undeniably falling apart.

Day 10 landed us in Iowa City at the children's hospital. Oh, sweet friends, it downright stinks to see your new perfect little person being poked and pushed on and examined over and over. And the crying. Oh heavens. I wish I could talk to my 25 year old self and tell her that some days are more than hard and how God's plan is so much bigger than anything she can see and that everything that is taking place is His the very BEST plan and that she did nothing wrong as a mama and that God loves her so much.

The following days and weeks are a blur. I know I cried a lot and sank into a place of feeling extremely lost and weak and defeated. People told me "pray more...pray harder". I couldn't. I just became frustrated. With people. With myself. With God. And on top of that I was still a pastor's wife and felt as though I couldn't really share any of those feelings with people because they would know my true unbelieving and untrusting heart and no longer take me seriously (which is funny to write now, because I realize how impressing people and holding up a front was much more important than being a real person with real fears. *Sweet girl, no one put as much pressure on you as you did on yourself*).

When Lanie was two months old, test results finally came back. She was diagnosed with Cystic Fibrosis. First of all, when your child is diagnosed with something DO NOT read everything you can on the internet about it. I think after parents get news like this, they should be locked in a room with people who love them and delicious food and God's word and so SO much chocolate. I'm not even kidding. It should be law. The doctors immediately wanted to have Jackson tested as well. We literally laughed at the idea. Jackson was never sick. Like never. We did as we were told and had him tested anyway. Yep, you guessed it. Positive. Both kids had now tested positive for this disease that I had read everything in the world about and there seemed to be no hope in sight.

6

Even though Luke and I had been believers for a solid 6 years or so at this point, there was a lot we didn't understand.

We didn't understand the idea of God's sovereignty.

We didn't believe everything that God said about trusting Him.

We didn't know that circumstances didn't have to rule us and also didn't declare who God was.

We didn't seek counsel of people wiser than us.

And we didn't see prayer as an all the time relationship with the Creator of the universe. We saw it as a way to ask for things or complain or share gossip in a church setting (bless).

What we DID do was let fear completely overtake us and let our emotions choose how we made our next decisions. I knew there was no way I would be able to bring another child into this world that had a 50 percent chance of being incredibly sick and probably not living until their 30th birthday. Even the idea of getting pregnant again felt irresponsible and uncaring. So together, Luke and I made the decision to make the 'wise' choice and not have any more kids. Looking back, I honestly feel like I made the bulk of the decision and Luke, because he's so incredible and saw the state I was in, lovingly agreed. Maybe that's not what happened, but also maybe it is.

The kids were treated at University of Iowa hospitals for CF for two years. Two years of blood draws and hospital visits and support groups hospital stays and vests the kids wore twice a day to shake up the mucus to cough out. Two years of raising money and awareness for CF and fighting alongside families who were going through the same struggles. We had come to terms with the hand life dealt us. Or maybe it was the hand that God dealt us. We weren't really sure.

At the end of the second year we decided to seek God more, but weren't sure as to what that even meant. Our hearts longed for our kids' healing and we knew God could do it. We knew that God could change our circumstances and we promised that His name would be known because of it. We would tell everybody. It seemed perfect. We decided to pray and fast for 21 days (eating only fruits and veggies the way Daniel did when he was given the kings best food, to prove that God was bigger and could sustain him better than a king could). We would start on January 1, 2009. This would be the year that God would be known as a Healer. Provider. Lover of His people. Answerer of His peoples' prayers. Miracle worker. Forty eight people from our church decided to do it with us. Those people. I can't even begin to tell you about their strength and wisdom and love. Oh do they know how they love.

After 21 days we KNEW God had done something. We knew that our kids had been healed and that God had listened to His people and He had healed. Our next appointment was not until March and oh we're we confident in the work God had done. The doctors were going to be our witnesses without even knowing it! We were so excited. The day came and we went to Iowa City with our heads high and our hearts lifted. And as we sat in appointments and heard that the kids were actually getting worse, all of our hopes fell. Not only did they fall but they hit a hard concrete floor and smashed into unimaginable little bits. How could this happen??

WE PRAYED! WE FASTED! WE MADE DEALS WITH GOD AND HE FELL THROUGH! I wish you could hear Luke's side of this. I was mad and in disbelief but Luke, sweet amazing Luke felt crushed. And he struggled so hard under disbelief of who God was. He came to the understanding that either God was all powerful but He wasn't good OR He was good but didn't have the power to actually do anything. There was no way God could be both. And Luke had to try and preach every Sunday not actually knowing what was true. Those were hard times, friends.

That year the kids kept getting sicker. Actually Jackson was staying consistently even and Lanie was getting sicker. Much sicker. She started having trouble with high fevers and lethargy. Our amazing local doctor referred us to a kidney specialist. For those of you that know anything about cystic fibrosis you know that CF doesn't affect the kidneys. It just doesn't. The doctors were baffled. The kids had CF and that was for sure. But this, this was new. And no one knew what to do. All hope seemed lost everywhere. We struggled with bitterness. With our faith. With our view of

God. And with our idea of church and what we should be teaching. The one thing that we did know is that we loved God's people. And they loved us. We didn't feel like we could share the actual feelings that we were experiencing though. I mean, we were PASTORS after all. We should've been filled with strength and knowledge and unending belief. We should've been stronger and unwavering. And we knew in our hearts we were living a double life with what we believed in one hand and what we told people about God in the other. *SIDENOTE RANT: You guys. Your pastors are incredible. They pour out their hearts for you. Counsel you. Hold your babies. Intercede for you. Sit through meeting after meeting that may or may not be relevant. They visit the hospital and homes and coffee shops and spend so much of their time seeking God and trying to figure out how to care and love and discipline His people. They are stretched so thin, friends. And so are their families. And it can be an incredibly lonely place. Please pray for your pastor. Lift them up before God. Get to know them and their families. Like really know them. Pray both with them and for them. They are people. They have real issues and demands and probably naughty kids that they are trying to figure out by the grace of God how to parent when they are gone so much giving of themselves to the rest of the world. Thank them and love them and please give them so much grace. Because, for the love...they desire it.*

In the fall of 2009, the same year we fasted and prayed to God for 21 days to change our circumstances, but never asked Him to change our hearts, we were referred to Amplatz University of Minnesota Children's Hospital in Minneapolis. This was and is known to be one of the top CF hospitals in America. The guy who invented the vests that Jackson and Lanie wore twice a day was from this hospital. We were ready for some serious answers but I still cried the day we went. I felt like I was betraying our sweet doctors who worked so hard in Iowa to understand the kids, especially Lanie. I felt like a traitor and like I was giving up. We met with so many amazing doctors that day though. They were all interested and intrigued in the way the kids presented their symptoms and decided to try something I perceived as especially risky: take them off of the vests and all their CF meds and see what happened. They also wanted to keep Lanie in the hospital for four or five days to run different functionality tests on her liver and kidneys and pancreas and lungs. That was November of 2009. The same year that we

9

prayed and circumstantially asked God to change things. And to heal. You guys. The kids have NEVER been put back on their CF vests or meds. CF is an incurable disease. Except they used to have it and now they don't. The doctors call it 'asymptomatic CF'. Whatever that means. We call it gone. Or healed. Or a miracle that only God could have performed. I can't say this enough. God did not have to heal the kids from CF. He would be just as good and just as sovereign if he didn't. My brother in law, Joe, told me once that he believes that God doesn't care as much about our circumstances as He does our hearts. And that God can be more glorified when we walk through unchanging bad circumstances with the joy and knowledge of who God actually is. I never believed that fully. But now I think that I might. God would be the same God if the kids still had CF. I don't know why God chose to heal them from that. I don't really know why God heals some and doesn't heal others. Or why He does anything the way He does. But looking back, I can see His bigger plans. I can see how what He does is better than what I want Him to do. And because of that, my hope is restored more than I could have ever understood it to be.

Because of that week in November that Lanie spent in the hospital, though, she was diagnosed with many other things affecting her little body.

Caroli's disease. Don't look it up. The internet can be a jerk for real.

A kidney disease called FSGS.

Chronic pancreatitis.

Hypertension.

Pulmonary Stenosis. That pesky heart murmur found at one day old.

And asymptomatic Cystic Fibrosis.

Whew. That's a lot more than one disease to be scared of. Our fear could have plummeted. It could have sent us into a world of hopelessness and despair. But weirdly, it didn't. We had seen both kids freed from the terrifying diagnosis of CF. AND WE FELT VICTORY YOU GUYS! God started changing our hearts. We saw Him differently. Instead of viewing Him only as an answer to our circumstantial prayers, we began to see Him as a lover of His people. As a Father who delights in His children. As a Creator who desires for His name to be known among the nations. And as One who is constant and all-knowing and whose name must be praised.

The next four years were hard. I won't even tell you they weren't. They were filled with so many hospital stays and blood draws and PICC lines and antibiotics. And so many doctors saying 'I don't know' and 'Lanie is special/unique/hard'. It was filled with frustration and so many miles on our cars and tears and definitely some fear.

And finally, in November of 2012, Lanie was added to the transplant list for a new liver, kidneys, and a pancreas. A triple transplant. In December of 2012, we got our first call from her transplant doctor. It was at about 11:30 on Christmas. We had gone to Kirksville, MO to see my husband's family. Seven hours from Minneapolis. We weren't supposed to be that far away but we thought there was no way we would get a call a month out of being put on the list. We were so wrong. Oh you guys. I accidentally body slammed my sweet mother in law while running around her house trying to get stuff together to leave. I'm not gonna lie. I wish we had a video of that night. It would be hilarious to watch now...after the fact. It didn't seem so funny at the time. Also, after like 15 minutes on the road the doctor called back to tell us that he didn't like the way the kidney looked and to not come in. We headed home the very next morning, never to leave the four hour Minneapolis radius again.

The next call came at the end of April. 2013. And this is where the rest of our story begins.

A story of how God constantly changes the heart of His people when they seek after Him.

A story of love and grace and joy. And mercy. So much mercy.

Chapter 2: The 1st days of transplant. Written by friends and family

THE DAY WE GOT THE CALL: April 28, 2013.

It was a Sunday morning. We had just spent the weekend with friends at an indoor water park, which was awesome. We had gotten back on Saturday night so that we could attend a meeting at church the next day and so that the kids could get some adequate sleep (yeah right) before school on Monday. Luke was leading worship that morning, which is so fun, because in a big church he doesn't get to do that very often. After church was over we were standing around talking to some friends. Who knows where the kids were. They feel so at home with all 400 people there and disappear to go hang with college students the moment they are 'released' from their seats.

Apparently my phone rang. I hadn't heard it. And then Luke's phone rang. He happened to have it in his pocket. Let's all say a big thank you for that! It was the transplant doctor. My heart still skips a little when I think about every feeling that happened in that moment. We found and grabbed the kids and told them we had gotten the call. They cheered. Like they were at a Texas football game kind of cheering. They were so on fire. Poor sweet things had no clue as to what was about to happen and change in their lives. I am sure they had no idea what this really meant except for the fact that Lanie was going to get a transplant and feel so much better. We knew a little more. And I'm not sure how a person can feel joy and fear and grief and excitement and doubt in the same exact second, but I sure did.

Our bags were already mostly packed and so we just grabbed a few more things from the house and hit the road. You guys. Luke is a speed limit driver. He is a rule follower. I wish I could say the same for me, but…well.

Yeah. I wanted to drive but Luke insisted. And oh man. The guy drove like he was Vin Diesel. It was amazing. On the way there we called all of the people on our list who were planning on meeting us at the hospital. I thank God every single day for the love and support of people in our lives. There were so many of us. Together we prayed. And laughed. And waited. And ate. And cried. And shared. Seriously. It was such a sweet time for us. And that is where the rest of the story picks up.

This chapter is written by my sweet friends who wrote when I couldn't. Or didn't want to.

Apr 28, 2013 7:43pm

Currently Lanie is in surgery to have a port line put in and then will have some of her plasma "cleaned" so that current antibodies in her blood will not attack the new organs. Anticipated time for the transplant is 3am and the surgery may take anywhere from 8 to 12 hours.

9:06pm

The doctor just met with us and said that they will only be transplanting the liver and kidneys since it is so much more complicated and risky to include the pancreas. They will deal with it at a later date.

9:46pm

Lanie just returned from having the port put in. It took longer than they expected because she had a vein spasm when they first tried so they had to wait for it to relax to try again. Otherwise, things went well. The plasma exchange which will take a couple of hours.

11:51pm

Just finished her plasma exchange procedure. Now waiting for the actual surgery. Please keep praying!

Apr 29, 2013 7:16am

After a long night of delays due to foggy weather to fly the donor organs here, Lanie was taken in to surgery at about 5:30am. Actual surgery procedure has just begun at 7am. It will be a long and tedious procedure and the doctor has stated that it could take longer than the estimated 8-12 hours. They will keep us posted each hour or so as to how everything is going. Thank you all for your love and prayers!

8:13am

They have told us that they will try to update us about every hour. Just got the call that things are going well and they have removed the liver already.

9:48am

Just got word that the new liver is in and they are beginning on the kidneys. They may only put one new kidney in. They will leave her original kidneys in for the time being and will remove them later when things are stable.

10:53am

Still working on the liver to get it functioning. This is very normal. It takes some time to bring it to functioning properly. So we continue to wait. We know it is a long and meticulous process. Please pray for patience for us as we wait and extra strength and endurance for the surgeons.

12:06pm

Call from surgery tells us that they did decide to remove Lanie's kidneys (not sure why the change of decision yet) and are putting in the new kidney. Liver is still not functioning yet. Please continue to pray.

1:31pm

Still finishing the kidney. Told everything is going fine.

3:15pm

Surgery is finished and everything went well!! Liver is functioning and kidney looks good! She may have to have some dialysis while the kidney restarts, however. She will be sedated for a couple of days in ICU before they bring her to consciousness so that she can heal faster. Praise the Lord!!!

Apr 30, 2013 8:27am

God has made Lanie so strong! She's awake already - but uncomfortable! Her ventilator is out, she's breathing on her own, and communicating what she wants. Pray she will have no pain, relax, sleep, and heal! Her kidneys have been responding some - it is progressing slowly - which they said is normal. She had a fever through the night (101), but it has now dropped to 99! Taking the ventilator out is good - but she is thirsty and her stomach is not ready for anything. This is a time of uncomfortableness. In our helplessness He is strong- God is at work in her! Thank you for your prayers!

9:33am

She was able to ask for things (ice chips!!) and talk some. She is finally resting well!!! God is so good and amazing! Your prayers are felt! Thank you all so much for spending this time with us waiting and crying and rejoicing and thanking our gracious and good Father!!!!

12:31pm

Dialysis is starting now - we are praying that this will really jump start her kidney. She has extra fluids that her body needs to processed and drain. Goal for the evening is that she will have some sit up time by 8. Pray that she will be comfortable until then and continual progress in healing. Praise God - Liver is doing what it is supposed to!

8:26pm

We still aren't sure as to how Alaina's new kidney is functioning, and they are still working hard to manage her pain but at 8pm Alaina sat up! She first tried sitting up around 6:30 but after getting half way the pain was too much. As many of you know, however, Alaina is certainly not one to give up

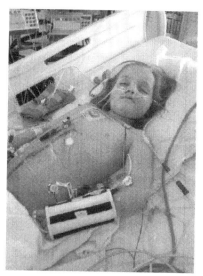

after she has decided to do something. Although today has been a long day, and Alaina is still at a critical stage in her recovery, we are continually in awe at the bravery, strength, courage, and determination of this little girl! I would include the picture here but can't figure it out so if you'd like to see her triumphs go to the living thru Lanie page on Facebook.

May 1, 2013 7:58am

Last night was a bit rough. Poor Alaina just could not seem to find a position that was comfortable for her. She would cry, the nurse would give her something for the pain, she would sleep for 15-30 minutes and then she would begin to cry again. On the positive side of things however, she is continuing to sit up, and the nurse told us that they were able to take her off of the blood pressure medication which is a major step towards leaving the PICU. The nurse did say that it would not be uncommon for them to have to restart the medication, but we're just praying that doesn't have to happen.

6:00pm

Heading to the OR now for surgery. Doctor just informed us that there is a possible blood clot that is restricting the blood flow to Alaina's new kidney and he wants to open her back up to find the problem and fix it. They also told us that Alaina has a lot of fluid around her lungs, due to the fact that her new kidney still hasn't "woken up", and so they will also be working to drain the fluid. Please pray. She is already struggling with recovery and everyone here has had little to no sleep, so emotions are maybe a little high.

8:42pm

The surgeon just came in to let us know that the surgery went well. He said that there was actually no clot, but because so many people on the team believed that the ultrasound showed a clot, his policy is "when in doubt, cut it out." Tonight could be a long night, seeing as how Alaina is coming back to the room with a breathing tube, which they want to wean her off of throughout the night. Our surgeon hopes to have Alaina walking by tomorrow evening, so please pray that this operation isn't too much of a setback for her recovery.

May 2, 2013 5:58am

I woke up this morning to Alaina's bright beautiful eyes. She slept peacefully for most of the night and was ready to watch some TV this morning. She's already sitting up today, and the plan is to have her walking around soon. Her kidney still hasn't woken up but the doctor keeps telling us that kidneys that have been on ice usually take a week or longer to start working. This morning I am just praising God for a restful night, and I'm looking forward to a great day. God is so faithful! - Luke

8:41pm

In the beginning of the day, Alaina was so alert and comfortable, but as the day went on she began to wear down very quickly. I think it was probably a mixture of dialysis which took 4 hours, and physical therapy, during which she was able to sit in a wheel chair that was just her size. The PT was really painful for her, and it was pretty heart breaking to hear her poor little voice saying "I don't like it!" over and over again as big tears rolled down her face. At the moment she is sleeping peacefully, and I'm praying that it lasts through the night again tonight. Thank you for your continued prayers and encouragement!

May 3, 2013 7:07am

Although the sky is a bit gray, and the forecast includes some snow here in Minneapolis it really is a beautiful morning! Last night before bed Alaina really had to use the bathroom, and they brought in a little red toilet that's

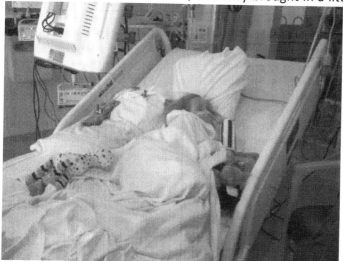 just her size. Like a trooper she sat without a complaint. Throughout the night Alaina was up at least three times, but each time was really good. She would wake up needing to use the toilet, so we'd get all her hoses and tubes gathered up, her bowls would do their work, we'd get her back in bed for some ice chips, and then she'd drift back to sleep. Around six this morning, we woke up to see her already sitting up in bed, needing to use the toilet again so I think it's safe to say that her bowls are moving. Another exciting thing is that what is coming through her catheter is becoming much less red, so this means that either her kidney is beginning to wake up, or the fluids they have been using to flush the line are just starting to come back out. We are going to pray that it's the former. At the moment she is watching cartoons, and feeling really good about the prospect of getting out of bed and walking today.

8:24am

The doctors just came in and told us that there is going to be a lot happening today. First the catheter is coming out, in a few minutes PT will be in to get her up and walking, next . . . I honestly can't remember what they said next but the plan now is to have her moved to the 5th floor by this evening!

9:15am

Alaina was able to go for a little walk today!! It was only from the bed to the door but the nurses said that it was an incredible feat for her to accomplish. After walking we went for a short ride in the wheelchair, and when we got back to the room she crawled back in bed all by herself.

10:50pm

Well, we hoped to have a little different view by the end of today but here we are, still on the third floor. With that being said though, today has been a full day. Alaina went on a walk, she sat up in a chair at least four different times, she climbed back into bed all by herself, had another round of dialysis, and had an ultrasound. Although her kidney still hasn't shown any sign of waking up, her blood pressure has remained stable, her catheter is out, and she has been weaned off of a few of her meds. She had a procedure done tonight to check the blood flow in her new kidney, but we won't know how that went until tomorrow. I feel like her spirits are pretty low tonight and she's incredibly sad about the way she feels physically. Please pray for encouragement for her. She hurts but she's so strong and never complains. We honestly haven't seen her smile all week...

10:22am

Last night was another good night where Alaina was able to sleep most of the night except for a few trips to the portable potty, where she did a great job of getting out and in her bed. The doctor told us this morning that the

19

procedure last night showed that blood was flowing into her new kidney, but there still isn't any urine coming out, which is what they expected. They're still having a hard time managing her pain, but they have a plan to get that under control today. She'll be having another round of dialysis, and the doctors are pretty sure that we'll be able to move to the fifth floor at

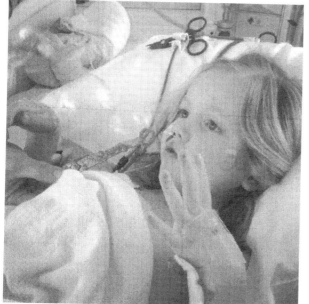

some point today as well. Her spirit still seems pretty low, but Jackson is on his way up for the weekend so I pray that will help. Thank you so much for going to the Father on our behalf. We rest in the fact that He is a good God, and although things don't seem to go the way we want them to, He has control.

Chapter 3: God's Mercy Wins. Always

10:07pm

So I (Ali; mama of the sweet and strong Alaina) have to admit that I have done a terrible job with keeping everyone up to date. My friends, and the last few days my husband, have been so amazing at letting all of you amazing people know what is going on. So please don't mind me. I'm not a writer and this is my first time posting really anything. So, man do I appreciate all of you. First, I want to say that I've read through the guest book and the posts on Lanie's Facebook page and am just so humbled and amazed at God's community and how loved and cared for we are. Thank you a million times over. I am so blessed by all of you.

So let's see. A recap of today. This morning Lanie walked really far! She had to stop and rest a few times but she rock star-ed it out and we cheered and cheered for her. By the way, cheering is apparently not allowed in the PICU. Noted. Soon after that she was so tired and once again CLIMBED (rock star right?!?) back into her bed. She had plasmapheresis in the morning and then soon after that had another round of daily dialysis. Man, dialysis just drains her. After that happens she is usually just done for the day.

Luke had to leave and head for home today as well. It was hard for him and for us to let him go, but I am so proud and honored to be married to such an amazing man. He is leaving today so that he can go and speak to a couple places in Iowa about God's heart! (I just love my family!!!)

Jackson came not long after Luke left and it was the first time that Lanie has seen Jackson since her surgery. Oh my heart...best reunion ever! Lanie has had such low spirits but when Jackson came and she woke up and saw him she reached her arms out for him and sat up to give him a huge hug. The dialysis nurse said she needed to lie down because her heart rate was so high!! She didn't smile but her heart was SO HAPPY!!!! I cried in true mom form.

Tonight Lanie has been mostly resting...still in PICU. We're a little bummed about that, but trying to see it as only a short time period that will be over soon. Please still pray against discouragement for our sweet girl. I keep talking to her about fun things that she'll be able to do and she just shrugs her little shoulders and says she can't do anything anymore. Break my heart...

Thank you so much to Luke's mom Joyce, my mom, my sister, and our visitors today. And thank you, thank you to all of you who continue to love and support us as well as pray! God is so good!!

Ps: Sorry I wrote a book. It's my first time :)

May 5, 2013 9:15am

I love mornings.

Lanie had such a good night. She woke up five or so times to go to the bathroom and then fell back asleep pretty quickly every time. At 5:45 she was up for good and asked if I would come and snuggle her. Of course I did! It was the first time I got to lay beside Alaina in a week and have her head resting on my shoulder...so incredibly amazing. By 8:00 she had already started slowing down a little again. One of her favorite nurses from unit 5 came down to tell her good morning and when Alaina saw her outside her room she cracked a smile. The first one that I've really seen this whole week. Praise God from whom ALL blessings flow!

She wanted to go for a walk but also wanted to wait until Jackson got here so she could show him how strong she was getting. He came about 8:30 and she almost jumped out of bed. She didn't make it as far walking today and tired out really quickly.

Getting some more sleep in now...

Praise God for mornings. Praise God for pain being low in those early times of the day. Praise God that no matter how hard and frustrating the afternoons and nights are...there is always the next morning to look forward to.

9:06pm

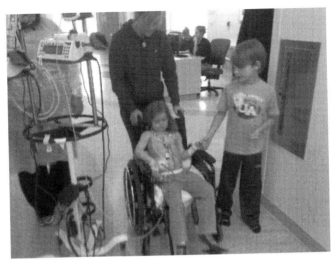

Well we moved to the 5th floor! Lanie's favorite nurse had been holding a sunset room for us throughout weekend and we finally got to see it today! A sunset room might not sound like a big deal, but to me it's watching the sun set every night over downtown Minneapolis, which is such a sweet blessing. So beautiful! Thankful we had lots of company at the time to help us move all our stuff out of the PICU (which it turns out was a lot of stuff, not sure how in the world that happened). We got everything in our upstairs room (not organized in the least thankfully) and found out that the TV wasn't working. Not a huge deal but...yeah it was kind of a big deal. The amazing nurses on unit 5 transferred us to the next room over (still sunset side) and here we have stayed since.

Lanie also walked again this afternoon. She did so well!! We would walk for a while and then she would ride in her adorable little wheelchair to rest. I thought she would be so done after that walk and just go right to sleep but she laid down for a bit and then wanted to sit in her wheelchair in the sunlight! WOOT! Today was also the first time she's done any sort of activity that she wasn't made to do. She colored!!!! I know, I know. Doesn't seem that impressive, but it so is, you guys. She hasn't felt like doing much of anything so the fact that she wanted to sit ... In her wheelchair... In the sunlight... Coloring... is AMAZING! Let me be a mom and have this moment.

23

I'm so proud of our little champ!! God has poured out so many good and sweet blessings today. Thank you for your prayers. Thank you for your encouraging words. We are falling asleep resting in God's goodness tonight folks.

And there is no way I can make these short like Luke's were. I tried. It's not gonna happen. Night sweet family :)

May 6, 2013 10:28am

So thankful for a positive mind set and day of blessing and gifts yesterday because I needed that to make it through the night with a good attitude. Lanie was up for quite a bit of the night because she was so itchy. She has quite a few little sores on her face and upper body from where she has scratched so much. Normally her mornings are her best time but today hasn't really followed suit. She has been pretty uncomfortable today and hasn't wanted to get out of bed or even sit up.

The doctors rounded this morning and are content with her liver function, although her levels aren't 'normal' yet and she's showing signs of mild pancreatitis. Kidney still hasn't 'woken up'. The plan is to do plasmapheresis this morning and then dialysis later today. The doctors have switched a couple of her narcotics hoping that the itching will subside throughout today. I think today will be pretty low key trying to get things a little more under control.

My plan for today is to take a shower and maybe, just maybe, wear something other than sweats AND if I'm feeling crazy...straightening my hair. Hope that you're all enjoying this awesome sunshine and feeling God's sweet love!

6:17pm

Dialysis was so rough today...never in my life have I seen her in so much pain. You guys. I just feel so done...

10:30pm

Wow. It's has been such a long day. Lanie is so strong and amazing. Dialysis was rough. She was uncomfortable through most of it but toward the end she had so much pain and anxiety. Her heart rate raced to about 180-200 BPM and she kept saying 'I just can't calm down!' She seemed so scared. And I was definitely scared. It took a long time to get the pain under control, but finally we did about 9:00 or so.

HIGHLIGHT! We got such a sweet video today and Lanie laughed when she saw it. Out loud. And asked to watch it again. And then laughed AGAIN! It made everything else sort of fade away.

Plus we've had lots of people hanging out today! Shout out to the Iowa City ladies and Grandma Joyce for bringing the party. The hospital, at times, has no clue as to what to do with us and all of the made up fun we can have.

Doctors are still confused as to what happened today. The plan for tonight is: blood work and X-rays within the hour. Hoping to get to the bottom of all of this and have an awesome day tomorrow...

Btw...sunset rocked again tonight. Thanks for the sweet present God!

May 7, 2013 10:17am

Better news? I wish.

Last night Alaina was up all night. For all of you who know Alaina and her personality and spunk and strength, you know she doesn't complain about pain. For her to hurt means that she really REALLY hurts. This one time, the doctors called me at home to tell me that Lanie's labs had come back really terrible and it looked as though she was having trouble with pancreatitis.

They said she needed to be hospitalized and put on IV antibiotics ASAP. I actually had to call her in from playing on the trampoline and she was so upset. She told me that her tummy was only hurting a little and asked if she could just play a tiny bit longer. So yeah. This was what I was dealing with. When this girl says she hurts, we listen.

Last night she would fall asleep for maybe 10 minutes and then wake up crying. All night. Nurses were in. Resident doctors were in. It seemed like people I don't even know came in (but in all honesty when it hit like 3 or 4 am I didn't pay as much attention to them). At 5:15 I let her turn on the TV and she just stayed awake, sitting up when she needed to and repositioning when she started to hurt. And of course she's been wide awake ever since.

X-rays and blood work came back decent from last night. Her blood showed her phosphorus and potassium were at high levels which I figured wasn't good or they wouldn't bother to mention it. The main thing that it means to us is another round of dialysis today. I'm not gonna lie. It strikes a little (OKAY A LOT) of anxiety in my heart after what happened yesterday.

This morning she's had an ultrasound and right now she's having a hydro scan (some kind of liver function test). She hasn't really been complaining of pain much this morning...thankful for that blessing. They are also thinking maybe a CT scan and then dialysis.

On a side note, my sweet mother in law had to leave this morning along with our Iowa City crew. It's funny how much I miss everyone when they go. So, so incredibly thankful for all of the people who come and hang out with us, send food, and just take care of us while we're here. Also blessed to know that Jackson and Luke have their own little (*not actually little at all*) crew doing the same for them in Iowa City.

We are all so loved...

5:05pm

Well our day has been filled with tests, tests, and more tests with a side of dialysis. Lanie started feeling a little better today but pain control has been an issue. Still waiting to hear back from the doctors on how any of the tests came out. Thanks for the love!!

May 8, 2013 8:08am

Yesterday was another rough day with pain control. Alaina just never seemed to be comfortable. They would give her pain meds and she would be ok for maybe ten minutes and then cry again. It was such a frustrating feeling to know that nothing was really working and that I couldn't do anything for her. Last night they finally decided to put her back on IV pain meds and let her give herself a "bump" when she needed it with a push button pump. That seemed to help a lot. Until about 3am, anyway.

She's sleeping again now but is still scratching a lot in her sleep and whimpers pretty often. Waiting on the doctors to round to give us the plan for today. Hoping for a free day with no dialysis or tests so that she can just rest. And feel good. And maybe color a little...

2:11pm

Pain and itching is out of freaking control...meeting with specialists today. Needing more shots than normal in my coffee this afternoon. Take that statement any way you like...

Chapter 4: What Does Healing Even Look Like?

May 8, 2013 10:25pm

My daughter is stinking amazing!

Lanie had a bit of a rough day with itching and pain. She had an allergic reaction to plasma which gave her hives on her eyes and we found a bed sore on the back of her head. But even though all of that happened...tonight was a huge blessing! Lanie was able nap a little this afternoon/early evening and woke up just 10 or 15 minutes before we had new visitors tonight...visitors who brought sweet little kids! And I don't know if it was the kids being here, Lanie showing off a bit, or just feeling pretty amazing tonight but she told me she wanted to go for a walk. Oh my word! She walked and walked and walked and walked. Two laps of that walk were without holding onto me at all! Whoa! Not gonna lie. I cried. I was just so overwhelmed with how good she was doing when I haven't seen that in her yet at all! Can those people and their two little kiddos come back and stay from now until forever?? Do you think it's okay to ask them that?

I was just talking to my friend Rachel about how the good stuff overshadows the bad stuff a million times over. All the stuff that happened earlier today feels like a bad movie I watched and all I can remember is how amazing Lanie did! Thank you Jesus for that protection of my mind!

I feel way more ready for tomorrow and whatever comes along with it...

Ohhh and I almost forgot to mention how she bent down during one of her laps and grabbed apple juice from the bottom of the fridge! Strong healthy abs, baby!

May 9, 2013 4:26pm

Ummmm. So God just healed.

I know this seems like crazy news but Lanie just PEED!!! 60 mL to be exact. And it's not TMI so just stop. She's been struggling a lot with pain today and just went through 4 hours of brutal dialysis so she's having a hard time still ... But she peed! The only way she can pee is if her kidney is working so yay for God's healing hand!!!! Our hospital room just turned into a party! Literally a party...except for Lanie's sleeping again, so it's a bit of a silent dance party. But really a party is a party, am I right?!

May 10, 2013 1:27pm

Sorry I haven't posted much since yesterday. Lanie was so busy last night walking around and sitting in the playroom and being a kid and all. She did pee a little more last night and the doctors keep telling us not to get too excited because there's a chance it still won't really function well. Ummmm too late. She slept ok last night but pain and itching still aren't under control. I finally woke her up this morning at 10:45 after a few attempts earlier in which she started crying about it being too early and not wanting to get up and to leave her alone for just a little longer and then would go right back to sleep. She's not bossy at all.

Once she was awake she took two bites of pancakes and then laid right back down. First solid food in a while though, so there's that. Once she let that ' settle' we all went on a nice long walk to the library and gift shop, and then played in the playroom for a bit. Overall it's been a pretty calm day. Playing with meds some more to get them all figured out.

Ps. I realized this morning I haven't felt the outside air on my skin in about a week. This southern girl is struggling for real. I'm hoping to get outside sometime soon so that I don't go absolutely crazy.

8:37pm – Luke's post

Since about 2:00 Alaina's pain and discomfort just seems to be increasing and she's been retaining more fluid. The doctors are switching up some medications and trying different things for pain that will hopefully cut down on the itching as well. Bottom line, she just really hasn't been herself today. Praise God that she has continued to pee, but we're praying for a night of rest. (and just so you know, this is Luke)

May 11, 2013 9:53am

We're such downers sometimes...

So yesterday we talked about how Lanie kept having more belly pain and how she was sleeping way more than normal. That definitely continued to get worse as the night went on. By 9:00 or so the pain spells got a lot worse and the sleep spurts were a lot less often. The entire night went like this. Lanie was trying to lie down, sit up, anything to make her tummy pain go away. She would start to try and rest but the pain would keep her up and crying. Throughout the night her temperature also started spiking- sometimes as high as 102.6. There were quite a few things we tried but nothing seemed to help he for lessen her pain.

At 8 am she finally started to sleep some, but even then would still cry in her sleep. The doctors ordered her a CT scan first thing this morning which came out decent. The doctors tell us that they know for sure that she has an infection but the question is where. Because she has so many places infection might be, finding where it is can be tricky. There's always the possibility of her port being infected. Or her drain. Or her incision site. Or her new organs. Or maybe she has a UTI. Or maybe it's just plain old pancreatitis (does that sound a little weird to anyone else??). The doctors are hoping that it will be an easy treatment plan once they find the cause. If it is her port or drain or site or even a UTI the antibiotics will have her feeling so much better in the next couple of days. If the problem is an abscess, or an infection within her tummy or new organs, treatment will be much more difficult. I don't even know what that means. Everything right now seems like it's difficult.

They still plan to do dialysis today which is a little like 4 hours of awful for Lanie, but will help so much with the liters of excess fluid that she has on her little body right now.

30

Ps. the doctors told us this morning that if it's one of the latter things, we shouldn't be surprised if we have to move back down to PICU. That one phrase sank my heart and we're praying against this pretty hardcore.

We'll update more as we know things. Thanks for seeking God and His glory with us friends. I'm praying right now for all of you...that you would see His love and grace so abundantly today!

May 11, 2013 11:44pm

Tomorrow will be better. Tomorrow will be better. Tomorrow will be better.

I figure if I keep saying it enough it for sure will be. But seriously, I feel like God has been teaching me a lot in these last couple of days (especially today) in that it's not at all about the circumstances we live in and are a part of, but instead about our perspective and belief about the circumstances. *CBT anyone? Any counselors out there that have had this drilled into their brains in class theory?* And our perspective and belief flows directly out of who we think we are and our belief about so God is.

So...

Even when Lanie and I don't sleep because her tummy hurts...

Or her temp hits 103.9...

Or the doctors tell me that they know that there is infection but they can't find it yet...

Or when I feel like a bad mom to Jackson and a nonexistent wife to Luke...

Or I feel like this period in the hospital is too much or overwhelming and I miss home...

I'm reminded that every time I look back God has chosen a better story for me and that He's good. And that He's trustworthy. And that He cares about Lanie (with her sassy personality, strong will, smile that melts my heart and right now fragile body) more than I ever could. *I am not actually sure how in the world that can be true but I KNOW that it is.*

31

I'm so overwhelmed tonight friends. Yeah. Today has been 'bad'. It's actually really and truly sucked. But that's not the reason I'm overwhelmed. I'm overwhelmed by love. And grace. I'm humbled by the people who have spent their precious time sitting at the hospital with us. I can't believe, or sometimes even understand, the amount of people that we have gotten letters, notes, gifts, food (the list goes on), some of which I have never had the privilege to meet. And I'm overcome with gratitude by the way people have laid aside other things or time and fallen on their knees for us.

Remembering tonight that this is just a season (one that I will openly admit that I'm ready for to be over).

So tomorrow will be better. It will be because I'll choose to be thankful and that alone will make it better.

And also maybe a little bit because its one day closer to Lanie and Jackson running and playing together... and feeling great.

10:46am

Hey all...sorry that I never got an update written yesterday. It was quite the busy day. In a good way. I mean...mostly.

The morning was pretty rough. Lanie had high fevers all night and when she was awake she complained a lot of her tummy and her head hurting. I turned off my phone because the ring would wake her up and she would cry. I lowered the shades because the light made her cry. I stood up from sitting in a rocker by her bed and she would hear that and wake up and cry. Fevers stayed pretty consistent between 101 and 103. Doctors are still looking for the source of infection. Her tummy has a lot of pain in one spot more than others and the doctor said during rounds that he is concerned about that because that's right where her kidney is. A biopsy is scheduled for Tuesday.

She did start to perk up yesterday evening though and even wanted to sit up and color. Her fever started to go down and she started talking a lot more and even smiled a couple of times. Fevers returned after she went to sleep, however. She also started having a cough yesterday that progressed throughout the day and even more into the night. Her oxygen saturation levels started dipping quite a bit so an X-ray was ordered and oxygen was placed (which was a lot less of a battle than I thought it would be, Praise

God!).The x-ray showed she has some fluid around her lungs but not much else...which I'm pretty sure is a good thing. Why didn't I go to school to be a doctor so that I could understand their language?? Oh yeah. Because that sounds terrible.

She woke up in a pretty content mood this morning and kind of surprised us all with her demeanor. Her cough is getting worse but other than that, I mean...she looks great (relatively speaking compared to the last couple of days). We are heading into dialysis this morning hoping that the kidney will fully wake up. (Did I tell you guys that she only made pee for one day and she hasn't since? I can't remember sometimes what I say and to who I say it to. UGH sadness.)

Ps: we had so many visitors yesterday! What an incredible blessing! Thank you, thank you!

5:09pm

So I have to admit, I wrote an update out to you guys this morning but the doctor came in to talk to me and I then somehow lost everything that I had typed. Since then I haven't even opened my iPad out of frustration. And I kind of wish that I had invested in a bulletproof/waterproof/disaster proof case so that I could throw the darn thing against the wall.

Before I update, I just want you to all know how thankful I am for you. I'm so incredibly encouraged after I read your comments on the CaringBridge website and on Living Thru Lanie's page. You guys are so amazing! And so full of love and grace and life.

Ok. The update: probably much shorter than my first one because I still feel a little grouchy about it unfortunately. So yesterday was a little rough. After dialysis Lanie's fever shot up to 104 and she was so teary at everything that was said to her. I felt so broken hearted. They moved her Tylenol from every 6 hours to every 4 to help kick her fever. It did help it go down to between 100 and 102 or so. Even after feeling so bad though she agreed to go for a walk! I couldn't believe it. I mean, when I have a fever of 99.6 my body is so achy and I barely feel like I can get out of bed (ok, maybe a little bit of an exaggeration but still...you get my point). Here she is, my little world changer, running a 102 temp and being agreeable in going for a walk...she is truly amazing. God is truly amazing.

Last night was fairly uneventful. She had to get plasma in order for the doctors to feel comfortable enough to go through with her biopsies today, but that was no big deal and something we've done quite a bit since the transplant. We did have an ' I don't know what the heck just happened but it scared me to death' moment this morning. She had an unexpected reaction during a procedure, but within moments was fine again. They came and got Lanie at 9:15 for her biopsy and by 10:00 she was ready to go in. The idea was to do both a liver and a kidney biopsy and drain the fluid that was outside her liver and find the source of her infection. They decided against the liver biopsy because they said it was doing really well.

While she was having her biopsy I had the chance to get outside and play with Jackson and my friend Rachel. I was a little disappointed in how chilly and sprinkly it was but hey, outside is outside. So therefore it was good. Who knew an hour later it would be 120 degrees outside! Now that weather calls me by name!

Lanie was only in the procedure room until like 1145a or so and when she came out the doctors said it went really great. It didn't appear like she was going to bleed (which is huge!) and they added a drain by her liver to make sure and get out all of the fluid that was there. They sent of samples of that fluid for testing to see if that is what is causing her to be so sick.

From biopsy until now she's still been feeling pretty crummy. She says quite a bit that her tummy hurts and even whimpers in her sleep. Fevers are still going strong as well. Her last one that was taken was 105. Is that even real?!?! Hoping that everything that was done today will help find and get rid of any infection that is hiding in her beautiful, sweet body.

ON THE BRIGHT SIDE----> doctors first allowed Lanie to have a popsicle tonight and when she did well with that they told her she could have oatmeal! A lady here also made her a cake so they allowed her to have a piece of that...she hasn't wanted the oatmeal or cake though. Not yet anyway. Also the kidney doctor came in and talked to us tonight. Rachel and I were a little unclear with some of what he said but the main things we understood is that the biopsy showed that she's not rejecting the kidney— such awesome news. And that she has acute tubular necrosis (ATN) which I am not an expert at yet, but I know that kidneys can recover from it. There is still a lot of unexplained stuff and a lot of frustrating moments but the light outweighs the dark. Sigh. Thanks again family for sharing in all of this with us.

May 15, 2013 9:36am

So I know you're all really shocked that I'm updating again, but my goal today is to do better so that I don't get overwhelmed. Last night taught me more about myself than anything else. Lanie was up almost all night crying about her tummy and her head hurting. It broke my heart and left me and her sweet nurse feeling pretty helpless. Although I was feeling so bad for her and helpless in the situation, I also felt tired and frustrated. We haven't really been sleeping. Like even for a second. I kept reminding myself that this wasn't a big deal to be up and that this was a sweet time to serve my beautiful little gift but nothing in me wanted to do that. I just wanted to sleep. And dream about all of the wonderful people in my life. And of hugs and love and other little sweet things. And preferably back in my own bed and Lanie back in hers and all things right back where they were before.

I maybe threw a little pity party. And we already had cake, so why not? (Don't worry...I haven't eaten the cake...yet). As I watched the room get brighter and brighter this morning I remembered the song 'Your light breaks through' by Adoleo. -- SHAMELESS PLUG -- if you have not heard their new music check them out on iTunes. You won't be sorry to have those songs encouraging you during frustrating moments and pity parties.

So thank you God for sunrises! (Mike Wild you'll be proud). And thank you God for new starts. And for reminding me that Your light does break through and that I can choose how I react to a circumstance.

I am also adding the lyrics to the song so that you can see how sweet it is and be blessed by it even if you don't go download the album (which you should do...just sayin).

"Your Light Breaks Through" - out April 2013
written by Ally Maloney, James Laugerman, Adoleo
lyrics:

There is no ocean too deep
No depth or distance to keep you away from me
There is no valley too wide
No past or failure or shame where I can hide

There's nothing you cannot change
No hidden place in my heart where you should not reign
You're turning ashes and pain

Into a sunrise, a song, and a brand new day
And when Hope seems so far away...
Your light breaks through
Your light breaks through
You have come and rescued me
You have come in victory
Your light breaks through

Oh death where is your sting?
You have no power to take hope away from me
For when the walls are caving in
I reach the end and it's there Lord, you begin
And when hope seems so far away...

And I will come into your light
Let my heart be seen
Let my sin be exposed
For I'm tired of the shadows
I'm through with keeping secrets
I want you, Jesus
I want you Jesus

Can I get an amen??

10:56pm

Today was a good day. Despite the fact that Lanie is still hitting high temps and she felt horrible and I was so, so tired, today was still a good day.

During dialysis we received such beautiful and special visitors! Thanks to the sweet Lynch family and their generous hearts, Lanie was able to meet Andrea and Danni - 2 cheerleaders from the Minnesota Vikings! I got to talk to them before they met her about how brave and strong Lanie is and the activities that she loves. The Lynch family and the cheerleaders presented Lanie with some incredible gifts including her own American Girl doll with a one-of-a-kind Vikings cheer uniform! And yes I got teary. I'm kind of a cry baby these days - but almost always happy cries. Lanie didn't smile a lot at first, but when the cheerleaders let Lanie hold their pom poms and play her smile was so big and sweet! Thank you guys so much for bringing cheer and love to my sweet girl today. Such an awesome blessing.

After dialysis Lanie struggled quite a bit with pain. She probably cried for about an hour and then was able to sleep some. We had fun friends come this afternoon and then more visitors this evening. Friends make the time

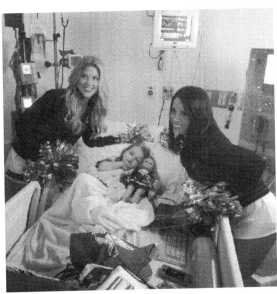

fly by! Also, everyone who comes here should know that I'm being an incredibly terrible host so I have to apologize a lot to the amazing people that take time to come and see us.

During the afternoon Lanie's NJ tube in her nose got kinked and after a lot of tries (Nurse Josie is a rock star but the line was not going to be overtaken) the line had to come out. It was so great to see her face tube free for once! I couldn't stop staring at her! Unfortunately the tube has to be replaced tomorrow afternoon but we'll take the short break that we were given.

Some more great news...

Luke came back tonight, which I was so thankful for. No pity parties tonight. This girl is sleeping while her husband gets to be on night duty. Once those sweet twins I've been hanging out with and our little family saw the sun set over the city, we had ourselves a little party. Luke's idea of a party was lying in bed cuddling Lanie (awwww) and my idea of a party was to talk and laugh a lot with friends (I know, lame compared to Luke. I never claimed to be a super mom). Either way, the day ended on such a fun and rejuvenating note.

Thankful tonight for friends. For people taking time to visit even when I'm doing a terrible job of entertaining. For sunrises. For sunsets. For glow bracelets. For family. For smiles. For cheerleaders. For generosity. For big pink squishy bears named Ginger (Shout out to Belinda! You rock). And for lots and lots of laughter.

Chapter 5: What the heck?!?

May 16, 2013 4:53pm

Alaina had such a great morning! She played games with the occupational therapist, laughed with Jackson, and went for a walk/wheelchair ride outside. Oh my word. The wind was blowing through her hair and she was smiling so big. The NG tube is out (only until this afternoon though) and I teared up watching Jackson push her around. That image is forever in my head. Thank you Jesus for that.

She started not feeling feel well again this afternoon and her fever started going back up. She started complaining of arm pain, but honestly we kind of ignored it thinking that it was just from her feeling bad. She was supposed to have her lowest drain taken out, fluid removed from her right lung, a new NG tube placed, and an ultrasound of her port so see if there is a clot or infection that is causing all of the fevers, all scheduled at 3:00p. We took Lanie down at 2:45p for all of these things to be done. At 3:45 we were still sitting waiting for them to get started when we noticed Lanie was breaking out in hives on her legs and back. When we asked the nurses about it, they brought us out in the hallway to talk. NEVER A GOOD SIGN. The anesthesiologist and doctor both told us that they were pretty sure Lanie was going septic. Umm huh??

I don't even know completely what that means and I have never had my heart drop so much. By the time they hurried her back to the room, I noticed that the hives started spreading to her arms. She was again complaining of not being able to straighten her arms.

Please pray for Lanie. Please pray for us as we sit and wait for the doctors. Please pray that my very anxious heart will be relieved soon.

Thank you. We love you

May 16, 2013 11:28pm

I just so happen to hate today. I'm not kidding or exaggerating. I just really don't like it.

Rachel and I talk most every night how we are able to love the day even if really bad things happen because we can remember so much good about it. And to be honest a lot of really good things happened today. This morning Lanie looked and acted like she was feeling so much better. I was able to get a decent 3 mile run in. The sun was shining. Our visitors were great and both Lanie and Jackson had won in Bingo. By the afternoon she was starting to wear down but she still seemed ok. Maybe she had just overdone it.

Once 3:30 hit though, things changed. She got sick so quickly and without much warning at all. When the doctor came out of the OR to talk to us, he told us he had put another drain in at her lung, tried to put the NJ in, but couldn't get it past the stomach causing it to be an NG. They looked everywhere in her abdomen for any sign of infection. They also ultra sounded her dialysis port to see if there was a sign of a clot. They didn't think any of those things showed infection. Nothing! Her fever was back down to 97.4 when I finally got to see her and talk to her which was awesome. But within 15 minutes it had already risen to 99.0 and then continued to rise even more quickly peaking and holding steady at 103.2. The red patches on her body spread very quickly covering her right leg, right side, most of her left leg, onto her arms, and finally onto her chest. The only thing the doctor (who we've never met before) said to us is 'this is not good'. Wow. Really?? That is not a helpful thing to say to parents unless you have a freaking solution! I lost my patience a bit here and had to walk away and let Luke (who is more level headed than I am) deal with her. Better to walk away than lose my temper, or so I've been told. Also, I realize an apology will be needed there.

Right about that time the doctors decided that Alaina needed to be moved back down to the PICU. Her fever was getting out of control, even with ice packs and a cooling blanket (she was shaking so hard because it was going up so fast), she couldn't unbend her arms, the redness was now covering most of her body below her neck, and she was complaining of so much tummy pain.

Once we were moved down to the PICU, the plan was to sedate her, place a breathing tube back in, pull the dialysis catheter, add a new catheter in her leg, and place a new Foley catheter. All of those things are now done.

Now we sit. On the 3rd floor. On the sunrise side of the hospital. All the while Lanie lies in her bed, her chest and abdomen completely covered in bruises, staples, 3 different drains, IV lines, and bandages. A breathing tube in her mouth which she really wants out as shakes her head no at pretty often while all of this atrocity that is happening around her.

And in all honesty, I'm frustrated. Why on earth can't we figure out this infection? And I'm fairly angry. I mean, the girl is 7. And she is so strong. But as her mom I feel so tired of her having to be strong. It's not cool that she had such an insanely good morning and is laying in the PICU tonight. And it's not fair in any sense of the word.

So yeah. I don't really like today. I feel like all of this is worse than the transplant. We knew what to expect for the transplant, but this...this caught me so off guard. And I feel like we just took 20 steps backwards.

The plan for tomorrow is to leave the breathing tube in, at least until they are able to do a CT scan in the morning. If the infection start was in the fluid off the lung or in the line, she should be better by tomorrow late morning, early afternoon. Antibiotics will take care of the infection in the blood and we will be able to move back up to our room 5. If for some reason the fever stays around until tomorrow afternoon, our transplant surgeon will reopen her stomach and try to find any abscess causing all of this.

Praying for good news tomorrow. Praying God will replace my anger with peace. Praying for my sweet Jackson who had to see his sister crying in the PACU waiting to move up to the PICU. And praying for God's healing hand to move a mountain.

May 17, 2013 11:18am

Good morning from the sunrise side of the PICU. I sound cheerier than I actually am, but I'm better than I was last night. I took a long, hot shower this morning and cried and cried and cried and then I felt better.

So Lanie had a decent night last night. Thanks to some hardcore meds she actually slept - I was gonna ask for some myself but decided against it (Actually Luke said no to me before I could ask my favorite resident doctor). Luke stayed the night here with us, which is awesome because the boys were planning on heading to the Ronald McDonald last night, which I'm pretty sure they'll do tonight before they head home tomorrow so that Jackson will be well rested for school on Monday. I think he's pretty annoyed that we're making him go back when he just wants to be here - mostly because he's been staying with Rachel and Leah — my sweet twin companions here in Minneapolis and they are way more fun than Luke or I will ever be :)

Overnight Lanie's fevers did start to trend down and have been pretty stable at 100.9. The redness is also fading in color. Praise God!! Our good healer! She's still having a lot of tummy pain and hates...I mean hates...the breathing tube in. She was trying to talk to us this morning using her fingers and writing in the air. Oh, if that didn't make me cry. She just was getting so frustrated and we just weren't getting it. She finally gave up and fell asleep... Feeling like a bit of a failure in this right now.

Her CT scan didn't show anything abnormal this morning. So that was good. Our transplant doctor isn't sure that it's completely accurate though. And maybe still wants to reopen her abdomen. No infection has presented itself as being 'the loaded gun' causing all the problems. Everyone is stumped. Everyone is frustrated. The plan for today is to extubate her and see how she reacts.

Thanks for the prayers sweet friends. And thanks for all the encouragement. I love your comments. I sometimes read them more than once. We are so blessed by your faith and love...

May 17, 2013 10:10pm

How many days in the PICU until I go crazy? My bet is on 1.

It's confirmed. My attitude on the PICU sucks. I've tried to choose joy but I'm having a really hard time finding it here. I was just telling my friend Tara (who came up and surprised me today from Iowa City!) that before when we were on the PICU, I knew that we were always headed in the right direction. Lanie was getting better every day, not counting that impromptu surgery that we had 2 days after transplant. We were on schedule to amaze the doctors and nurses with how God heals. I'm learning a lot lately about my time and how it's different from God's time. And trying to be patient. And joyful. And encouraging, but y'all...I'm struggling.

Lanie actually held a really low grade fever of 99.5 - 100.9 all day which the doctors were pretty pleased with. She also started peeing a little again!! About 5 cc's an hour actually which is a party in and of itself! C'mon kidney...you've got this! They decided to hold off on dialysis all weekend trying to force her kidney into kick starting on its own, out of necessity. Maybe it's working!

Man, after writing all of those really sweet things, I should be in a pretty happy mood tonight. And maybe I'm over-exaggerating the negative things in my head and that's the problem.

Lanie has struggled a lot with tummy pain today. She got her breathing tube out about 11:30 and has been mostly crying about tummy pain ever since. She does have good 15 minute breaks here and there where she feels good but for the most part...no. About 5:00 tonight I noticed she was feeling really warm while lying against me. When we took her temp it was 101.4. The next time we took it, it was 102.5. She started crying again of foot and elbow pain and how it hurt to move. Her tummy and her head have been the biggest complaints though.

Our transplant doctor told us that he was going to watch her closely tonight and if she continued to stay febrile he would reopen her abdomen tomorrow and clean everything, looking for pockets of abscess. Honestly I think that this, and this alone is the dark cloud over my day. Yeah. The PICU is hard. The nurses don't know Lanie. As stupid as it sounds, the 5th floor feels like home. This feels like a strange and unknown place. And we have to be quiet and reserved and trapped. Being here reminds me that we are farther away from home. But even that has nothing on this overlooking statement that we still might not know the source of her infection and that we may need to take quite a few steps back and reopen her almost healed abdomen.

I want to choose thankfulness in today's blessings. And I will choose to be thankful in those things. But to pretend that my attitude is good would be a lie. There is always tomorrow. There is always the freshness of a new day. There is always the knowledge and understanding of a good and faithful God. And there are always the millions (I don't feel like I'm exaggerating here!) of notes, letters, texts, messages, phone calls, and visitors that make every day that much more awesome. Seriously you guys...thank you!

Ps...I get all of your emails and messages and I've read all of them. Sorry that I am slow to respond. I will. And soon! Thank you for your patience!

May 18, 2013 10:27am

Hey sweet family! Thanks first and foremost with putting up with my crappy attitude the last couple of days. You guys are so humbling to me and it's just incredible how faithful and strong you all are.

Last night was so good! Lanie's temp went back down and stayed stable all night between 98.0 and 99.3. That is awesome! The lowest it has been in a week!! ALSO she peed quite a bit last night into the catheter. This is so incredibly huge guys! I've been singing the song "Fighter" to her by Gym Class Hero's (well the chorus anyway because everyone who knows me knows that I screw up the lyrics to most songs) so I'm pretty sure she's getting better because she's just so sick of hearing me sing.

Our awesome transplant doctor came in this morning and said he wasn't going to reopen her abdomen today because her night was so good. He said not to be surprised if he still ends up doing it tomorrow but I don't feel concerned about that at all. As of right now, the doctors are pulling her line that's in her groin, pulling her staples, pulling her bottom drain, and adding an IV on her arm instead of another dialysis catheter. All really sweet steps that are so, so, so much closer to home than last night!

Dude, you guys. God is so faithful and so good! I don't know why we had to come down to PICU. I don't know why she had to be intubated again. I don't know why she had so much tummy pain the last couple of days. But I'm remembering more and more that the 'I don't knows' are fine. I don't have to know. I may never know. It's ok.

So yep. God moved a mountain last night friends. Not only did he move it, he picked it up and threw it so that there would be no mistaking that it was Him and nothing else. Praise God who is the giver and sustainer of all things. A good Father who knows better than when we do.

Ps...My little side note praise. The two days we've been down in the PICU - on the sunrise side - the mornings have been grey and overcast. Ahhhhhhhh beautiful. Thankful today that God loves us in the little things too. I'm still praying to be back on 5, sunset side, very, very soon! And I also know that all of my prayers are circumstantial and small. Thankful that God sees my heart.

Love love love you all.

May 18, 2013 8:16pm

Right after I updated you guys last time, the doctors came in and told us that we could move to 5 today sometime after 3:00. She was having such a good morning and hadn't complained much of pain at all. I just felt so overjoyed!

Around noon I noticed her cheeks getting really pink and her body felt very warm...ok pretty hot but I didn't want to admit it. The nurse took her temp...103. I've felt that sinking feeling a lot lately and today was no exception. The nurse let the doctors know and the transplant doctor called me right away telling me that he had already called the OR to get ready for her surgery. My heart sank deeper.

Once the transplant doctor arrived Lanie's temp had gone down and she was feeling a little better. He asked me to step outside to talk with them. Sigh. I honestly felt like I was in an episode of 'House'. All of the different doctors were throwing in their opinions and ideas and looking at her trends in fever and in med changes. To be honest though, no one knew what was going on. No one knew where the infections were. No one knew what to do next.

Because she was starting to look content again and because her fever had gone down, they decided to wait until tomorrow morning to add another dialysis catheter and maybe reopen her abdomen then. SO MUCH WAITING!!! Doctors also said we'd be at least 3 or 4 more days in the PICU. Trying to not be discouraged...I feel another long hot shower coming on tonight (I sometimes need all those tears, though). The boys left today about 2:00. That was harder than I thought that it would be, but so thankful that Jackson will get back into routine. Hoping I can talk one of these sweet girls that are visiting into cuddling me up tonight - as Lanie would say.

On another bright note, we had sweet visitors again today and that helps everything to be way better. I just love you guys! Thankful that even though I'm a terrible host, people are so forgiving and they just keep coming.

Heading into the night with a super heavy heart and dreading the morning. But hopeful that tomorrow will bring answers and peace.

Goodnight friends. Hope that your weekend is restful and full of family, love, and joy...

May 19, 2013 9:47am

Ok. I usually love adventure and never knowing what is going to happen. I crave it actually. I love adrenaline and change. The 'usually' I was referring to is that I've found I don't appreciate it as much in the hospital. Not that I ever need to know a plan. I don't. In fact, my friend Tara is here now and we were talking about what we would all do last night after Lanie fell asleep and I realized I don't even like to think about that because we never know what's going to happen. By the way, we had a lot of fun after Lanie was finally resting, just so you know we're all still having fun here. Back to how I don't love adventure in the hospital...

Lanie had a really good night! She was only up a few times and her fever stayed at 99.8 and under. The anesthesiologist came in to talk to me about 7:30 to prep us for the OR. Right as we were getting ready to leave at 8, the doctors came quickly into our room and stated that she wasn't going in to surgery this morning. Wait. What? I mean, I'm for the change of plans, but why?

The reason, they said, is because Lanie is teetering on needing dialysis but not desperate for it so the kidney and transplant doctor decided to cancel her operation to see if we could wait this out one more day. They are all so stumped. Every doctor that comes in tells us that everyone knows Lanie and they all talk about what to do with her and how she's just throwing them for a complete loop. Well I know the girl is unique and amazing, but I kinda would like to know the doctors have seen some of this before and know what to do. I'm pretty sure they don't.

So today we wait. The good news is I've become an expert on waiting. I might even write a book on it. Hahahaha who am I kidding. I hate to write. My friend Meggan will write my book on waiting.

Lanie's only plan for the day is to eat and ride around in a wagon. I love that this is her plan. It sounds like a plan we would all enjoy on a Sunday afternoon so I don't think she'll complain much about it - oh and I think I forgot to tell you the reason Lanie isn't walking again is because her right leg is pretty swollen. They are thinking she has a small clot in her vein and are working to get rid of that today. Sorry if I totally forgot to tell you. Just found out about it late last night.

I can't foresee anything else happening today but literally have no idea from one minute to the next in this crazy hospital life. Thankful that God knows that I have an adventurous heart that longs for more than day to day. Thankful that he carries me through the adventures that he continues to bring me to.

Make sure and tell God all of the things that you are thankful for today!!

May 19, 2013 12:07pm

So I've met this amazing family here and I would really love for y'all to pray for them! They are the sweetest family from Saudi Arabia. They have been here with their 4 year old little girl - in the same room - for over 9 months! Their other 2 kids are still in Saudi Arabia being taken care of by friends and family. The little sweet girl has a Berlin heart right now, and is waiting on a heart transplant. Pray that this beautiful family will see the healing hand of God. Pray that they will find comfort and peace as they are here. Pray that staff and other patients will love them well.

10:00pm

Hey friends and family! I was trying to think through what our day looked like and believed for like a few solid minutes that nothing had really happened. As I was talking to my girls here tonight, though, I realized that actually a lot went on here.

For starters, Lanie went on her first walk since being in the PICU. Well I guess it wasn't really a walk because her legs are so swollen from the clot (just in the vein) in her right leg and from being fluid up because of not having dialysis. We started her out in the wagon but realized pretty quickly that her body was sitting in a perfect little V and that she was incredibly uncomfortable. Go figure. The girl has a foot long incision down her little body and sitting in a V hurts. As quickly as we put her in, I took her out.

We put her in a giant wheelchair instead, which was fine as long as she had pillows and blankets all around her. We went quite a few laps around the PICU...Lanie and 4 adults. It was like a parade, Lanie in her wheelchair. Tara pushing. Grandpa holding the portable monitor. Lindsay rolling the oxygen. And me walking backwards with her giant sized IV pole. I wish we had a picture. I'm sure we were hilarious. Or ridiculous. Either way, that picture would have won some kind of award.

Right as we were finishing her walk, Lanie started getting so tired and crying that her tummy was hurting. By the time we got her back in bed she was crying much more. We took her temp. You guessed it - 101.8. Darn it! I just feel so frustrated by it. She had a fairly rough afternoon following that temperature, as well; going from feeling ok to almost instantly crying that

48

her tummy hurt. I just feel so helpless when that happens, and like I should be doing something, but then I'm not. She did finally get some rest later in the afternoon and then woke up feeling really good! She had a few really great hours again tonight where she played with our visitors and laughed and read books. Only a few times complaining of tummy pain.

As I'm writing this, she's laying in bed with Lindsay watching movies, crying here and there about her tummy and how much it hurts. I'm constantly amazed by her strength. She had to get poked twice tonight for blood draws and she did it like the stud that she is. She doesn't really complain. She asks if her pain button is 'available'. She asks for steri-strips to be put in places that she knows she picks at on her incision and she likes to wear her oxygen. She knows when she needs breaks. She knows when she wants to push herself. She ate like 4 bites of food today and I've never been more proud.

I hope that I can be half as strong as she is. I pray God continues to use her compliance to teach me patience and grace. I pray that when she isn't discouraged, I don't bring her down with my frustrations. Tonight I am watching Lanie with amazement and awe. I love this girl.

May 20, 2013 2:05pm

Lanie had a pretty decent night last night. She woke up on and off complaining of tummy pain, which confuses the doctors even more because she shouldn't be having tummy pain this much still 3 weeks after transplant.

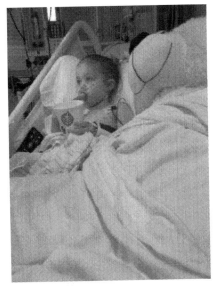

The doctors cancelled her space in the OR again this morning during rounds because she had a fever free night and is still only teetering on needing dialysis.

Lanie slept a lot this morning. She's been so sleepy the last couple mornings and hasn't wanted to stay awake. I was hoping for a great afternoon after such a long nap but around 12:30, the nurse took her temp and it was 101.6. We just took at again and it's 102.4. When her temp spikes in the afternoons she cries and cries about her tummy. I don't feel like there is a lot that we can do to console or distract her. It is just so incredibly frustrating. Earlier this morning they told us that they didn't see any reason we couldn't move up to 5. Last night was decent and fever free for like 20 hours. And then this afternoon happened.

I'm literally just so frustrated. I'm frustrated that the doctors don't know what's going on. I'm frustrated that I don't feel like I know how to take care of her. I'm frustrated that afternoons are this hard. And I'm frustrated that no one has any idea what's going on. AND NOW THE NURSE JUST TOLD ME HER TEMP IS 104.7

GRRRRRRRR.

Letting the doctors know now so I'll guess we'll see what happens next.

Going to go sit next to her and tell her that I'm sorry and that I'm frustrated just like she is and this is just a season. A really really crappy season.

Chapter 6: Learning curve

May 20, 2013 10:03pm

So as an update and change of mood tonight I thought maybe I would talk about all of the things we learned today...

1. Don't tell people to come at such-and-such time because Lanie is 'better in the mornings'. Truth is, come at any time. There is not a lot of predicting this girl's behavior anymore. A girl after my own heart.

2. Don't eat more than 5 cookies in a 24 hour period. Ever. Stomach ache the size of Texas.

3. Lanie is so funny after her morning dose of pain medication. She asks the most random things like if I know certain people from her school or who is holding her hand (really she was squeezing her pain button). Another quote from today...'why do I have to wear this dress if we're not going anywhere' - she only wants to lay in the bed naked for the most part with a soft blanket covering her.

4. She doesn't like when we laugh "with" her when she says silly things.

5. Don't try and write an update when Lanie is going through a fever spell...I read it. It was a mess. My apologies.

6. Visitors are one of my favorite things in the world and keeps me engaged with anything and everything going on outside of the hospital. They lift my spirits, laugh with me, cry with me, and don't ever judge - at least not to my face. I'm kidding. I think...

7. Just because a few hours in the middle of the day are super rough doesn't mean that the day itself is bad. Trying to keep perspective and take lots of deep breaths. I also realized at like 3:30 today that I hadn't really been out of our PICU room at all. I walked around the PICU circle once and realized that things were happening outside of my own frustrated little world. The clock was still moving. People were still going about their daily things. And this little stint in the middle of my day was nothing more than a crappy little section of time and life would inevitably go on.

8. My friends Tara and Lindsay stayed the night in the PICU last night with me. I really like to snuggle. Tara doesn't. 2 chair/beds in our room, and we all 3 still fit perfectly. We're really good at improvising.

9. Lanie loves her grandpa. It has been such a sweet thing to have Grandpa Darrell here for the last few days. I love to watch her kiss him goodnight and ask where he is in the morning. Every day she tells him to stay another day. It does the greatest thing to my heart.

10. Lanie is a for real stud. I already knew this but it has hit me so strongly in the last 24 hours that it's unreal. I only share a bit of what she puts up with and her attitude but if you guys saw her...it would take your breath away. She is so sweet to all of the nurses/doctors/lab techs/PT/OT/and millions of other people that are constantly waking her up and poking and prodding her. She also has so much going on that it's been really hard for her to walk or use her legs last couple of days. Although I know she's in a lot of pain, she went for a long walk/wheelchair ride with her entire entourage and would get out of her wheelchair constantly to prove she could do it. That is the picture that's connected and at the end of the walk Lanie asked me..."I'm doing so good, can I go to 5 now?". Kill me now. If only I had the authority to say yes.

11. God knows more than I know. You would think I have this down, but I realize that sometimes I don't. Actually a lot of times I don't.

Trying to overlook the hard stuff tonight that breaks my heart and the fact that my family is living in two separate cities. And the positive truth is I am learning a lot about myself, Lanie, others, and God in this process. Thank you for walking this with me. And for constantly showing how much you care. And thanks for not judging, to my face.

May 21, 2013 12:03pm

Lanie had another night of some sleeping and some crying. She usually isn't up for very long during her crying spurts and God is giving me plenty of energy to not be sleepy during the day. Having friends here definitely helps!

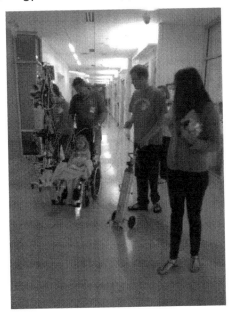

This morning doesn't look a lot different from other mornings. The doctors round and tell us that they are watching her so closely and we'll just see what she does today. There has been a lot of mention of going back up to 5, but it sounds like they're pretty full right now (which also means that maybe Jesus is just waiting for a sunset room).

Lanie did go on a walk this morning, so that was new! She walked so much more than she even walked last night, and we, of course are her cheerleaders the whole entire way. The PICU has to be annoyed with us right now so I'm sure they want us on 5 as much as we want to be there.

She's back to sleeping now, on her pink bear, Ginger. So incredibly adorable! Praying against fevers as the afternoon starts to creep up on us. My heart starts to show signs of anxiety when I look at the clock, so praying against that too.

I feel like there is such an unknown line between hoping and believing and also being content with knowing that our time in the PICU might not be quite over. Praying mostly that I will be able abide in Him and his timing.

May 22, 2013 12:04am

So yep. Still writing from 3rd floor PICU. But deciding to choose joy instead of frustration. Lanie's first fever spiked at 12:30 today at 102.5. I was bummed, but still had hopes for going to the 5th floor. At 3:30 she spiked again at 104.4. The fevers lasted a lot longer today but the crying was much less...mostly I think because we took her on a long walk this morning and so she slept through the 'bad' part. I was actually pretty productive during her sleeping times. I paid bills, made like 10 videos with the girls, did like 5 minutes of yoga, and laid in a chair. Impressive, I know.

Her attitude was so sweet today too. She still complained of some tummy pain, but was so incredibly kind with her words and loving to the staff that I almost couldn't take it. I smiled a lot today.

After Lanie woke up from like her 4th nap we decided one more walk was called for. We played hide and seek throughout the unit and Lanie walked more today than she has in the last few days combined! We know how to have fun. So thankful for the amount of time I spent laughing today.

There still aren't any changes that we know of, but there is a lot of talk in the air about new plans of what we should do. I'm starting to get used to the third floor, which I'm hoping is me just being content and not me feeling like I'm losing hope or giving up. It's weird how those are hard to separate sometimes.

I feel like there has to be a reason that all of this is happening and we can't get back up to the 5th floor. God knows it, so I don't have to.

I guess I don't have much else to say tonight. I guess we'll just see where tomorrow takes us...

And thanks for the prayers for my Saudi friends! Some amazing girls that came to visit today brought them in a gift also and the little girl just lit up when we gave it to her. It's such an honor to be able to share God's love in this place...Goodnight friends

May 22, 2013 10:51am

It's 10:30?!? So it's been a crazy morning here already. In a nutshell...

-we woke up 9 times during the night with tummy pain

-labs were taken 3 times between midnight and 7am...yep a poke every time. Grrrrr. Lanie is such a doll though and holds her arm still and talks to the lab techs through it. Stud

-nurse came in at 8am and told us we were moving up to 5 by 9:00 and that Natalie would be our nurse. I LOVE HER SO MUCH SO YAY!! Lindsay and I packed up Lanie's little room

-we made coffee...which is a big deal because Lindsay and I have no idea how to do this. It was a mess. Coffee everywhere. I'm sure I drank lots of grounds. But in the end it was just so good. PS - someone please teach me how to make coffee! It's getting embarrassing

-doctors rounded at 830a. Good news, bad news. The bad news is thatLanie's fevers are getting higher and lasting longer. What the heck? Ideas: that there is medication causing the fevers (although she isn't given any meds around that time whatsoever), an infection pocket somewhere, another clot, something in her heart, or something going on in her brain (I was too scared to ask more about that), although they didn't seem too scared. The good news is that she peed over a liter last night! Yay!!! Her creatinine dropped from 5.2 to 1.8 in three days. That is honestly amazing. Every time she pees we tell her how awesome she is. I think Lanie's starting to believe that the hospital is making us crazy. There's a chance she could be right...

-the charge nurse told us that they had no indication that she was getting a room upstairs today. Ugh. They had already told Lanie she was moving so I definitely spoke up again at this point. Man, you can't tell her we're moving upstairs when we don't. Frustrating. She's already asked at least 5 times this morning when we get to go.

-X-ray of her chest and echo done.

- I drank so much coffee that I'm shaking while writing (don't mind me and my scattered thoughts)

-and the doctor told us that we would be at least 4 more weeks inpatient. I may need lots more coffee with that kind of news. We definitely need some positive things to happen to get us through this kind of morning of ups and downs...

May 22, 2013 11:55pm

Wow! What a crazy afternoon/evening it has been! Lanie slept most of the morning today. I guess she had to make up for all of the time we were awake last night. Grandpa Darrell had to leave around mid-morning and Lindsay left about lunch time...sad, sad day, but so thankful for the amount of time they got to spend here!

About 1:00 I was cleaning up around our little PICU room and happened to look out the window to see a familiar face! I thought for a minute I was having a desert island experience and was hallucinating but after a few more seconds I realized more Iowa City friends came to hang out with us today! I can feel the love, guys! I cannot tell you all enough how much you all mean to me and the fact that people are driving from all over to see us is beyond humbling.

About 1:30 I was talking to my friends, and realized Lanie hadn't had a fever yet! I got so excited. Maybe this was the end of the horrible afternoons. The nurse took her temp about 2:00 and it had risen a little to about 100.3. By 2:45, she was at 104.5 again. That 45 minutes that her fever raised she had such terrible chills and told us her tummy was really upset. About 3:00 she started coughing and throwing up (except there is like nothing in her stomach, so she could really only throw up once or twice until she was just coughing and gagging). The next few hours were long, but not as bad as past afternoons. Lanie cried a lot about her tummy pain. I was talking to my friend, Gail, who was also visiting during that time about how everything must be so sensitive on Lanie right now. She complains of things that would have never bothered her in the past. It just seems crazy.

Lanie started calming down about 5:00 and about 5:30 the nurses told us that there was finally a bed on the 5th floor! The doctors were a little hesitant to give it to us after the events from the day but finally sent us up. Moving upstairs was such a whirlwind (and I had no idea we had so much stuff. Seriously...where is it all coming from?!).

And then I started getting texts about 7:30 or so asking about moving up to 5 and realized it was already online! Oh social media. We have a love/hate relationship.

Since 7:30 it's been a little crazy with getting things up to 5, getting Lanie situated, talking with doctors, talking with nurses, organizing a bit, getting old IV's out, putting new IV's in, and writing a few thank yous. Lanie has had a really good evening. She walked a ton around 5th floor with me and Rachel and is glad to be able to go whenever she wants without having someone carry a monitor and her oxygen alongside us. I think she feels so much better and happier just being up here. I know she does actually.

In spite of all the positive things that happened today there is something else happening in my heart. Now that we're up on 5, I feel like I should be breathing big sighs of relief, but for some reason I'm not. I should be feeling joy and thankfulness, but instead I feel frustrated and despondency and I don't even really know why. I can't think of any good reason to be unsettled and maybe even a little sad, but yet here I sit...confused by my own emotions.

Asking God to help me walk in contentment and joy, without worry or disappointment and choosing to soak in thankfulness tonight despite how I feel...

May 23, 2013 1:53pm

Good morning from 5...plus it's not morning

It took me a while, but I think that I'm over the slump from last night. I didn't sleep a lot last night...I don't know why (no psychoanalyzing) and so I think that left me still a little disheartened.

I've had 3 cups of coffee for breakfast now, though, and feeling ready to roll. I just looked at the clock and realized it's after 2:00 so I guess my coffee was brunch. Where do the days go??

Lanie slept pretty good last night. She's on a heparin drip because they've found two little clots now, which is awesome (the heparin, not the clots) except for when her IV gets pulled and we get up in the middle of the night to clean up blood that's seeping out of her bandage all over her bed and her. Crazy. Still hoping to talk the doctors into a PICC line. Labs 3 times a day plus switching around IV's is a lot for my little doll. Even if she doesn't complain about it...I will on her behalf.

Lanie slept most of the morning. I felt somewhat productive. I have to record Lanie's labs everyday, which I do a terrible job at because everything distracts me and you guys, it just isn't a fun task. I caught up on most of those today, though...thank you coffee.

I heard Lanie starting to cry in her sleep about 11:30 and came over to the bed to sit with her. She didn't feel warm yet, but she was acting a little strange so I asked the nurse to take her temp. 100.1. Dang it. I kinda knew what that meant and within minutes Lanie started to shake and cry harder. When they took it 15 minutes later it was 102.7. I don't like that I know how she reacts. I don't like that every day for a few hours she feels so terrible.

She's finally coming out of it now and is letting Rachel play with her some (even though she won't let me leave the bed yet).

Plan for the day: well who really knows the plan...it changes all the time. POTENTIAL plan for the day: switch a lot of her IV fluids to the NG so that we can save her IV lines and not go through them so quickly. They're still worried about infection so they really push back on the idea of a PICC. We'll tackle that issue again on another day and time.

PS - lack of sleep means I worked out, showered, straightened my hair, and dressed myself up a bit. That makes me feel better already. And by better I mean human.

10:54pm

Hi friends! Well today has been another day. Wow. That statement isn't really helpful at all for you. Last time we talked I had drank coffee for breakfast and lunch, Lanie slept and slept and slept and then woke up spiking a temp, and I was somewhat productive.

Well, I guess some stuff has happened since then. Lanie's fever came down to almost normal about 2:30 and then spiked to 104.8 at 3:15. She had already had Tylenol so we just had to wait this one out, until we could give her more at 4:30. That was kind of new. Usually she spikes once in the afternoon and then nights are good for her! Today she spiked twice, which means from like 11:30 to 5:00 she felt pretty bad. She cried on and off, but mostly on, about tummy pain. Times like these make me feel like I'm going to lose all my senses. I can do absolutely nothing for her when she's upset and in pain. There were times in that period when she was distractible. Examples...she played 3 man tic tac toe with me and Rachel (which is actually more fun and more stressful than regular tic tac toe, you should totally try it), she painted some (while sitting on the floor!!!!!), and she would talk about a couple things in between her cries.

Rachel and I took her for her second walk outside in 25 days! This is torture for her I think...to be inside for so long and not running and playing with the other kids. By the time we got back upstairs, she wanted to sit by our window and watch the construction guys work on the park that's almost finished. She sat there forever. It was honestly so sweet and she hadn't really wanted to do anything like that yet.

She was so exhausted after all of that she laid down in bed to rest for a bit before her and Nurse Natalie were going to build a fort for the American girl dolls. She was so excited about it but fell asleep within minutes of lying down. Rachel and I just had some down time (which was actually running around looking for food and choreographing a dance to a song my friend Boswell wrote for Lanie). We're getting really good at the dance by the way. And I wish you could all hear the song!!! We listen to it at least 10 times a day and I've heard the nurses and doctors humming it as they work. Bos...you're awesome (Kelsea, you too!) You little Jack Johnson you.

Lanie didn't wake up again until the boys got here. Oh happy day! It was so fun to look out the door and see them standing there! I wasn't, however, ready to see them head to the Ronald McDonald house for the night, but thankful that they're in the cities. It makes my heart so very happy. Plus a four day weekend! Score

Heading to bed for the night as soon as Lanie starts to settle down again...tummy pain go away! Last night's lack of sleep has made me one sleepy girl. Thanks for all the encouragement friends. I'm blessed by you guys constantly.

Chapter 7: So long sunrise

May 24, 2013 12:35pm

Wow it's been a crazy night/day. I feel like it's been days since I've updated because so much is going on and we have been busy here on the 5th floor. It took me 2 hours yesterday afternoon to write the update (I told you...easily distracted) so today I'm reverting back to list form. Here's what happened at a glance...

- Lanie was up all night with spiking temps to 104 - 105 and having tummy pain. I'm not even exaggerating here with the up all night thing. The first time we fell asleep was when I crawled into bed with her at 630a to help her hold her tummy. The nurse came and woke us up at 730a to go downstairs for her scheduled procedure. Here is a warning to people who come to visit or have to see me today: I'm not my best on an hour of sleep. Proceed with much caution and even more grace.

- Lanie started spiking a temp again when we got downstairs into the procedure waiting area. And after being down there for 20 minutes, she was already back up to 104.6. We then had to wait for it to start coming down before the doctors would even touch her, which was another half an hour or so.

- Procedures done: Abdominal tube removed. Chest tube removed and a new one was placed to try and get more fluid out. Midline PICC line placed. Abdominal scan to try and find more sources of infection. None were found.

- We met the boys and a sweet visitor from Iowa City back upstairs at like 10:45a. Doctors rounded then also. Amazing news is that Lanie's kidney continues to get better. Her creatinine levels are lower than they have EVER been. Yay God!! Sometimes I forget that he moved that whole mountain and need reminders that His hands have *already* healed... In other news, no one can find the source of infection and her fevers went crazy yesterday afternoon/last night/this morning. Something is happening there. The girl is a sweet beautiful mystery.

- Our sweet nurse Josie came in the room with great news right after that...we were getting moved!! I know that you guys may have a hard time understanding the significance in where we are in the hospital, but to move from sunrise to sunset side was like a piece of sweet hope in my heavy, tired heart.

- so right now, I'm sitting in our sunset room feeling God's love flowing over, while my baby girl and amazing men (plus sweet visitors) are chilling over in our sunrise room - me being over here writing was their idea (easily distracted, remember) - aren't the people in my life amazing?!?

- I don't know a plan for the day, but do I ever? Not so much. I'm feeling the itch to go for another run since the boys are here now, and my heart is bursting with hope and thankfulness. (And I know it's dumb that something as little as moving rooms can change my outlook on everything, but it does. It really really does). It also may have to do with the lack of sleep.

Thanks for hanging in there with me through mood changes, bad attitudes, and pouting faces. And I'm sorry to the nurse last night that I got a little sassy with. I know things aren't your fault. And if I see you tonight I'll apologize in person. Love you guys ~ Ali

Ohhhhh PS: I wanted to add a picture of the amazing sunrise this morning from our room. The sunrise was amazing, not the picture. Don't want any disappointments. Thankful that I was able to see it this morning and even more thankful that I won't be seeing it from now on.

PPS: I'm not a sunrise hater. I love sunrises. I love them when I'm running, or out on a lake, or camping. Mostly anytime that I'm already awake and not in the hospital. 'Already awake' being the key word :)

61

Thank you God for today! And here are some specifics in just some of the ways I'm thankful...

1. Lanie has been fever free since 12:15pm!

2. Although she slept a lot...and I mean a lot...Lanie had such a good night. She ate a couple bites of grilled cheese and some Jamba Juice smoothie (thank you Darcy and Chloe!!!!!). She also went on a couple walks without holding onto anything. Get it girl!

3. Her PICC failed to work tonight and when the team who put it in this morning came and looked at it, they said that maybe there was a hole in it or maybe she was having spasms causing the PICC to not work. After thinking through some different plans, it was decided that she just needed a new IV. Doctors never loved the idea of the PICC anyway. In this I'm thankful that our doctors talk to each other and care. They are cautious, beautifully caring, and brilliant. I trust them so much.

4. Soaking up the sunset side of life. Just sitting in here tonight makes my heart glad.

5. Nurse Brittany is back after way too long of a vacation (a week) and running a marathon, no big deal. That girl is awesome. I love the unit 5 nurses. They are so incredible and caring and I just want all of them to come and live in Iowa City with me. They have my heart. Thank a nurse in your life today. These folks are serious rock stars!

6. The boys are here. Amazing how much more freedom I have when Lanie wants someone other than me when she's feeling horrible. I will admit, though, it's hard to not jump in and console her or tell Luke how I've been doing things. Ugh. Please don't let me be that person.

7. Pizza Luce gluten free pizza with light cheese and so much meat, adorably named "The Bear"--> I literally love you

8. Visitors that bring Monster energy drinks and cold press coffee. Tomorrow will be a fun day

9. Looking through all of the cards/letters/notes that people have sent. I get teary thinking about it. Talk about encouragement and generosity. I'm so sappy when it comes to those things. Tonight I'm thankful for YOU!

10. I got to go on another short 3 mile run. West River Parkway is an amazing route. I saw signs today marking the Minneapolis marathon route and thought of my sweet friend Leah who is running that race for Lanie. That thought made me run much faster and harder than I have in a while. It felt so great. I will be cheering so loud for Leah on June 2nd! After a mile or so, I took the trails that led down to the river, which slowed me down but made me so happy. God creates beauty.

11. Lanie just fell asleep and seems so peaceful...I think that's my cue to follow suit

G'night sweet friends. We'll share more sweet memories and thanks tomorrow.

May 25, 2013 11:48am

So, I've been dragging my feet writing this morning because I just don't have a lot to tell. Lanie had an awesome night of sleeping...such a big deal friends! She literally just woke 10 minutes ago. She was given IVIG last night in and was watched super closely with vitals and whatnot, but slept through everything. She woke up with tummy pain and her face is pretty puffy, so the plan for today is to deal with those things and to pray against fevers.

We are almost 24 hours of being fever free! Holding my breath this afternoon!

Wanting to get in another run today while the boys are here and things seem calm. It's funny how I seriously cherish the times I get to work out and try to take advantage when I can because I never know when the next run will be. Funny how that is...

63

May 25, 2013 4:37pm

Just chillin on this fever free day with her big brother! Today has been so good y'all!!

Chapter 8: You take the good, you take the bad

May 26, 2013 3:41pm

Sometimes I'm not sure what to write at all. If I celebrate a good day, what do I say about a bad day? If I complain about a bad day does it mock the good hours/days we have. To be honest I'm not really sure. In saying all of that, I'm sure that you can kind of see where this update is going...

Lanie did so great yesterday. You guys know...

So last night, when she woke up at midnight crying about her tummy, I was thinking that it was just going to be a short little spurt and then off to free and clear healing from there. Not really the way it happened. Lanie was up off and on (mostly on) throughout the night crying about tummy pain and looking so puffy. When they weighed her this morning, I could see why she looked so puffy...up 2 and a half pounds from the day before. Four pounds from 2 days ago. All from fluid. About 5am I asked the resident doctor some questions about her puffiness and what was maybe going on and he had no answers. I don't know if it was because he was new to us, or he was grouchy, or if I was just so tired (probably mostly this one) but I need to add him to my list of people that I have or will apologize to in the hospital.

At about 6, I felt her skin and she seemed pretty warm. I tried to live in denial for a while but realized that probably wasn't the best way to handle the situation. I called in her nurse to take her temp...100.4. Not terrible, but I know what this means.

I didn't take it too long to climb up and then remain somewhat stable, with the help of Tylenol, at 102.4. 40 hours. That's how long she had been fever free and I was glad to see the light at the end of a month long tunnel. And now the light seemed further away than ever. She had a lot of tummy pain this morning, along with feeling crummy with a fever, oh and also being fluid up with 4 pounds. Lil champ! She still wanted to try and walk around to feel better. Literally I'm amazed every single day at the choices she makes. It's humbling to realize I complain more than she does.

After all morning of her tummy hurting and fevers, it was such a sweet blessing to see her come out of it this afternoon. She started talking to us again instead of crying and asking to go on more walks. As my friend Rachel would say, the sparkle came back in her eye. And it was beautiful. And I realized that even when things are hard or frustrating...there is always that moment where they're not. And we wouldn't realize how great something is, if there were never times when it wasn't great.

So I can take the bad because then good is so much sweeter. I can go for nights without sleep because the times when I do sleep all night are all the more glorious. Thankful today for a new fresh perspective and hoping that it holds out the next time this happens.

May 27, 2013 11:02pm

I wish that no news was good news. But to be honest last night was another sleepless night and today was another rough day.

Lanie was up another kilo this morning (2.2 pounds for all of us that never learned the metric system, ie EVERY SINGLE AMERICAN). That makes 3 EXTRA kilos of fluid on her in the last 3 days. 6 and a half pounds of fluid. I can't get over this. On her little normally 40 pound body that is so much weight.

On top of the fluid she's holding, she ran another high temp last night, a 104.6 temp today, and had quite a bit of tummy pain. When she wasn't sleeping today, she was either getting an ultrasound, getting X-rays, trying to do OT, or crying. We didn't go for a walk today. We didn't color. And we didn't play.

So because today was pretty hard overall I was so thankful for person after person being here. Luke and Jackson came early this morning and left about 2:00p, and then we just had so many people in and out throughout the day. I seriously love visitors. It makes every part of the day seem brighter.

So really, that's what happened in a nutshell. Sorry for such a short report today. I'm a bit discouraged...and tired...and grouchy...and Lanie's fever is starting to go back up as I write.

I know what the phrase "I'm feeling done" means now.

May 28, 2013 2:42pm

Today is one month. Really? Yes really.

I've been waiting to update today until I knew a little more about what's going on. Although I don't know the entire plan...I have a general idea and can tell what I do know.

Lanie had a rough night; a lot of stomach pain and fevers throughout the night. The plan today was to get a PICC line placed, pull the NG tube, pull the chest tube, and eat! Dude. That's a sweet plan. Even though I was tired and frustrated last night, that's a plan I can totally live with.

All morning Rachel and I sat (and by sat I mean, held Lanie while she was upset and crying...but like a champ) through a CT scan and ultrasound. I could definitely feel something in the air - the doctors and nurses acted different around us...

While we waited to hear more and why we weren't following the plan from yesterday, our favorite PICU resident came to hang out and Rachel and I worked hard to entertain Lanie. She's feeling less and less amused by us by the way. We're going to have to up our game.

Finally, I heard the knock on the door that I know so well. Our amazing transplant doctor. When he called me out into the hall, I felt my heart go up into my throat. This wasn't normal. He wasn't smiling. And then neither was I.

The news I just got was that we are heading down to surgery. Maybe this afternoon. Maybe tonight. Maybe tomorrow. Lanie's not getting better and her good days are few and far between. His plan is to reopen her incision and wash out her abdomen while also looking for sources of the problem. I'll admit it. I cried. First time to ever cry in front of our transplant doctor. I was just talking with Rachel and resident Luke about how amazing her scar

67

looks and how it's healed so beautifully! And I feel like this is 200 steps backwards... because...well...it is.

I keep trying to remember that this is a good thing to do. She'll heal so quickly once this is done. But the thought of packing up our sunset room on 5....heading back down to the PICU....and seeing her have to heal all over again feels like a bit more than I can take.

And to top it off...a stupid but disheartening thing is today is one month. A month ago today we got the call. Right now I'm sitting in the exact same room as I sat in one month ago today. #5125. My feelings are much different heading into this surgery. I know it's not a big deal, this surgery. I mean, it's not a transplant. But I'm not happy about it either. I would love to say that I'm excited because we'll find answers, but I'm not excited. I'm a little mad. I'm actually really mad. Not at people, not even necessarily at circumstances. Just because. Life today is stupid.

I feel done. I feel defeated.

And then I feel selfish because it's not even me it's happening to.

So God...reign! Pour your love out on Lanie. Fill her with love and peace. Help her to not feel bitter or sad. Let her be uplifted!

And don't let me bring her beautiful little self down.

May 28, 2013 4:41pm

So, about 30 minutes ago, Lanie headed into surgery. Yellow blanket and unicorn in hand. Already asleep from the hectic-ness of today - no pre medication required.

Doctors said it would be anywhere from 2 to 4 hours. Sitting in this OR waiting room, once again, thinking about the craziness of this last month...

Chapter 9: PICU - round 3

May 29, 2013 12:21am

Hey guys...

Sorry I haven't been able to write yet. Lanie got out of surgery around 7:00p or so but pain has been so out of control that I haven't been able to write. I feel like I'm in such a helpless state tonight. Pain still isn't under control, but Lanie doesn't seem to mind Rachel sitting beside her so I can write this quick.

Surgery went well...I mean, I guess. Dr. C, our transplant doctor came to talk to me when it was over and told me that he decided not to use her old incision because he was worried that if he opened even part of it up, all of it would be open. Instead he made a new incision on her right, front side diagonally. It's maybe 3 to 4 inches long. From that site, Dr. C was able to wash out her abdomen and take off a piece of her liver that looked problematic (he said that it maybe hadn't gotten as much blood supply to it and died, which isn't that abnormal). He also wanted to see if there was an abscess there, but didn't find anything. They also replaced a chest tube and added another drain in her abdomen, added a PICC line, and replaced her NG tube.

We've been sitting in this PICU room for a while now, hearing her cry and cry and cry, all the while I was thinking it will be better tomorrow. This will all be over soon. And then we took her temp. I realized then that it never occurred to some that there was a possibility that she would have fevers.

I thought that the only place to go from here is up.

First temp taken: 100.4

Second temp taken: 102.3

You have got to be kidding.

And I would be lying if I said I was feeling ok about it. I'm not. I'm so tired. Emotionally. Physically. Mentally. (Are there more ways I could be tired? If so, please include those in this list).

On a much, much happier note God has reigned down love on us today. Like so much. It's easy for me to believe that I'm not doing a good job and that I should advocate for her more or be selfless in my decisions (which I'm totally not...sometimes I don't want to move to the PICU because I hate the idea. I don't want to move things. I don't want to sit in those rooms. I don't want to be quiet). And just after I had a huge meltdown - sorry for everyone that had to see that - God brought food and visitors and encouragement.

And I remembered that we would get to see sweet our sweet little Saudi friend, who we loved so much. And her faithful parents. And that God really hasn't forgotten them...or us.

So yeah, I had myself a pretty good size pity party this afternoon/evening. And I feel like I've cried a good portion of today, which has not really been my style of handling things. And I have definitely had to bite my tongue when talking to nurses that don't know us. -- 6 cups of coffee, no sleep, and an emotional roller-coaster of a day is NOT a good mix. It's downright brutal, y'all.

But the night will end and morning will come. We'll wake up in the morning, drink coffee (but not 6 cups...ohhhh my stomach), listen to the doctors in rounds, thank God for a new day, and try to live it up in the PICU.

May 29, 2013 2:13pm

When today sucks, I will still give thanks.

It was such a long night. Rachel decided to stay with me when it was clear things weren't going to get easier for Lanie. She literally cried all night long with no handle on the pain. Rachel and I would get up and then as soon as Lanie even looked a little more asleep/comfortable we would jump back in our chairs, cover up with our blankets, and within minutes fall asleep. Just to be back up doing it again 15 minutes later. Lanie finally fell asleep for real at about 10:00p. Longest night/ morning ever. Help us all.

Also, her fever hit 104.2 this morning. Gross.

The plan for today is mostly to get her pain under control, get her fevers down, have her try to eat or drink a little, and maybe sit up in bed. It's gonna be a big day folks.

Because tonight and this morning was bang my head on the wall cruddy (I even dreamed of running through one of these walls and knocking myself out) ...I thought I would revisit making a list of thankfulness just so I don't spend my day staring out the sunny window and falling apart (don't feel that bad for me, it's mostly just deprivation of sleep).

Oh...and if things aren't bad enough, she tested positive for AFB. One of the bacteria that cause TB so we are in precaution, even though the doctors think that the test was wrong.

And by "in precaution", I mean that we are in a room that I was only sure was fit for ET. We're pretending that it's really awesome and fun instead of annoying.

1. The sun is out and that makes me happy. Even if I can't play in it, I'm glad that others can.

2. We were able to get 2 chairs instead of 1 in our room. Actually, this is Rachel's. I like to snuggle.

3. We got to see little bits of the old Lanie. There were times when she would talk to us that she seemed completely pain free and was just hanging out. One time in the middle of the night she was calling out for our nurse

Todd and I jumped off my chair to see what was wrong. She said "oh I'm sorry mama, I didn't want to wake you up. I just need Todd because my tummy hurts". TALK ABOUT HUMBLING! I have been so grouchy about getting up and here she is in pain and apologizing. Break my crazy heart.

4. Living it up on sunset side. PICU or no PICU, sunsets are amazing. Can't wait to see one again from outside these windows. A glass of wine might also be appropriate in this circumstance, however, I heard that the hospital might have a rule against that.

5. The team working with her is growing and growing. We are so cared for at this hospital! Already this morning, Lanie's resident doctor from upstairs and 2 nurses from 5 have come to see her and play. She is so loved!!

6. Bos, Luke, and Scott surprised us today! They only get to stay for the afternoon/early evening but I am so thrilled. Love these boys. Plus we've been able to introduce Boz to all the nurses. (He wrote Lanie an incredible song that I listen to at least 20 times a day. Every now and then I hear the nurses singing it too!!) How do I know so many amazing people?!?

7. We got so much mail today!!! We've only made it through half before Lanie fell asleep but still...exciting!

8. I'm about to take an incredibly long hot shower. So excited!

9. Her pain is a little more under control, temp is down right now, blood pressure is down, and she's sleeping. Ahhhhhhh yeah :)

10. And friends that are here that keep shouting out things to be thankful for. So I'm thankful for them :)

10:58pm

I'm laying on my chair in PICU tonight watching the storm out my big window. It's so quiet in here. No one's crying. No machines are going off. And Rachel's asleep in the other chair. The only sound is the rain and occasional thunder.

Lanie's had a good afternoon given her circumstances. She slept for like 3 or so solid hours before waking up and when she was awake, she wasn't really complaining of pain - except for an every now and then wince or little cry. When she woke up she wanted to color and play with some new books she had gotten in the mail. It was so fun. We kept saying that we could see little pieces of Lanie! And man do I miss that girl! Even now she is sleeping so soundly, her blood pressures have been good again, her heart rate is good, and pain has been really well managed! Her body is still so filled with extra fluid so she is pretty uncomfortable the majority of the time, but overall, things are already looking so much better! Lanie also sat up in bed today, with help. So sweet for one day post op.

More good news: the piece of liver that was taken out yesterday grew bacteria on some of the cultures. We now have a reason behind the fevers friends and sickness friends. Surely now, the only direction we can go is up. On top of all of that, I got to see Luke and the boys today for a couple hours. That was a really sweet surprise that I wasn't counting on.

Overall, this has been a pretty fantastic day. Especially for it being a PICU day.

Really the post should end here and I should snuggle into my chair and fall asleep (I can't believe I haven't fallen asleep standing up today). Filled with joy and rejoicing in thankfulness and a heart that is overflowing. And I almost want to end here instead of writing more, but I don't feel like I would be true to myself if I did.

In all reality, I'm lying here in the PICU chair feeling fairly sad. Or overcome. Or defeated. Or I don't even know what. And as I'm writing all of this, I completely and totally realize that today has been so good, maybe even better than good and for that I really am thankful, like I mentioned earlier today. I realize that it's silly for me to feel so fractured tonight. But I do. Maybe I can blame the lack of sleep or my longing to spend some time outside. Maybe it's because I feel super selfish in the things I do feel. Or maybe it's just because I'm having an off day. Nevertheless, it's there.

Praying that God will pull me out of this slump. Praying that God will pull away discouragement and bring joy that I know He has already given freely. Praying for refreshment and sleep for us, ready to take on the day tomorrow in our usual optimistic and excited for adventure way. And praying that I will fall asleep without over analyzing myself or the day and just leave it how it is...ready to wake up to a brand new day, where the light really does break through....

Chapter 10: A new day

May 30, 2013 2:12pm

Good morning! Or afternoon I guess. How has this day gone by so crazy fast? Last night was the first time in what felt like forever that Lanie slept. And I slept. Sweet glorious sleep. Thank you pain for finally being under control.

I finally woke Lanie up about 10a or so to see if she wanted to try to go to the bathroom. She didn't. But I'm persistent and asked her to try anyway. She's persistent too and kept saying no. Long story short, I won. We got her up to go to the bathroom and then she wanted to sit at the end of her bed for a bit. That was new...and awesome. After a couple minutes she wanted to lie in bed again so I let her. And she wanted to eat. So I, of course, let her do that too! After a few bites she was done. I was still happy.

Our PT sweet girl came in while Lanie was eating and I was a little unsure on how Lanie would do. I had just gotten her up. Once again I asked Lanie to sit at the end of the bed. Once again she said no. And once again I won. She didn't like it and complained most of the time. Then I asked her to stand so that I could just hug her and I told her how much I missed hugging her because I couldn't do it well when she was laying down. She still wasn't buying it, but once again, I was pretty persistent. I had her scoot off the end of the bed and stand. Once she stood up on her own for a bit, I something in her changed. I think she felt empowered. After that, on her own she took a couple steps to give me a hug...

And then walked to her little potty...

And then walked to the back of the room by the windows...

And then sat up in a chair to play computer games...

And then started to play with other things, which is what she's doing now.

And as she did all of these things, my heart reacted the same as it did when she took her first steps after transplant, and every other victory she's had since. Except this time, it overflowed more with the thought that she was determined and strong and believed in herself...

And all the frustrations I had been feeling lately have started to melt off my heart to make room for the hope that her persistent little attitude brings now.

It also sounds like we're moving up to 5 today. Not to our same room because of all of the precautions she's on, but 5 nonetheless. Amazing how things can change so quickly.

And now they have found two different types of bacteria that they can treat.

1. In her liver – enterococcus

2. In her lung fluid - NTM (non-tuberculosis mycobacterium) --- at least they are assuming from everything that they've seen it's this and not tuberculosis. They said it's really rare to find this and they're taking precautions for her but will just see how it plays out. Labs are still pending.

Wow. The first time in a month that we know what to treat. Such a relief. And I feel like we've finally turned a corner. And I want to be all in, but there's still caution in my heart that I wish wasn't there.

For now, I'm embracing the joy of today and feeling like a heavy load has been lifted from my shoulders. Thank you God for your wisdom, answers, strength, love, and mercy.

PS...y'all are awesome. My emotional state hasn't been so great these last couple of days and you just continue to encourage and uplift me. Thank you a million times over!

May 30, 2013 9:20pm

It's so early for it to be quiet around these parts. I'm used to having people here late and hanging out or Rachel staying with me the last few nights while in the PICU. This just feels so different. How did I do this all the time when we were inpatient before transplant? No idea. But thankful that God knows my need for people around and thankful that I am able to see that because no one is here now.

On another note, we got to move up to 5 this afternoon/early evening! We are still in precautions, so we are occupying a room on sunrise side while all of our stuff is occupying our room on sunset. So blessed by this hospital and how much they value people and their silly little needs. After we get off precautions, we'll live all in one room again.

In all actuality though, I'm starting to appreciate all sides and floors in this hospital. And starting to not complain about all the moves and switches and craziness. After all, I think it has helped to make this month fly by like it has.

Today is the first day since...well I honestly can't remember when...that Lanie hasn't taken a nap. She's been awake and mostly content since 10a when I woke her up. Praying that she will be nice and tired now tonight and will sleep well and pain free. She also got up and walked again today. I feel so bad for her every time she does. Her sweet little body is so swollen with around 6 pounds of fluid. Her legs are so tight I cringe with every step she takes. But she takes step after step after step with perseverance and determination. I love how much she teaches me.

To be honest, I can't think of much more to update. Today has been a good day. A day filled with activity, moving, friends, BBQ, fingernail polish, and peace. And I mean, really, what else can you ask for in a day?

76

May 31, 2013 10:02am

Once again, Lanie didn't sleep at all last night. So much tummy pain. It's because of God, and God alone that I am able to hear her cry night after night and not go crazy.

But something was different last night while she was crying. Normally when she cries of tummy pain, the only thing she says is "ohhhh my tummy, my tummy" and cries and cries. Last night she was TALKING more about it. She was saying things like "it just hurts so much when..." or "can you help sit me up so it won't hurt so much?" Don't get me wrong...there were lots of tears between us, but she was different. She was expressive. She was Lanie.

We've actually had a decent morning. Her tummy is hurting a lot still (mostly where her new drain is) but she has smiled at me when I was asking her questions and offering ideas about where to sit that won't bother her so much - she picked the rocker btw...adorable.

The doctor is a little concerned about her drain because bright red blood has been coming from it since last night, but not overly concerned because not a lot has come out and her labs are stable. Doctors haven't rounded yet this morning to let me know more.

And I'm honestly surrounded by peace and hope and sunshine. I've been able to read this morning, play with Lanie, watch Johnny Test, have some breakfast, help Lanie with her breakfast, and take Lanie on a walk around the room. It really is amazing how productive I can be when pesky sleep doesn't get in the way.

So my hopes are high today. I know I 'should' be cautious, but I'm not. I'm excited. And thankful. God continues to remind me that Lanie is His. He takes care of her. He knows everything that is going on her body because He created it. It's His hands that hold her at night when she cries and His strength that gets us through those rough nights.

And in all of this I've been thinking. I don't think that it's true that God doesn't give us more than we can handle. I can't handle this. I can't be thankful, on my own for sunshine and soft blankets and forehead kisses and big pink bears that I get to sleep with on nights that Lanie doesn't notice. I'm not strong...or gracious...or even kind when I use words for the most part. And if God did only give us what we could handle, what would be our need for Him? It makes more sense to me that God allows us to be involved in circumstances that we CAN'T AT ALL handle so that He can shine through. He can be exalted. And I just get to spend the morning sitting in the sunshine and being excited for the day...

Jun 1, 2013 7:19am

Happy anniversary to me!!! Good morning from the 5th floor...Room 25...Sunset side. Yep. We moved back to our room on the other side. We have gone full circle. I wrote out yesterday how many times we've moved rooms in the almost 5 weeks that we've been here. It was 9 times. For some reason that was so funny to me and I laughed about it a lot. I blame the lack of sleep and the large amount of junk food I ate yesterday for no good reason at all. Btw--that will not be happening again for a very long time. I feel so gross today.

So highlights from yesterday/last night:

- Lanie had a fever pretty soon after I wrote the last update. I was so incredibly disappointed. It stayed below 101 with Tylenol, though and I just tried to blow it off and pretend that it didn't happen. And that actually worked really well except the doctors kept reminding me.

- although Lanie's morning was a little bit rough yesterday, she started feeling a little better as the day went on. By afternoon she was playing with OT and PT, walking around a little more, and giggling some. Yep. I said it. GIGGLING! Be still my mama heart! That is the first time in honestly like forever I have heard her laugh! And she was playing. Ad shooting little gun discs and nailing targets (ok...I know this isn't pertinent information for y'all, but I love that the girl has aim. Lil Annie Oakley. I was both proud and impressed).

- I talked Lanie into washing her hair. This is a ridiculous job that we have not yet mastered. We've tried like 3 different tactics because her body can't get wet, but I think yesterday was the best so far. It was hilarious. We all got pretty wet. Lanie came out with a dry body and clean hair. Score one for Nurse Jill and I.

- we got off isolation! Which meant no more masks and moving back over to our room on the other side. And we can go for walks again, including walks outside. Which makes me very happy seeing the sun this morning over

Minneapolis and how the city is starting to wake up as the sun runs over the buildings. I'm pumped.

- Luke and Jackson came! Yay. Weekends are so fun and I love that they get to come and I can remember that we are all 4 a unit. They stayed in a really sweet hotel last night...which is a really funny - I made a bad choice story that I'd love to tell you at another time.

- Lanie was still so great by evening. She just kept livening up more and more throughout the day and by last night I was overwhelmed by her beauty and joy. This was not the Lanie I had spent the last month with. This was the Lanie that I knew pre-transplant! I couldn't stop staring at her and commenting on how great she was. It got annoying, I'm sure, but I didn't care.

- Lanie started having tummy pain again around 845. It came on pretty quick and it took me a bit by surprise after our day that we'd just had. She complained on and off for a couple hours, but nothing like before. A sweet girl from Iowa City showed up about 1015 and the 3 of us talked (well Lilli and I talked, Lanie watched 'good luck Charlie') until midnight. I know, I am in no way winning any 'mom of the year' awards. I've accepted this fact.

- Lilli stayed the night with us and it was such a good night. Lanie only woke up a couple times and even those times weren't a big deal. I decided to just sleep with Lanie last night just in case she had a rougher night and we both slept so well. It was a short night - in bed by midnight, up at 530 - but it was good.

- Lanie woke up this morning and she even looked better. She got up and wanted to sit in the big recliner again. Yay! And when the nurse came in to weigh her, we noticed that she had lost a kilo from yesterday! Plus you can just tell by looking at her that she isn't so full of fluid! I guess she still has 2 kilos of fluid on her but a whole kilo gone in a day?? Yes! C'mon kidney!!! Keep peeing out liters of fluid!

I have nothing but great thoughts toward today. The sun is still shining and we may even venture outside. My friend Lilli is here and some college friends are coming to hang out later. The boys are here and Lanie is having a splendid morning. Yep...my hopes are staying high.

PS: it's June 1st. Quite a few years ago today I married my best friend. Since that time, our lives have been a serious adventure. To have seen what was in our future, there is a good chance that I would have run and hid. But looking back, I can see how God has just weaved Himself throughout, tangling in and out of our choices, both good and bad. I'm so blessed and thankful to have shared so many years of my life with the same person, who knows me better than anyone else. I would say 'I do' over and over and over again. (Maybe next time, on a beach). Luke...I would follow you anywhere. Thanks for choosing me.

Jun 1, 2013 7:48pm

Hey friends!! I've had another 'lesson learned' day and I thought I would share it with all of you...in chronological order of course, because otherwise it would all be a blur in my mind...

Lesson #1: 4.5 hours of sleep has become a full night's rest. This whole 8 hours thing is so overrated and it turns out there are a lot of things you can do with all that extra time like....hmmm...okay yeah, I'd rather be sleeping.

Lesson #2: I love love love sleepovers! Just having someone else in the room with me at night makes all things better. I know. I'm ridiculous, but it's true.

Lesson #3: I'm so clumsy in the mornings. I don't know how I usually work out as soon as I get up at home. Here I'm tripping over everything and bumping into random things. This morning topped it off when I fell in the shower trying to shave. But really hospital showers are like long standing boxes. I'm only so flexible before it all falls apart.

Lesson #4: I haven't spent this much time 'getting ready' in over a month. Being a woman can be hard work. Showering. Straightening my hair. Moisturizer. Makeup. Getting dressed. I actually had a lot of fun though. I should do this more often in the hospital. Crazy how much more alive I feel when I don't spend the day in yoga pants.

Lesson #5: Ronald McDonald is much different in person than I anticipated. Don't ask me how, because I don't know. Just different. Also...he's huge! I didn't even come to his shoulders! Lanie and Jackson on the other hand were very entertained. I was impressed by how much they loved having their picture with him. I did not.

Lesson #6: if you keep asking Lanie to walk farther, she will. And she won't really complain about it. I sometimes worry that I push her too hard, but then I remember that she's a beast and that people cheering her on, or doing something 'better than her' is her best motivation. We are almost the same people, me and her.

Lesson #7: College friends are amazing. I love how we may not see each other for a while, but when we do we laugh and laugh and laugh. You can always pick up right where you leave off, just as if you are in each other's day to day life. Brent and Sarah. I love you. Not many people make me laugh quite like you! Side note - how is everyone I know and that comes to visit me 7 feet tall??? I looked at our picture today and realized how short I really am. It doesn't seem like that in real life. Pictures obviously distort things.

Lesson #8: I love elk! And I realize what a precious commodity this is. So if I share it with you, it means I have a special place in my heart for you.

Lesson #9: I am physically able to leave the hospital and the world will not implode. Luke and I were given tickets to the Twins game today by some sweet folks. I just happened to already have a twins shirt with me, so hey. Thanks God for helping me to pack for the unknown. I had to take deep breath after deep breath when we finally started walking out of the hospital.

Lesson #10: Fear is a jerk. There is a reason that God said over and over 'don't be afraid' or 'be strong and courageous'. There is nothing good, or true, or noble about fear. In all actuality, fear pulls us away from God...not towards. And that's exactly what happened when I stepped outside of those hospital doors. Fear crept in. Fear that Lanie would start feeling worse and I wouldn't be there to take care of her. Fear that the doctors would come to tell us something so incredibly important and I wouldn't be there to make a decision. And fear of what the world (as in the doctors/nurses/our friends/all of you/and every person outside of this hospital) would think of me, leaving my sick daughter in the hospital to go out and live it up in downtown Minneapolis, even if it was for just a few hours. It wasn't until I got back to the room I realized how silly I was being. The honest truth is that even if I was here, I still have absolutely no control over whatever situation happened. And God isn't a God of shame...or fear. And so just because I was believing that I was a horrible mom for leaving, doesn't mean I am one. I'm still working through this issue...hence the scattered thoughts.

Lesson #11: I love steak...and walleye. I was a chicken girl forever. But I have seen the error of my ways and am forever changed. Thank you to all who have made this realization possible. You know who you are... PS - I went with steak and veggies tonight and loved every single amazing bite.

Lesson #12: Lanie has had a great day...despite my fear of the world ending when I left. She giggled more tonight at Luke and Jackson than I have seen in a long time. Laughter really is the very best medicine.

Thanks for listening to all of the new things I'm learning about on this crazy adventure that we are on. I'm sure y'all are shaking your heads at these realizations that you've known for years and my naive self is just learning. Thanks for helping to teach me some of these lessons through your support and encouragement. I am literally blown away by the newness that comes with every day.

Chapter 11: Lanie...and also Jackson

Jun 2, 2013 7:38pm

Where in the world did this beautiful, sunshiny day go?? Here it is 8:00 and I feel like I was just drinking my morning coffee and stretching last night's sleep away. I think that honestly been a gift from God in and of itself...time flying. It's not that I don't love all the things I'm learning about and the time I've gotten to spend here in the hospital with my little Lanie Lou, but usually time in the hospital drags on and on and on and then I look at the clock and realize its only 11am. Ugh. Man, is that a killer. God has blessed us with the gift of a quick 5 weeks here. Crazy.

Well Lanie has had another great day! I was a little worried last night after I wrote. She started throwing up, actually quite a bit compared the small amounts of food she's been eating. And then having quite a bit of tummy pain. Just as I was starting to get really discouraged though, she started feeling better again. Her smile returned and the pain meds kicked back in. Nights are a little rougher anyway, so I try to always keep that in mind when the sun starts to go down. Grandma and grandpa also were able to come late last night. And they brought gifts. And that cheered her right up.

Lanie's night was decent as well. Luke stayed here with us and split his time between cuddling me and cuddling Lanie. That was a blessing in and of itself. She woke up a couple times with tummy pain, but with a new pain med we're trying, pain seems to be more under control than before.

And this morning was so good! My sweet friend, Leah ran her first marathon this morning here in Minneapolis! And she ran it for Lanie! I have been so humbled by this. Every time I woke last night and then this morning, I haven't stopped thinking about her and praying for her! The finish line was not even a mile from the hospital and I tried and tried and tried to figure out a way to get Lanie there, but nothing that I could think of would work. Jackson says that Leah is his best friend, so I figured if I couldn't get Lanie there to cheer her on, I could get Jackson. We made it maybe 10 minutes to our spot before we saw Leah coming up in the distance. Oh my goodness, y'all...I was cheering so loud! Jackson asked if he could run the last little piece with her and I said I didn't care (I hope that she didn't either!) and together they finished the race holding hands. 26.2 miles. I was so humbled and proud of her. My heart was overflowing. And there's a good chance she finally realized that I'm a bit crazy when I just started crying when sent her medal back with Jackson to show Lanie. I adore that girl...that whole family really.

Grandma and grandpa have also been here all day. Lanie has beat grandma in more games of crazy 8 than I can even count. And grandpa is trying to get Lanie to watch 'River Monsters'...which by the way, she usually LOVES, but I think she's playing hard to get. The boys left about 3p and once again it was hard to let them go. Jackson felt a little better when I told him that he would get to go to the farm tomorrow for a week or so with grandma and grandpa after his last day of school. That will be so great for him. That kid is incredibly and I don't get to brag on him enough.

My Jackson brag...

The kid is awesome. He takes care of Lanie better than any of us sometimes. He knows what she needs and just does it. Example...the lights were hurting her eyes for a while when she was still having bad headaches and he was always hold his hand up and shield her eyes. Or he gets her whatever she asks for. His heart is so kind and he cares so much about people in general. His future wife will be one of the luckiest women that walk this planet. I pray for her regularly.

He is also so incredibly creative. He can paint, draw, sing, and do anything in the world that has to do with innovative creativity. He also is a beast at dodge ball. He is his father inside and out. The one way he is completely different from Luke, Lanie, and I in that he isn't that competitive. He just doesn't really care about winning like we all do. He would rather just enjoy himself. Crazy, I know. And I love him for it.

He would rather have adventures than things and actually sold a majority of his toys (with the exception of his beloved legos and lizard) so that he could have money to visit our foreign exchange student from 2 years ago in Georgia. Ps. I don't think he realizes how much plane tickets to foreign countries are but his heart is so sincere. And he attaches to people hard. And hates to see them leave. Man, I love his sweet spirit.

Little Jackson fun fact...the kid LOVES coffee. He asks for a frappuccino every single day and hardly puts any cream in when we do allow him a little coffee. I tell him it'll stunt is growth and he told me once 'I don't care. I'm not playing basketball'. And I mean...how can you argue with that?

So here's to another fever free, sunshiny, feel good day. Living in thankfulness and pure blessing of God's abundance and grace. Love you guys with my whole heart ~ Ali

Jun 3, 2013 1:29pm

Good morning! I realized I should start updating in the morning again too. (Okay...I know it's almost noon, but I started this update at least 3 hours ago...thought that counts, right?) If for no other reason than to make the updates less lengthy and because the nights have been progressively getting worse.

Lanie started complaining of tummy pain about 9:00 last night and cried pretty consistently about it until she fell asleep a little after midnight. That time of night is a beast and I like to pretend all day that it won't happen, but then the sun goes down and reality kicks in. By the way, the sunset was incredible last night. I tried to distract Lanie but she mostly just got annoyed.

Last night was also the second night in a row that she threw up. This is new. Most of the time I like new. At the hospital, I don't necessarily like new. She was so stinking sweet through it though. She apologized for crying and for not being able to calm down. She also asked if I could hold her hair because she would've hated to throw up in it. And she asked the nurse if they wanted her to save it or if she could just throw it away. Sweet little doll. Side note: nurses don't want to see your vomit. I'm sure of it.

Doctors rounded this morning and didn't have much to say. Chest tube would come out today still leaving her with a drain over her liver, NG tube, and her PICC. It's so good to see more and more things going away...finally.

She also had a small fever again this morning. Such weird little things that we're not going to worry about but trying not to ignore either.

She's finally doing well again this afternoon. Coloring paper dolls and beating me at go fish. Did I mention before how I hate to lose? Yep. Even in go fish. And even to a 7 year old. This next game is mine...

Until later this evening...adios.

AND I'm sorry for the scatteredness of this update. It was written in between doctors visiting, tummy aches, coffee breaks, and hugging the grandparents goodbye. Thanks for your constant patience!

Jun 4, 2013 8:31am

So I started writing an update at least 3 times yesterday and then would get distracted. I'm easily distracted, so this isn't an abnormal thing. I'll just do a brief recap so that I don't drive you guys crazy with pages and pages of random talking.

- Lanie had a chest x ray done, which showed she didn't have any fluid over her lung meaning that we were able to get the chest tube out. That was so exciting to me. I love not having another piece of plastic in her, and one more out means one more step closer to outpatient.

- She ate so much more than past days (still not near where she needs to be eating but still). This is a huge deal and brings us closer to getting the NG out.

- Physical therapy went so well. She's been getting more excited about playing with the PT and OT and I love that

- So many sweet visitors came yesterday! First we had two sweet little princesses that came to sing songs from 'Wicked' and 'The Sound of Music' to Lanie. At first while they were here, she just watched and watched them, somewhat hiding under her yellow blanket, but the longer they stayed, the more she opened up to play with them. By the end of the time, the girls had colored, played games, and played with her AG dolls. So sweet for Lanie to have some girls to play with! Thank you, Shawn, May, and Kenzie for such a fun time!

- One of our favorite resident doctors, Luke, came by too, which was a surprise to us because he had the day off. Lanie had been asking every day for lucky charms (gross, but that's what she's really craving) and Luke came bearing the gift of cereal. Lanie was so happy and perked up so much after that. She talked about it all night. Luke...you are awesome. Thank you!

- The return of Rachel! Man I missed that girl this weekend! Just so incredibly thankful for her mere presence. She embodies joy. And she brought me a Jimmy John's unwich...so yep. I love her.

- More visitors! Russ, Ann, Bruce, and Nancy! We love love love visitors so every single person that comes is such a great gift.

- Last night went ok, which is much better than the last couple of nights. The doctors gave her Zofran which I think helped with nightly 'throwing up' episodes. They also gave her some meds to help her sleep, which also helped. She did start complaining of tummy pain around 6:30 but it was much more intermittent than the last couple of nights. It lasted til about 10 when she finally fell asleep. She woke up a few times throughout the night, but nothing ever major and she went back to sleep quickly after each time.

- And now we're caught up to this morning. Lanie was up earlier this morning complaining of tummy pain, but has just recently fallen back asleep. Waiting on more doctors to round to see what the plan for today is and what the morning X-ray showed.

Chapter 12: Best. Days. Ever!

Jun 5, 2013 12:01am

Oh my goodness you guys! Day #37 will officially go into the history books as one of the best days ever... Why?

1. Someone else made me coffee (i.e. Rachel) and it was delicious.

2. Lanie got to eat her Lucky Charms for breakfast. She hasn't been eating that well but she ate the whole bowl! Her transplant doctor also brought her a box today so she is more than set on cereal. Maybe now she'll eat better!

3. Mail day! Lanie loves mail day! We got to open cards and notes from friends. So incredibly sweet y'all! ALSO! In one of our moves to the PICU, my insanity DVD's were lost. For those of you that know me know that I LOVE insanity. And I can do it in the hospital so that's awesome (well I haven't really been able to do it much this time because it has been CRAZY and then they got lost). Today Insanity came in the mail!! Oh my word. Thank you thank you thank you Jill! What an amazing mama you are and from the bottom of my cardio loving heart -- I love you! Rachel...suit up. Tomorrow we are going to own this workout.

4. At like 10:30 this morning, Lanie told us she wanted to go for a walk. We couldn't go right away because doctors are literally in our room all morning discussing and creating plans, and trying to figure this sweet little girl of

mine out. Once she was able to go for a walk though she has not slowed down. We literally walked this whole hospital today...like 7 times.

5. Not much for plan changes today. We did stop 2 of her thousands of antibiotics (what do you mean exaggerate?) and upped her diuretic because she's holding onto fluids again, but other than that...plan = walk, eat, play, pee, PT, OT, be a kid...easy enough

AND THE BEST FOR LAST...

6. She was so 'Lanie' today! She talked, giggled, played, walked, got sassy, was bossy, was generous, was so sweet with the nurses, hugged me, sat on my lap, ate grilled cheese, played in a fort that she made with our nurse - Natalie, crawled, squatted, climbed, reached, washed her hair, rode a trike, and even jogged for a split second. WHAT?!? Alaina is a STUD!

7. No crying, throwing up, or staying up late tonight! She fell asleep around 9:00 and has been sleeping really well since then!

I can't even believe we had such a great day! It's been so different from any of our days here. Usually we have a good 10 minutes/half hour/couple

hours etc. but TODAY has been good. You could see that she was starting to wear down a lot tonight, as completely expected. She worked and played so hard today! She was out of her bed from around 11a until 8:30 tonight. And she was busy.

Thank you God for today. Thank you that I got to see my little Lanie Lou. Thank you that her confidence was built back up throughout the day. Thank you for all of the people cheering her on. Thank you for our nurses and doctors...always taking care of us. And thank you for sweet gifts. Praying against worry that tomorrow won't be just as wonderful...

Jun 6, 2013 9:30am

Day 38 - 39:

Another good day yesterday and today! And such a busy day that I forgot to update. Sorry you guys!

Highlights from yesterday (by the way...I hope to never forget to update again. Time is like a blur here and I forget what happens from day to day)

- woke up early yesterday morning early with some tummy pain, but once I laid in bed with her she calmed down and we fell asleep again for a bit like that. I love holding her. I know that since her kidney is working like a champ she'll start to grow and I'm honestly feeling so weird about that, but also excited for her. I guess she won't be little forever. Better take advantage of every single sleepy second of cuddling I have now.

- Rachel and Lanie decided to throw a birthday party for her AG doll. This seems like no big deal, but let me tell you. The planning that went into this...it might as well have been a wedding. Once Lanie was up and feeling better yesterday, the party planning commenced. We cleaned the room, decorated, made invitations, made popsicles, made cakes (I'm not crazy into Pinterest, but thankful for cake that takes water and a microwave. AND are delicious. Everyone was impressed), passed out invitations all around the hospital, and dressed up the dolls. - By the way, you guys...you can so tell that this was Rachel's brilliant idea and not mine. My ideas usually have nothing to do with dolls, planning, or creativity. The CAKE however was my only idea. This whole thing literally took until the party started at 3.

- Lanie felt so good. There was even a time when she ran a bit holding on to her wheelchair. AMAZING.

- So many adorably sweet people came to her birthday party for her doll, ate her cake, and sang happy birthday. I was pretty shocked, actually. I mean. It's a doll. But Lanie was so happy!!!! Oh my goodness. She just took her picture with all the staff and played and laughed. Doing real things and being able to get her out of this room has been so good for her.

- John Sullivan (center for the Vikings?) came to the hospital yesterday also and had the grand opening for the new park that he paid for. Oh my goodness, there are slides that kids with IV Poles can go down and different things to play on for everyone! Lanie was a little skeptical at first because she thought it would hurt and she was worried about the pole, but within minutes was going up and down the ladder to go again. This is the most movement she's had in...Well...close to 40 days.

- My sweet friend Suzie came! And brought cookies and coffee cake and all things delicious. Shame on her!!! We shared with the nurses.

- Lanie literally played almost until she fell asleep. She did cry for a bit before bed time, saying her tummy was hurting, but fell asleep pretty soundly not long after. Last night was ok. She was up but not really crying. Just up. I almost gave in and told her she could watch cartoons at 3:00a but something inside me shouted no. I went with that, but promised myself that if she woke up again in the next 30 minutes she could have whatever the heck she wanted. No questions asked. Thankfully she didn't. She slept til 5 and then I got in bed with her and we 'slept' until 7:00am.

- This morning was fairly rough. Lanie didn't feel great at all and cried a lot about tummy pain. When doctors rounded they told us that her hemoglobin was pretty low and the she would need another blood transfusion. The later part of the morning was spent getting ultrasounds and X-rays trying to figure out why and where she was bleeding. I haven't heard any results yet.

- After the transfusion Lanie started to feel so much better. She got a trike today and has literally been riding it all afternoon. It's a two-seater so I have ridden on the front, on the back, and ran beside her. Her favorite is for me to drive and pedal. Let me tell ya, that works some muscles I didn't know existed. So that was fun.

It has been so good for her to get out of her room and enjoying the people and things in the hospital. She is so much happier and I am just standing back in awe of her and her sweet spirit, hoping that we are all that much closer to going outpatient.

Lanie still has her NG tube, liver drain, Heparin drip, and narcotic IV drugs that we need to get rid of before heading out, but I feel like every day we are so much closer. The last few days have been a party. Literally 24/7. Yep I definitely party in my sleep. And I don't know just how much longer she can be contained by these walls.

Thanking God today for his millions of miracles. Oh how He loves us!

Chapter 13: Overwhelmed with love

Jun 8, 2013 12:21am

Yep. It's day #40. It really looks similar to the last couple of days so I'm always unsure if I should update or not. Last night was ok at best, sleeping wise. God has granted me the sweet gift of being able to sleep anytime, anywhere. It's coming in so useful now...oh, and also in college. Lanie woke up this morning at about 2, 3, and 6 am and cried some until she fell asleep. At 7am she woke up again and cried for a while, until about 830 or so that her tummy and head were hurting, but mostly tummy. She finally fell asleep around 830 and didn't wake up again til 1030 and then was feeling great! Doctors decided not to change anything today (ya know, cause the weekend and all) and see how she does with eating on her own, peeing and getting rid of the 4 - 5 extra fluid pounds that she's holding onto, and managing pain and sleeping. It's actually a great idea, I think, to hold steady on everything and see how this plays out. Doctors were a little concerned about her breathing and coughing, but attribute it to the excess fluid... That sounds like an easy fix so I'll take it.

Lanie felt well from around 1045am until about 745pm! That's awesome and a huge improvement! We need to get nights and early mornings under control and then we'll be golden.

A few highlights during that time...

1. Lanie and Nurse Brittany played a lot this morning together
2. We had a picnic lunch
3. A baby (lil James) came to visit us (he brought his amazing parents too of course)
4. Luke and Calie came to play.
5. Everyone rode on Lanie's trike that is here for physical therapy. I don't know what they all complain about. My knees fit pretty decent :)
6. Lanie played forever in her fort - props to nurse Natalie!!
7. Lanie got to play at the new park IV free for a few hours!
8. As I'm typing this, Lanie and her daddy are sleeping together in her bed

So yeah. It's been another good day. We MUST get nights and mornings under control...

And Wow. It really has been 40 days. That seems so crazy and I just keep wondering 'how in the world did we make it this far?'. I thought about this hospital visit and how it was a little different from other visits and tried to figure out why. The biggest reason I can think of (other than God's amazing grace, of course) is you! Your cards, emails, texts, visits, gifts, thoughts, generosity, food, and prayers have been insane and beautiful. Rachel and I started writing thank you cards for everything, and then honestly we got so overwhelmed by the generosity, time, and money of others and just couldn't honestly keep up with all of the thank you's and do well with every day hospital life. So until we can get your thank out...please consider this incredibly informal thank you from our family to yours.

And thank you all for keeping up with us. I hope that I can do just as great of a job sharing the love you have given to us! WE LOVE YOU!

Jun 9, 2013 9:02am

Day 41 - yesterday
Day 42 – today

Literally nothing medical has happened this weekend. Medically, Lanie still has the JP drain in her liver, NG tube, PICC line, 6 antibiotics, 9 oral meds, Heparin drip for the blood clots, and still wears occasional oxygen. She also, as of her weight yesterday, has around 7 extra pounds of fluid on her. She still has some trouble in the evenings with tummy pain and early mornings until about 10 or 11 are somewhat rough as well. So really, she is really good for like 8 hours out of the day!

How we filled those 8 hours yesterday...

1. We had visitors all day. Like seriously. All day. The days fly by when people are here and we could not be more excited for people to come! They started coming to visit around 9am or so and our last ones left 11p. Thank you God for fully understanding my need for people!

2. We're walkoholics. Lanie is anyway. After being kept in a room (well actually 9 different rooms, but who's counting) for over a month, the girl wants out. She walks around our unit, down to the lobby, to the library, to the gift shop, to the park outside that just opened this week, and out to the walkways. If she's not walking, she's riding her trike around all of those places. Also! Her trike is a double-seater. So I'm pretty sure that almost every single person that has visited and gone on walks with us has ridden that trike as well. Let me tell you, those are not made for adults.

3. Luke and I took a walk over to Starbucks and then walked around the park for a bit while Lanie played with our friends (thank you Calie and Leah!). It was only like 45 minutes but it was so nice to get out again and just be outside. By the way, Minnesota. It's June. I should be basking in the warmth of your sun when I'm out, not wearing a sweatshirt. Let's get it together already.

4. Besides lifting heavy things, Lanie has no physical restrictions. (Well our kidney doctor was a little nervous about her running but...) she's now mastered walking, running (shhhhhh), stairs, squatting, kneeling, bending, crawling, reaching, climbing, and all sorts of other playing. Because she has so much water weight on her though, there are some things we have to be careful of. Yesterday she was playing in the fort in her room and she crawled out and we noticed blood all over the front of her shirt. I was trying to not make a big deal out of it, but she definitely started to freak out. The bottom of her midline incision opened up just a little from all of the pressure plus the added activity. A few steristrips and a big bandage (as well as a shirt that had be thrown away) and she was good as new. I did make her rest and watch a movie for a bit after that though.

5. Entertaining ourselves when Lanie no longer thinks that we're fun or funny. I know that this is incredibly hard to believe but sadly it's true. Entertaining ourselves however is great fun. These last 41 days have helped me to perfect my dance moves, singing abilities, how high and far I can jump, as well as uncover many other abilities I didn't even know that I had. Sometimes it takes being stuck somewhere for a while to discover all the hidden talents we possess. Thank you, hospital, for that.

And that pretty much sums up our yesterday. I also started cleaning out our room yesterday - high hopes for going outpatient soon - so that I could start sending a lot of our things home with Luke today. I feel like Lanie is doing so much better and my hope and prayer is that we would only have another week or so inpatient. I know we have a lot of tests and whatnot (ultrasounds of her legs, abdomen, and heart, EEG, EKG, X-rays, liver and kidney function tests, and classes for me on how to take care of her) this week to see how everything's doing. After all of that we should know quite a bit more about what discharge to outpatient will look like.

We are still so humbled by all of you. When I stop and think about you guys and how God has used you to impact our family, I am blown away. I'm wrecked by it, actually. God's love is so real you guys. And you are all just one way that He speaks it to me. I was thinking about this so much yesterday and this morning. That this story isn't about a brave, strong, amazing girl. It isn't about spending time in the hospital and what that looks like. And it's definitely not about me and my ramblings about how to make

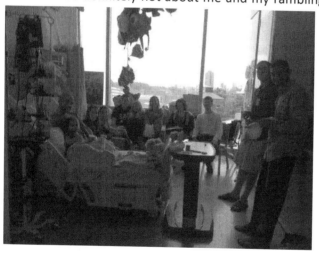

sense of it all. It's about God's provision, and His character. His love and grace seeping out of the envelopes you guys send and the food we eat. His mercy abounding in the experiences and times we spend with friends, not entertaining them but enjoying them. His heart that breaks when I walk around the PICU and unit 5 and see His little children crying and in pain...our little sweet Saudi friend spending almost a year now in a hospital room, mom's and dad's with weary faces and sweet little guys and girls experiencing life - all the hardships, joys, struggles, laughter, and tears while living in the hospital. Stories are good because they're about God. Not because they're about us. Donald Miller wrote a book called 'A Million Miles in a Thousand Years'. - I'm not even ashamed of this plug. It's so good and talks about the elements of story and how God gives us stories to live that people would actually like to watch...because it's about Him in the end and not us. And as I look around me, there are millions of those stories. Going on around us every day. It's incredible. Pieces of God interwoven in daily lives. It's beautiful y'all!

Thank you for reminding me of that these last few days. I'm stronger and wiser because of it. Love you guys and so happy to be able to live this story with you...

Jun 11, 2013 10:43pm

Hey guys! Sorry! You probably thought that we disappeared there for a while. I think that I assume that if we are having good days then I'm just really repeating myself a lot, even if it's good repeating. And who really wants to hear a repetitive story? No one. But then I realized today that it's not completely repetitive. The good things that happened today and yesterday are way different from the good things that happen on other days and even a little update is better than none. Moral of the story is that I'll buckle down and do a better job.

Yesterday was another day of playing for Lanie, Rachel, and I. Seriously, John Sullivan. You built the best park and I will cheer so much louder for the Vikings because of you. They can thank you and Chad Greenway for that. And also Adrian Peterson because that kid can for real run.

We really thought yesterday that we were going to be clearly out the door, living it up in outpatient world, maybe as soon as tomorrow. Lanie's had quite a few good days of playing. She's 'graduated' from both PT and OT and we can hardly keep up with her. That IV pole is nothing short of a nuisance. Last night, however, was a little rougher than the previous few. She had tummy pain again before bed and didn't fall completely asleep until midnight. Once asleep, the night was good. I woke up this morning about 7am, wanting time to just be thankful for a night of sleep and excited for another good day bringing us closer to tomorrow...discharge to outpatient. This is how the day went from there...

745 - Our favorite Resident Doctor, Luke, came to talk to me about such a sweet surprise he's putting together for Lanie. She is so loved by the doctors and nurses here. I am in awe of their compassion and generosity and just how well the team here connects with patients. We really do love this place.

From whatever time Dr. Luke left until 1030 – I showered and actually spent a little time on my hair and makeup for no reason except Lanie was still sleeping...and why not? That time also included a dance party in the bathroom while getting ready session with Rachel and there's no telling how long that lasted. Time flies when you're having fun. Doctors also rounded sometime in there but didn't say much. I mean the plan was to go home tomorrow.

1030 - Transplant coordinators come, embarrassing us only a little because we were still dancing it up in the bathroom. They refreshed me on all things transplant and meds and I remember why I'm scared to go outpatient. Still not completely certain that I know how to take care of Lanie well. I had a mild panic attack in my head that I'm gonna screw all this up and then reminded myself that I can act normal now and read all the literature over and over again like crazy later.

12p - Finally got Lanie to wake up. She literally slept all morning. Crazy. I just assumed it was because she was up so late with belly pain last night.

12p - 145 - Lanie cried that her right side was really hurting. She didn't want to get up and play or really do anything. This is so unlike her the last few days. The only thing off on her labs was that her platelets were low. We also noticed small red pinpoint looking bruises on Lanie's back. All the doctors came in to look and then said that they were going to order another X-ray and an ultrasound just to see. Ok.

145 - 645 - Sweet visitors! It was so fun to spend our day with the Lynch/Golly family! Oh my word they are such a blessing to us! They brought their sweet daughters Mary and Katie who just livened Lanie right up. They came with us to ultrasound and kept her entertained the better part of the afternoon. Those girls were seriously the medicine Lanie needed today! She also got unhooked from her pole during this time! They stopped the heparin until we knew what was going on from this morning so we were good to go. We were so overwhelmed by love both for and from this family. God is using them in sweet and beautiful ways to show His compassion and

love! We played in the room, on the floor, in the library, in the new park, and then all got to enjoy dinner together, and then said goodbye to our sweet visitors - PLUG - The restaurant 'Crave' located in beautiful downtown Minneapolis is awesome. Twice now in the 46 days that we've been here they have catered in food to patients and families. Good food. Luke and I also went there for our anniversary. I recommend the steak and veggies. You will not be disappointed. And if you do go, please tell them thank you for being generous and providing such an incredible gift to all of us here...

7pm - Came back up stairs. Good news, bad news. Good news - Lanie doesn't have this thing they were really concerned about with her platelets and clotting. Blood work showed everything to be A ok. Bad news - the ultrasound showed a pocket of fluid below her spleen, which is on her side, which is where she was holding and crying all morning. More bad news - we're not going outpatient tomorrow. With all the different changes today and now this pocket of fluid, she needs to really be watched closely for the next couple of days to make sure she's still good. I made myself feel better by telling myself that I am so glad this happened inside the hospital so she can be watched and I'm so thankful we're not going outpatient yet. In reality, it made me both want and fear outpatient all the more. Go figure.

730 - I told Lanie her NG tube got to come out today. She was scared to have a nurse pull it so I just told her that I would take the tape off and let it fall out, hoping that made it seem less scary. And who can blame the girl for being a little worried. I mean, it's a tube she can feel both in her nose and in the back of her throat. Gross. Gag. Ick. She let me take the tape off and then realized the tube was just hanging there. She didn't like that either and started to pull it out. That a girl! Through a little gagging and choking (on my part just as much as on her part) the NG tube was out in no time. Oh my word, y'all. That thing was long. Goodbye gross tube!

8p – we finally settled in for the night and rested some...and yes I let her watch a movie. Around 845 she really started struggling again though saying she thought she was going to throw up and that her tummy and side hurt so bad. I honestly have no idea why this is happening again for her but I guess we'll know more in the morning. She finally fell fully asleep around 11p

And now it's 2am and I'm still wide awake. My mind literally trying to just process the day and Lanie over sleeping not at all soundly (crying, whimpering, and moving all over the place) on her bed...feeling a slight bit of concern for the things going on with Lanie so close to outpatient and

99

nervous I'll go a little crazy, even though I love our little 'studio room apartment' and it's amazing view and family of nurses and doctors, if we have to stay inpatient much longer.

I'm taking applications, by the way, for people who want to come over to the hospital in the middle of the night when I like to process things and listen to me go on and on and on about how I don't know how to be a good mom and how I can't wait to go outpatient, but it's also scary, and how God is so so so good and just showers us with blessings and I how have no clue how to accept gifts well (I don't think it's an acceptable response to say 'shut up!' when someone gives you something, hmmmm...noted) and to tell me that it's ok that I'm a bit crazy and that I am loved and that this is just a season. And that person can give me a huge hug because that's how the end of talks like that go. And please...don't all jump up and apply at once for this amazing opportunity.

Tomorrow will be fine. In all honesty it will be better than fine because we'll keep on playing and dancing and praying and enjoying. We'll keep living this crazy adventure until it's time for a new one. And I can fall asleep easier resting in that.

Goodnight sweet friends! And sorry for my erratic ramblings. This is what happens when I go too long without writing apparently.

Chapter 14: So much fun. We're bound to get kicked out...

Jun 13, 2013 1:20pm

So yesterday...

Lanie woke up so early! And after going to bed so late the night before, I must admit, I was super nervous. Mostly we just played all day though! We played inside all morning because it was storming, had a picnic lunch in one of the family rooms, and then it got sunny and hot so we went outside to play at the park. Doctor Luke told us he had a surprise for Lanie, but I had honestly forgot about it and just had so much fun playing outside that it took us a long time to come back in.

When we got back up to our room, Doctor Luke was already up here waiting for us, and once we got a little settled, in walks Miss Minnesota, 2011! She is the most adorable thing, y'all. We had so much fun playing with her and hearing all about her sweet and generous lifestyle. And she was just so great with Lanie! They stayed forever and we all just played - We older girls maybe had a fun time trying on the Miss Minnesota sash and crown as well. How could we not??

After that, my sweet new friend Chloe came to hang out. I was so thankful for her company. Rachel and Sue had to leave a little early last night, so Chloe was a sweet little gift. She stayed and watched movies and hung out. So nice! We couldn't get Lanie to sleep for a while though...that pesky tummy pain! Another late night for her.

And then today...

This morning I woke her up around 8am. 2 reasons. Reason #1 - tire the girl out so she'll sleep normal hours at night. I know. This might not be great parenting, but with going outpatient soon, I want her back to some sort of schedule. Reason #2 - doctor Luke was coming to have breakfast with her (lucky charms of course) and to tell her goodbye. Neither reason was great, but that's how my mind functions.

She's been doing so well this morning too! We've already played a ton. We've heard a lot of chatter about discharge sometime between right this minute and Saturday. I started packing up our room just in case. It's funny how I know I should be so excited about discharge. And I am. I really am, mostly. Lanie is literally busting out of this place, and there isn't a lot holding us in. But also, today is day #47 in the hospital. I love this place. I know that I am always ready to go, but also I'm kinda not. My mind starts to swirl a little. I'm gonna miss my nurse friends on 5 like crazy. Literally we've spent every day together. And then there are those pesky thoughts that ask me what I'm going to do if Lanie gets sick? Or has tummy pain? Am I going to be able to give her shots twice a day ok? What if I mess it up? - I gave her the first one this morning, but what if something else happens with them? How do I know how far to push her physically? How do I make sure labs are done when they need to be? When will I know if we're ready for home? What if I forget to put on sunscreen and she gets burned because of her meds? What if we're out someplace and something happens??? Gahhhh! It's so much to think about.

But then there's the other side of me. The much much MUCH quieter side. This side tells me that things are fine. I'm aloud to freak out. And this is why there is such a thing as outpatient. If I have a question...call. Or come. It's not like I'm alone. And outpatient is gonna be a blast. Seriously! Hanging out at parks and having fun, having no responsibilities for a month all over this great city? Sign me up! And I didn't think I could do transplant either. And look where God has brought us...

The trick today will be to listen to the quiet side. And pack. Just in case...

Chapter 15: Transplant - phase 2 and Outpatient 101

Jun 14, 2013 10:05pm

So it's the end of day 48. At about 4:00p today we walked out of our 5th floor room, down the hall, out the double doors, in and out of the elevator, through the lobby, and then finally out of the front doors of Amplatz Children's Hospital. Outpatient. These last couple days have been such a roller-coaster and because I feel somewhat - fine....VERY - emotional for a million different reasons tonight (no worries, I won't go into detail on why I've spent 60% of today crying) I'm going to make another 'but I'm still thankful' list.

In chronological order again, because we all know my memory is horrible otherwise.

The things I'm thankful for...

1. Sunshine. Rachel, Lanie, and I literally spent so much time outside yesterday playing at the park (yep...been there every day), having a picnic dinner outside, and going for walks. I might have spent some of that time just laying on the ground and soaking up the sun. I'm not scared of those tiny little red bugs, so it's all good.

2. Our resident Doctors. Oh my goodness. I'm sure that doctors do these things for everyone, but one resident came to have breakfast with Lanie yesterday (just in case it was her last day) and then spent a long time just hanging out today, another resident came in on her day off yesterday and spent at least an hour playing with us both inside and outside at the park, and another resident spent time with us yesterday afternoon just playing and hanging out. I love our residents. And I am super honored that we just happened to be at the hospital (hint, hint God is awesome) at the same time that these amazing people are going through their residency. They all have a sweet little spot in my heart. And also please ignore that huge run-on sentence you had to read...

3. Rachel. I know I say it a lot, but I really am. Even when the doctors said no to leaving yesterday, Rachel helped to keep the celebratory party alive. She truly is an incredible gift. She left this weekend for a wedding and it was hard to say goodbye today to everyone without her by my side. It was insanely hard actually.

4. Visitors. I feel like I'm always repeating myself but I love when people come to hang out. I had such fun people around me yesterday, last night, and today (sorry for those of you that came today...I was a complete and utter mess of emotions. Eeeeek). And especially sending a shout out today to Ken and Sue who helped me move every single thing in our room to Ronald McDonald for the weekend and had to try to figure out what to do with my emotional self during the transition. I love you guys.

5. Little things like guacamole, watermelon, movies, tight hugs, coffee, Kleenex, sunsets, and distractions. I just secretly love being taken care of and all of those things fit into that category. PS - Rachel made coffee last night so that I just had to push the 'run' button this morning. And then she texted me and reminded me to push the button (which I of course had already forgotten). I'm hopeless.

6. The Lynch Family! Thanks for being such an incredible blessing to our family! The boys were so excited tonight when they called me to tell me about their day and it helped my emotional heart to find joy. I hope that our family can continue to spread the generosity that they have poured out upon us. I am so blown away!

7. Unit 5 nurses. I know I am always talking about the nurses on unit 5, but guys. C'mon. They are incredible. And I already miss them. I would list them and talk about all of the things I love about each one of them but my luck I would forget someone and feel like a horrible person for the rest of my life. So. Unit 5 nurses. I love you. I love that I can be real with you and honest. And I can laugh with you and cry with you. I love that sometimes y'all know Lanie better than I do, and that is a very, very hard task. I love that you advocate on our behalf. I love that you love your patients and their families with all of your heart. I am proud and honored to call y'all friends. And part of my heart will always be yours. Also Lanie has talked about you guys so much since we left I'm about to bring her back.

8. The Ronald McDonald house. Walking around here tonight, I have been so thankful for every dollar that people have given for these amazing structures that provide food, shelter, safety, and hope. Although we'll probably only stay here for a very short time during outpatient (no worries, we have people that are willing to take us in, even if they did offer without fully knowing the consequences of their actions) we are just so humbled by the time and effort that has been built in to every part of this construct.

9. Phone calls and texts today from people checking in and not being annoyed when I cried or complained via text about a day that was supposed to be so happy. I'm so thankful that you guys get me when I don't even understand myself.

10. And lastly Alaina. She asked me at least 3 or 4 times today why I was crying and would come over and hug me. She's a million times stronger than I am. Also, there were things I didn't even think about with being outpatient. Like the fact that doesn't sleep flat on her back (she still tilts the bed up a lot so she doesn't hurt) and beds in the outpatient world don't have the same sweet abilities. And that it would take me roughly around 45 minutes to do her meds tonight (including a shot that was the nightmare of all nightmares. Oh my word. Holding down my daughter is not my idea of a good time). And that we actually have to figure out food and I can't just run down the hall or get her apple juice or milk anymore. And through all of these things, Lanie loves me. And forgives me. And even takes care of me. She holds my hand and tells me how excited she is while I'm crying and feeling a bit terrified of whatever this outpatient thing looks like. I'm inspired by her and what God is doing in her. I'm thankful that she is strong and mighty. And I'm thankful that I get to share her with all of you and that you get to see the beautiful and amazing spirit that pours out of her.

Thank you guys for being so forgiving of my 'I'm sad but I should be happy' post tonight. I'm excited for what tomorrow and every day after that will bring. And am TRULY thankful that today is over and we made it to the end of the night alive and still intact. Inpatient, you have been so incredibly good to us and we are forever grateful for your love and support, but your chapter is over and it's time to start the next one with a bit of independence, freedom, and healing.

Peace out family. Tomorrow will be a new day full of new blessings and fun experiences. Excited to start this crazy ride... We love you. ~ Ali

Jun 16, 2013 10:42pm

With a couple days of outpatient under our belts, I am way less whiny. I know you're all very thankful for that right now. Friday was hard. Really hard. I really thought that I was going to cry my way through this second phase. Thankfully that was short lived.

Lessons from life on the outside...

- Don't wake Lanie up earlier than need be. Let the child sleep, unless of course, you would love to have your day filled with emotional outbursts and lots of pouting.

- Throw up makes me freak out. A little over halfway through taking her morning meds, Lanie threw them all back up. After freaking out a little, I remembered that if she threw up within an hour of med time, she needed to redo them all - because that's exactly what she wants to do after throwing them all up. She actually did it like a champ though and I suddenly remembered that she's the strongest girl I know.

- I still need people. Surprise surprise. Yesterday and today we had so many people around us and it completely melted my heart. And sorry to all of the amazing people that I didn't call Friday when I was having a cry-fest. I know you would've come and played with us, but I'm terrible at asking. I'll work on it. Probably.

- College friends put me right back into college mode. In such a good way. I had so much fun with you guys, even with being cooped up because of the rain.

- I love rain! I love to run, walk, dance and play in it - if it's warm. Mike and Shannon...it was my privilege to stand on the corner looking for you. Seriously.

- If I don't get out of here soon Girl Scout cookies will be the death of me. I'm not kidding. My willpower is only so strong people.

- I miss cooking and cleaning and all of that nonsense. I'm no Martha Stewart, but there's something about everyday things that I miss more now that I'm outpatient than I did when we were still in the hospital. Crazy, I know.

- Playing outside all day today in the sun was the most amazing medicine. It felt great to be active and playful and hot. Better make this medicine a daily thing.

- Goodbyes are hard. Even if they're only for a short time. It was really hard to tell Jackson to go home for one more week until I can get this outpatient thing a little more under control. It was like I was saying 'I can only be sort of a good mom to one child right now and if you stay here there's a good chance I'll walk into Target with 2 children and walk out with honey crisp apples and maybe some sorbet'. I feel like my mind is that scattered. And I hope that Jackson understands just a little that I'm trying to be a good mom and not a fun hater. Or that I'm someone that doesn't love him as much as Lanie - my actual fear of course.

- Without a car, I feel helpless. This is ridiculous. I don't need a car for anything right now. But I like the idea of going where I want when I want. Mine is being fixed at the present (what is a catalytic converter anyway and why does it cost so much to get a new one??) I don't think anyone really knows.

- If I can't sleep with a real person, I will sleep with stuffed animals. Thank you to all the sweet folks that sent them. No worries. They are being used.

- Ok. I know I said I would only stay in the Ronald McDonald house for a short bit, and I still will but you guys...this place has a decent workout area (going to get my workout on right after I finish this actually), a movie theater, and 208 living rooms. Not even kidding. Sheesh.

- Once I have this outpatient thing under control, I really think I'm going to like it. It will take some getting used to, but I'm pretty excited about playing around in Minneapolis for about a month or so until we can go home again.

I'm sure there are a bazillion more things that I'm going to learn during my stay here as well as when we go home. I guess I don't really know when to stop writing in this, so maybe I can just play it by ear...? How about when you are finally sick of my ramblings and nonsense you can just let me know. Until then, thank you for being my listening ear and honest encouragement. I don't know what I would do without you all in my life and being a part of this story.

I thank God every single day for you. And pray that He can teach me how to be as generous and loving as what you've shown me and my family. I'm humbled and amazed...still.

Jun 20, 2013 12:37am

Hey everyone! I've missed you! Things have been good here in outpatient. Because I know myself, I'm not going to let myself write and write and write all about the last couple of days (who am I kidding? This is gonna be long)...so let's just do a highlight reel (I feel like this would be much cooler in video form, but I don't have anything like that for you)...and honestly I was going to do a Monday, Tuesday, Wednesday thing, but I typed out Monday and had no idea what happened that day and most of the day today I thought it was Thursday. That being said, this will be a highlight reel of only things that I really remember...which isn't all that much. Be thankful. And if you understood any of that first paragraph, you'll make it through this just fine.

- Lanie slept so much on Monday! That I remember. We had labs in the morning and then she fell asleep on the way back to the house. Then we went outside and she slept for a few hours on the patio. Poor sleepy girl. (Labs came back decent, by the way, mostly just made some med changes). In the afternoon I took her for a run by the river. She loved it. I almost died. I'm sure the problem was that I'm not used to pushing a stroller 5 or so miles and not at all that I'm a bit out of shape. Lanie fell asleep again right after dinner for a short time and then was up and playing outside during the evening making all kinds of crazy messes with dyed bubbles, which don't really work all that well in the wind, just in case you were wondering. We had sweet visitors that night and Rachel came home! Double fun. I also remember that Lanie didn't sleep at all Monday night. Hmmm I wonder why. This mama has seen the error of her ways and will not let that happen again. I'm creating a no nap rule in this house from now on.

- Yesterday we didn't have any appointments so we took our time in the morning just getting up and around. Also, please remember the lack of sleep from the night before. Lanie wanted to show Rachel the run we conquered yesterday so that meant getting on our running clothes and going again. This time I only pushed the stroller half the time though and took a few more breaks to explore the river. There are swings...in the middle of nowhere... And one is so high that it took Rachel and me a while to even figure out how to get on it. Ali and Rachel - 1. Tree swing - 0. Of course there was a low swing as well. Lanie had no problem pointing out the fact that she was able to get onto a swing much faster than we could. Bully.

- After our fun little running adventure, we stopped into Jamba Juice for lunch (thank you Dave and Kelly!!!!). Yum. There's no shame in drinking your lunch. That place is a-mazing. That run and lunch stop took up a lot of our afternoon, but we all really wanted to go see the nurses on 5 too, plus we needed to pick up our mail there - you guys are awesome!! Getting mail at the hospital is the least creepy way I can think of to still get to hang out with my sisters up on 5. Thanks for helping a girl out! It was so fun to see them and have Lanie play in a place she feels so at home. I seriously love those beautiful ladies. And we'll all just ignore that Lanie asked for a room back on 5 and 'might' have said she wanted to be inpatient again. Sheesh.

- We got back to the Ronald McDonald just in time for dinner...tacos. Y'all, we've never been so excited. That really is a huge blessing. Dinner is served every night at 5:30 and it's awesome. Plus tacos...I mean, c'mon. After dinner we were all so tired. The sun takes a ton out of you! And I love it. (Thankfully Lanie has become the responsible little trooper and carries sunscreen, bug spray, her meds and pill crusher, Chapstick, hair ties, Kleenex, and a decently healthy snack with her in her little messenger bag). It's like hanging out with a Boy Scout. I have her and my pocket knife so I feel like we could get lost anywhere and survive, because we're tough like that. And we all went to bed at a really good time.
Having fun all day is tiring.

- We had labs again this morning. We also had a doctor appointment 3 hours later with our GI doctor who is just amazing and has been seeing Lanie since she was 3. In between appointments Lanie and I grabbed some

Starbucks and sat out in the warm morning sun. I loved every second of it. I had such a sweet little conversation with her as we drank our coffee/Izze and sat outside at those little tables that kind of make me feel like I'm way more high class than I actually am. I don't know why. And I think my life flashed before me a little bit. And all of the sudden Lanie wasn't so little anymore. And she was talking to me about things that she missed about home, and also about the things she loved about being outpatient with me here in Minneapolis. It made me sad for a really brief moment that she had grown up and I wasn't my little baby girl anymore and weird because I got to have real life conversations with her. But it also made me excited; because I could see many more of these happening as time goes on. And in that moment I remembered what a gift it is to be a mom. Thank you God for sweet little minutes like this.

- We had way more time than we knew what to do with between appointments so we spent the rest of our time playing at a park that is super close. I love parks by the way. I love spider-swinging. And running around. And playing tag. And follow the leader. I don't like hot slides however. And I also don't love tire swings that spin. We still did all of those things.

- Her appointment went ok today, although not as we'll as I would've wanted. Both her kidney and liver levels were elevated and I immediately blamed myself trying to think through all the things I had done and the meds I had given her. I thought I had done it right, but second guessing will get you every time. I was a little too scared to tell our lovely doctor that I'm sure it was all somehow my fault and just freaked out in my heart instead. The decision was made to get an ultrasound of the liver and kidney. So we waited around for what seemed like forever and then headed over to ultrasound. I haven't heard back yet. There is talk about doing a liver and kidney biopsy, also, but haven't heard about that yet either. Her next lab appointment is Friday.

- The rest of today was somewhat anticlimactic. Lanie has been so moody today since her doctor appointments and I feel like whenever I get near her I set her off into an emotional outburst. Bummer. Such a sweet time this morning and then emotional and dramatic all afternoon. I hear it's from the prednisone. It makes me want to throw that drug in the garbage (no worries, I probably won't). I'll have to up my game with her on afternoons like this, though.

- I got to hang out with sweet Iowa City friends tonight too! That was so fun! Lanie ended up having quite a meltdown, again, so she and I came back to our little room for the night to settle down. Seriously. Crazy mood swings. I can't handle you. Go as freaking far away as possible.

So, as you can see, outpatient has been good to us thus far. It's challenging. The meds can be difficult and a bit mind-numbing. And I still feel like I'm going to somehow break my daughter. But other than that we are having fun. The sun has been beautiful and amazing and I am excited to spend most of our days outside. We play at parks, go for runs, ride bikes, and have picnics. We're transitioning well. I think.

Thank you a ton for sticking with us through all of this. Thank you for the mail that allows us to keep spending time with our nurses (yeah...we're those people). Thank you for your continued prayers and love and support. I am still continually amazed by you! After all this is over can you just all come to either Minneapolis or Iowa City so we can have a big party together?? Yeah that would be awesome.

Chapter 16: Fighting discouragement

Jun 21, 2013 5:53pm

Hi sweet friends. I keep trying to think of what to say tonight but everything that I can think to write sounds whiny and frustrating...and honestly kind of pathetic. Because that's the kind of mood I'm in. Which is silly really. And it's all about perspective and not really about circumstance anyway, right? I believe that in my heart completely. Tonight I'm trying to believe that in my head too. And maybe also a little in my heart...

Yesterday was so fun. Iowa City friends came to hang out with us (you guys are awesome!) and it was a gorgeous day out so we decided to take Lanie to the lake. We got there about 11 and played for a little bit before getting in the water. Oh my word Minnesota! I could only stand getting waist high in your frigidly cold water (which lasted a total of 15 seconds before I got tackled) before vowing to never get in again. Ever. Of course I did, but not without a little complaint. We spent a good four and a half hours playing on the beach, at the beach parks, in the water, and doing all sorts of other beach-like activities. I remembered to put sunscreen on Lanie almost every single moment of the day plus I got her to drink a lot so I was feeling pretty proud of myself. After the lake, we took showers and walked downtown to my friends' hotel. You guys. The Millennium Hotel is beautiful. My friends had problems though with their room, the pool, and the elevator (get it together Millennium!) so we got to order free appetizers and go to the penthouse club suite for the kind of fun only people who buy expensive rooms can have (okay Millennium, you're now forgiven). We still had time before I needed to lay Alaina down so we decided to walk around downtown Minneapolis. I don't know how people can't adore this city. Lanie was pretty wiped out after that kind of day so not long after 8:00 I took her back to our quaint, sweet little room at the Ronald McDonald House. She took her meds and was asleep instantly. I haven't gotten her to bed that early yet. And it was very, very welcomed.

We had labs again this morning and had another Starbucks date (thank you to everyone who sent Starbucks gift cards! Such a great gift that we have been enjoying this week). And on lab days I don't ever have time to feed Lanie a good breakfast so Starbucks pulls through on that end too. We were in and out of labs in no time today. That girl is a for real champ. Labs 3 days a week and not one tear shed or complaint given. I don't even understand where that comes from, definitely not her mom. After labs and Starbucks, Rachel came and picked us up and we headed to Brooklyn Park to hang out our friend Nancy and her fantastically large black dog (in which Lanie is so in love with). Nancy seriously spoiled us this morning with ample dog-playing time, pedicures (Lanie's first one ever!), and a delicious lunch. So much fun!

After we got back from our super adventurous morning, I got a call from Lanie's transplant coordinator. Labs were bad. Creatinine (kidney function) is slowly but steadily getting worse as well as liver function tests. We heard this on Wednesday too, hence the ultrasound. I never heard back any results from that. What happened to 'no news is good news'? The coordinator wasn't completely sure what they wanted to do yet so she told us to stay close to the hospital until I heard. Noooooo. I didn't want to. The boys were coming. I made dinner plans. And date plans with Luke for after. And I don't love this idea whatsoever. So I went for a walk. A complained a lot in my head. And got some Jamba Juice. Seriously. That stuff makes things better. Usually. I got another call about 3:00 that she would have to go inpatient. Lanie cried at first. Then straightened up and said 'it's fine, because we'll be on 5 with all our friends'. Little champ! I was still upset and could not be deterred.

4:00 equals inpatient. Sweet Brittany set us up with a room on sunset side, because she's awesome. How can you guys not love these nurses?!? They are seriously like my sweet sisters.

The plan? Biopsies of the liver and kidney on Monday to see what the heck is going on.

What's happening in my head? A crazy mix of 'how in the heck could I have screwed this up in a week?' and 'well, at least we're close to the hospital'. Leaning a little heavy on the first thought unfortunately. So yep. I feel frustrated with a huge side of blah. Thankful that the boys are here to lessen the sting of tonight. And hoping that I pull myself out of this pit I dug (that I'm perfectly fine with sitting in tonight, to be honest) and find joy in all the blessings that God is still reigning down. Which is a lot people.

Time to change my perspective even if I don't want to...wish me luck.

Jun 23, 2013 9:18am

Warning! This morning I have so many ramblings in my head that I have no idea if any of them will make sense, but I'll give it a go, because well, I have nothing else to do this morning while Lanie's sleeping. You're welcome.

First things first, medical stuff. We are inpatient after all.

Lanie is un-confinable (I'm not sure if that's a real word, but you get the point). Yes she's connected to an IV pole, but apparently she could care less as she's running through the halls of the hospital and making laps on 5, giggling as she goes. Why are we inpatient again? Oh, that's right...labs. All of her labs came back a little better yesterday after some medication changes and with the help of IV fluids. We've been holding her aspirin and Lovinox also, just in case we need to do biopsies of both organs tomorrow sometime (i.e. blood thinners, i.e. shots, i.e. thank you, God that I have not had to poke my daughter the last couple of days and see her arms and legs bruised and believing that people who see us out on the street notice and wonder if they should call social services or if someone else has already taken the liberty to do that). Her labs were somewhat decent this morning as well, but kidney function has dipped again, making another day here inevitable. Drink, girl, drink! We'll see what tomorrow brings in terms of outpatient.

Otherwise, nothing is really happening here. Lanie spent yesterday playing with all of her friends on 5, giving hugs and high fives, and acting like she owns the place. Side note to the good people at Amplatz. Stop being so amazing to Lanie. Stop playing with her and bringing her snacks and toys, and letting her hang out with you while you work, and picking her up and loving her completely. I have to completely de-program her when we head

114

back out into the real world, where I make her walk up stairs and throw away her own garbage. You're killing me.

As for me, yesterday was much better than I anticipated. I was way less grumpy than I was on Friday and I know that Luke and Jackson and the rest of the Minneapolis world that I came in contact with were thankful for that. My sincere apologies to all of those who had to deal with my grouchy, ridiculous self on Friday. Thankfully it's rare for me to be that inconsolable. While Luke was here I had time to pay bills, go for a decent hilly run in which my legs and rear end are not thanking me for today, get some one on one Jackson time in, and make a Starbucks run. Starbucks cards I love you. And I didn't realize until last night that a skinny mocha for breakfast and another one for lunch, with another coffee as my mid afternoon snack makes me a ridiculously annoying person. Thankful for the beautiful people who brought BBQ from Famous Dave's last night. Why is there not a meat and coffee diet? That, even I could stick to. I'll try to not turn that into my next social experiment...

Luke left yesterday afternoon to head to the town we called home for 6 beautiful, sweet, but also hard years of our life. I'm a little jealous. I like to be there anytime I can. I miss those people so much and if I think about it too much my eyes start to tear up and my kids start asking what's wrong, in which I just look at them with an 'I don't care to talk about it' stare until they find something else that attracts their attention...which is usually about 5 seconds. Jackson stayed here with us. Rachel and I were talking last night about how sadly humorous this week might look. Jackson, who has the sweetest heart in the world and gets so upset if he thinks that he has hurt people's feelings whatsoever (did I not tell you guys he would make the best husband?) and Alaina who believes that everyone is out to hurt her feelings and is against her (prednisone, I loathe you) are going to spend this week together. Bleeding hearts unite. I'm legit scared.

And on top of all of these thoughts, I realized about an hour ago that it's Sunday. I know that doesn't mean that much to say, but today is my 9th Sunday in a row now being involved in corporate worship. Believe me, I'm so not that person that believes that going to church is a make it or break it to love God. There is no rule in the Bible that states that if we don't go to church, we are horrible people that deserve to be called heathens and have noses across the globe turned up at our outright rebellion of God and His plan to get everyone in church on a Sunday morning. Ok. I know I'm being a bit sarcastic here, but for real, I've had discussions like this. I don't miss corporate worship because I think God is mad if I don't go. Or less pleased with me. I miss it because there is something about lifting up myself before a Holy God while connecting to all of my beautiful friends and family. I miss deep rooted discussions with my group of Thursday nighters (who I'm told have switched to Tuesday nighters...unacceptable) about the character of God and why we do what we do. I really enjoy being a part of all of that.

And I think that being here has taught me even more about the church.

Things like...Americans are so enamored by time that we started believing somewhere that Sunday mornings (at least an hour of them anyway, because we all know that the hours before church are spent chasing kids around the house telling them to hurry up and asking everyone where I set my coffee and trying to straighten my hair and decide what to wear, and cleaning the kids' faces so that they are somewhat mess free and reminding them to not tell everyone we had Nutella - spreadable chocolate- for breakfast) are meant to be spent singing, giving, and listening to who God is. It's been pretty freeing to be here with no time constraints. Nothing that I have to really go to, or be at. I had no clue about this idea before. I mean, I liked the idea of being where I want, when I want, but we all know that's only how time works on that 1 week a year we take for vacation. The hospital has reminded me that worshipping God or learning more about who He is, or talking to His beautiful children isn't an hour long thing once a week. It really is about who we are and even more importantly, who He is. It's also taught me, though, for my need. Of Him. Of people. All the time. Not just on Sunday mornings, but also Sunday mornings. And how there's a reason to come together. To be encouraged, and encourage as well. To be challenged in thought and deed. To sing (joyful noise, right) alongside others, hearts lifted high. And to cry out to God on behalf of our world and those who have never met Him, as a community. A family.

So yep. I miss church. There I said it. and I'm not really sure if it's a good thing or bad thing that it's week 9 when I'm having this rant, but we'll leave that for another discussion. Or not. And I tried to go to the church here at the hospital once about a year ago and I'm almost positive that will be a 'one-time only' experience. And I hope that when I go home...I mean home, and not outpatient, because I use those two words interchangeably and it starts to get confusing...that I keep this perspective in my head. That we are free. And in freedom, I still like to choose some kind of Sunday morning worship, otherwise known as church.

I'm praying for you guys this morning. That you experience freedom. And love. And give it back in return. Love you guys and your sweet little hearts.

Time to spend the rest of the morning figuring out what to do with a child that feels decent but is still confined to a limited amount of space. This should be fun...

Chapter 17: And...inpatient...and outpatient

Jun 25, 2013 10:21am

Things are crazy here. As always. Here's what our definition of crazy looks like, just in case you were wondering.

- Sunday we played outside and inside all day and Alaina was seriously crazy. I mean, lost her mind funny. She was rolling around on the wet floor, dancing to Run DMC (who wouldn't?!?), jumping off her bed, and just acting insane. Rachel and I could not stop laughing. And it lasted for a while.

- Rachel and I tried to make a frozen yogurt run, because that's what we wanted for dinner more than anything else in this world. We're both lactose intolerant by the way. We got distracted while we were out on our excursion and we'll just say that frozen yogurt was not our best idea to date.

- No medical stuff whatsoever took place on Sunday besides the things the amazing nurses do. Biopsy was scheduled for Monday at 2:00 because kidney levels are staying elevated.

- Lanie woke up yesterday at about 10a NPO because of her impending biopsy. Which was cancelled at 11a, so she ate.

- Both kids were already going stir crazy in the room (it's still morning!) so we headed downstairs to find them food and then picnic-ed it up outside. Picnics on a somewhat windy day just don't work. The kids *tried* to eat. Fail. I chased plates and napkins. Fail.

- We were over the picnic idea almost as soon as it started and decided to play at the little park for patients. Lanie got mad at Jackson for taking off his shoes. Hers were off as well...hmmmm. Jackson accidentally bumped into her, touching her belly (which feels fine for her to lie down on and play hard, but apparently when it's lightly brushed is when disaster happens) and she fell apart. Jackson felt horrible. He fell apart as well. End of park experience.

- I had them pick out a movie in the library. They couldn't agree (of course) so I let them each get one. Then there was the problem of who's to watch first. Which was almost an issue, but Jackson gave in. Seriously. You rock little stud.

- They watched their movie. I drank my fourth cup of coffee for the day. Rachel napped. All seemed well. Then the movie ended. Rachel and I thought it would be nice to play a game, go for a walk, dance, anything really...which caused more problems than solutions. Insert second movie of the day. We are no longer entertainment for these children.

- Alaina started having pain, (in really weird places like her foot, her arm, her toe, her ear, her eyeball - you think I'm kidding) but only when asked by her nurses. She charted her pain at 9 or 10 on the chart while eating a Popsicle. Mmmkay. Rachel and I could only look at each other at this point.

- Rachel and I schemed for an hour how to leave the kids here with anyone and get a little break from the madness but thankfully God knows what we need more than we do. Lanie fell asleep (never ever ever happens without her trusty night meds) and woke up again about 9p so cuddly and sweet and wanted to be snuggled. Jackson and Rachel headed to Ron McDon's for the night and all things started to calm down. I went to sleep as soon as I possibly could.

- I woke up this morning early to order Lanie breakfast so that it would be here by 730, knowing that she'd go NPO by 8a. And to work out, which was surprisingly really good. And then I went back to sleep for 10 minutes.

119

- I woke up Lanie at 745 when her food came so that she could destroy all of the food on her plate in the next 15 minutes before she went NPO. She ate a bite of yogurt. Well that was worth it.

- Doctors rounded at 930a so that they could all round together. Which was hilarious. Mostly what this consisted of was GI vs. Renal on opinions as to what to do in regards of the biopsy. Both sides are legit. Don't do biopsy and let us go free today while watching labs or do biopsy and leave tomorrow or the next day. Doctors talked and talked and talked back and forth. I accidentally started laughing in the middle of it. Probably inappropriate but so incredibly funny. At one point the doctors stopped talking and everyone just looked at each other and one said, 'yeah, we still haven't decided anything'. I just started laughing again.

- They left and promised a decision within an hour. 15 minutes later they came back and told us we could go outpatient! We'll keep up with labs tomorrow and Friday, and depending on how those look we have a biopsy scheduled for next Tuesday with an impending inpatient stay this weekend. Oh my my my...

- so now, I'm packing up and waiting for discharge orders. And easily distracted (which I don't mind at all actually) so not getting any of the 10 things I'm doing done. This included (I've been typing this for over an hour and a half). I know. I'm ridiculous.

See. Crazy. Excited about outpatient! And getting this girl to drink. Peace out for today sweet friends!

Jun 29, 2013 12:34am

Hey guys. What's going on with all of you? I miss asking people that question. When people come to visit I realize that they literally know everything that's going on in my life and I literally know nothing about the outside world until people who live there come to visit (some of you have tried to call...I'm sorry for your experience. I'm awkward and weird on the phone and don't know how to fill even 2 second silences. My average phone conversation with my own sweet husband lasts roughly 5 minutes. On a really off day I'll talk for hours. There really is no middle ground here). Anyway, I hope that you are all good and I can't wait to hang out when we get home, or come visit wherever you are, which is I don't know when, but I'm sure it will happen.

So...outpatient. I've decided that living in Minneapolis during outpatient is like a super sweet little vacation (except for Luke not being here, and Jackson only being here a little, and Lanie getting labs a minimum of 3 times a week, and not really spending any money, and missing all my friends and roommates). But other than that, it's a good time. Here are some of the ways we are trying to keep the kids entertained...

- Tuesday we went outpatient. I had to literally peel Lanie off of the nurses while she repeatedly told me she wasn't ready to go outpatient and wanted to stay because it was more fun. Unit 5...you did this. Hire some old cranky nurses STAT. Rachel and I thought it would be fun to take the kids to the Como Zoo. Or Como Park. I don't really know what it's called. Anyway. It's fun. And cheap. And the kids were excited. After a slight meltdown from Lanie (arrrrgh), we headed into the park to play. This was the first time the kids really got to play together other than Father's Day. And they were so sweet (this can also be read, they had so much fun because Jackson kept giving in to Lanie). I had missed seeing them run and play together though. Seriously awesome.

- We went straight from the zoo to our first bonfire of the summer. If you know me at all you know how much I love this. Bonfires, camping, playing catch or frisbee or whatever object we want to throw at each other, hiking, swimming, and long walks under stars are all favorite summer activities. Tuesday night made it feel like summer was official.

- Wednesday is a blur. What even happened? Well it was Wednesday so Lanie had labs. They came back 'okay'. I can live with 'okay'. We had our weekly Starbucks date and Rachel picked us up and we headed back to the Ronald McDonald to do a little bit of laundry. My sweet buddy Amos came to play with us and completely schooled me in basketball (I know how surprised you all are, I'm 5'2 and a half...almost 5'3 really. Ok fine. I'm just 5'2). And also I can't shoot soooo, there's that. I can see my star basketball player roommate shaking her head as she reads this. The kids showed Amos all around and roped him into a million games. He'll think twice before telling them 'oh, whatever you want'. Rookie.

- Oh, also Wednesday I got my car. I haven't driven in ages! It's so fun. It was such a hot day (yay heat!!) and I still rolled down the windows and opened the sun roof and blasted some music. They kids thought this was fun for a whole 20 seconds, but they were so sweet and entertained me all the way back to the house. We decided to split the kids up for the night and give them some one on one time too. Jackson went with Rachel's twin sister Leah to Legoland in the Mall of America. The kid loves legos. And Leah. Most perfect date ever. Lanie had me. She was surprisingly ok with it. My idea was to take her out to dinner somewhere and go bowling or do something fun and then maybe get ice cream. What she chose instead --> eat dinner at the house (breakfast for dinner!!), play in the bouncy thing that was there that night (which really was fun), and get a gas station slushy. Interesting choices, but ok. She's going to keep her future husband on his toes.

- Thursday was packed full too. Rachel came over early and we headed to the Turtle Derby at Amplatz (a fundraiser for the hospital which has about a million different games for the kids and actual turtle races). You guys. I wasn't sure about this. But I watched those turtles race and some of them were crazy fast. I understand the now how that tortoise beat the hare. We ended up staying awhile. Plus we got to see a lot of our hospital friends (also known as the nurses, lab techs, doctors, ultrasound folks, etc). I can't help it. I just love them all.

- After that little morning party we headed to a park that was walking distance from the hospital with a pool. The kids at this point entertain themselves, so that's handy. Plus, Lanie hasn't gotten to swim very much because of PICC lines, drains, and wounds healing, so she was just so happy to be in the water at all. While the kids played, Rachel and I talked. Some of my best conversations happen poolside (or at a beach...water-side would be a better term). It maybe has something to do with the fact that I'm already feeling vulnerable wearing so little, but who really knows. We talked about fear...and going home...and people who are in our lives...and parenting...and lies that we tend to believe. And I left thanking God for long talks that are genuine and full of love and mercy. And for sweet siblings laughing together in the background.

- The kids were so wiped after being in the sun all day so I let them relax a little before dinner in the room. Lanie almost fell asleep instantly. I walked downstairs to talk to the office staff about a couple of things when they asked me if I wanted to go to the Twins game that night. My jaw dropped and they gave me 4 tickets, ensuring me that they were awesome seats (I stood the whole last game I went to. I'm just happy to be at a sporting event!). I went up to tell the kids. They weren't thrilled. Lanie was moments away from sleeping and Jackson was sprawled out on the floor. I told them that we would eat dinner and then they would feel more up to it. Nope. They were actually more against the idea (I almost had a meltdown and might have told them that they could stay in the room and lock the door and watch movies until I got back, which would be around 10p when the game was over). Rachel talked me down. And social services got a good night's sleep. Instead we let the kids watch a movie until they fell asleep (20 minutes), that we half watched with them but mostly practiced braiding our hair new ways (who says Pinterest is a time waster?).

- Lanie woke up last night at 4:45 with leg cramps. Booooo dehydration! I thought we were drowning her in water and Gatorade yesterday. And finally fell asleep again around 6. I was pretty wide awake after that and decided to get up and workout. I'm gonna be sore. I showered and laid back down (accidentally falling asleep again for 20 minutes) and woke up just in time to remember that Lanie had labs again today. The kids were bears to wake up, but after telling them a hundred times to hurry we made it to labs only an hour and a half late. I felt like that was pretty good. We had a pretty chill afternoon and then headed out to see a friend of mine who just flew into town from his home in Brazil. So good to see him and talk about how awesome God is. We actually got to stay there for a while. Aaron, you made my day.

- And tonight I'm just basking in thankfulness. For friends. For long talks. For being real with people. For the generosity of those who just take care of us. For a super comfy bed. And for the outpatient season so far.

Side note to my amazing husband Luke. I miss you. So much. And I know how selfish outpatient is for us here, getting to not have the responsibilities of home and everything. We get to play here while you're home providing for us and taking care of us. I am just so thankful for you. And sometimes I feel frustrated by things that are happening here, but I can't even imagine how frustrated you must be trying to deal with the same things hundreds of miles away. You are incredible. I'm so thankful for you. See you soon...

Chapter 18: So yeah

Jul 2, 2013 11:29am

Hi everyone! First of all it was so good to see so many of you on Saturday. My heart was so full!

Second of all, I already typed this caring bridge/Facebook post once and lost it as I went to post so now I'm feeling a bit grumpy about it. My tone might have changed since then but I can promise that the first one was awe inspiring and amazing. You'll have to take my word for it because I guarantee nothing with this one.

My attitude is mixed writing today. I feel pretty discouraged but also so incredibly thankful. The thankfulness list outweighs the discouragement list by ginormous proportions, yet I hold onto the most immediate feeling of the two...so yep, I'm pouting.

My discouragement list...

- I got a call last night that Lanie's labs are still off and she had to go inpatient today. Blah. As much as I adore this place...I love the freedom of being out. She has a biopsy scheduled for today, and although no one really thinks that her body is rejecting those beautiful little organs, they also want to be able to rule it out. I'm cool with taking that little gem off the table as well.

- Her biopsy was scheduled for 10a so we had to come in at 8 for labs and check in. Not all of her labs are back and there's a chance that they might not even be good enough for the biopsy today, so at this point it's been pushed back to 1p. Because sitting in a little room in the hospital on a beautiful day is fun.

- The anesthesia nurse who came in to talk to me is the same one who completely freaked out when Alaina had sepsis and had to be rushed into surgery and down to the PICU time number 2. My heart froze when she walked in. I'm sure she was just having a bad day before...or she's just a little crazy. Either way, I need to let it go.

- I had plans other than being in the hospital today. And they were gonna be fun. I mean, not actual plans (but anything would have been more enjoyable than this).

- I DO NOT want to be in the hospital over the 4th of July. I just don't. Since last summer, Lanie has been in the hospital every month for at least 5 days. We were also here for Halloween, Jackson's birthday, Thanksgiving, we got our first call Christmas night and came the next day, the week after Lanie's birthday, part of spring break, Easter week, and my anniversary. I DO NOT want to be inpatient over the 4th. I want to play at the park. And hang out with my friends and family that are coming. And eat BBQ. And lay in the grass. And watch fireworks not through a window (I warned you that I was pouting).

I also have a list of thanks. And you're thinking *'finally! Sheesh'*...

I'm thankful for

- getting to go to the benefit on Saturday. I did not expect so many of you amazing people and I couldn't believe that many people I love could all be in one place. I love you guys. And I can't even tell you how much it meant to see all of you (even if I couldn't spend as much time with everyone as I would've loved to!)

- the amazing folks that drove us down to Sumner and took incredible care of us (even when my alarm was on vibrate and they had to wait on us almost making Bruce late to the run...you guys put up with too much from me!). I have been so blessed by you guys and would road trip with you anywhere, anytime (if we listen to the Bible musical though, there's a solid chance I'll fall asleep, no matter how good you say it is). Next stop...mountains or ocean.

- My sweet friend Marcy and her amazing crew who put together the benefit and the Lynch family. I wish I had words, but I can't think of any way to express myself that seems worthy. I love you guys. And you will forever have a huge part of my heart.

- Friends in Sumner that put up with me or my husband just showing up at their house to hang out. People really put up with a lot from us. I'm positive that I know the most hospitable, generous people in the world.

- My friend Tara who came to stay with us after the benefit. Anyone who can pile 4 kids under 8 into a vehicle and drive them up to Minneapolis for a few days to stay in a tiny room is a superwoman in my book. Our kids will forever be little brothers and sisters, with the exception of Adisu, who is going to marry Alaina one day. And that's that.

- That Tara was here when I got the call about Lanie's labs and going inpatient. And that we got to spend a good part of the night in the bathroom (the room is small and there are sleeping children..sooo bathroom it is) armed with a glass (hahaha) of wine, dark chocolate, strawberries, and all things pampering. So much laughing and talking. I miss that girl like crazy and I'm honestly just honored to be in her presence most days.

- The water part at Como Zoo. That place was ridiculously crazy yesterday but we managed to keep the kids entertained and cool. The kids had a blast...and Tara and I might have had some of our own water splashing fun too.

- And then the millions of little things like the sunshine. Lanie's attitude. Our nurses. Ginger and her crazy adventures. Soft blankets. Free dinner. Gluten free/dairy free cookies. Huge warm solid hugs. Pools. Lakes. People who let me talk and talk and talk. Our friends at Ron Mcdon. The arcade and gym and game rooms and play areas. Starbucks Americanos. Or sugar free almond milk triple shot mochas (Hiba and Ben...don't judge, or come and make me some coffee). For playing in the rain. And texts. And good workouts. For being able to drive again. And for never feeling alone in any of this.

126

So yeah. I need to stop the pouting. And remember to be thankful. Because honestly this stay is a just a blip in our time here. And it's one day closer to home...

Jul 6, 2013 8:59am

I woke up this morning and realized that today is Saturday...and I haven't posted since Tuesday. Not cool, Ali. I've officially failed you guys.

I'll give you a brief (for me) rundown of the days I missed...

Tuesday --> Lanie had her biopsy at 1:15 pm. Since we arrived at about 8a I was no happy camper. I accidentally got punched in the chin bone by a nurse in sedation (it's still sore, plus maybe I'm a baby). Lanie came out of the biopsy already waking up and cried for over an hour. Not a hurting cry which I would've felt really bad for, but an angry cry where she kicked the blankets, threw herself around, and was just mad. At one point I just started laughing. Don't judge. An hour of that kind of fighting and crying is enough to make anyone crazy. Because she wouldn't calm down, we couldn't go up to unit 5 right away and had to wait until almost 4p. She was put on bed rest until the next morning. Thankful for visitors that night. I needed a little adult time.

Wednesday --> While we were waiting on results of the biopsy to say whether or not we could leave, we had sweet friends from Sumner come and visit us. They were so fun and I can't believe how fast they made the 'waiting' time go by. I could not be more thankful for the people God keeps giving to us! Around 2p a doctor came in to talk to us about the biopsy. Finally! She said that they weren't able to see the actual slide yet, but the biopsy showed NO REJECTION! We know there's still something going on because her Creatinine is still elevated and her labs are still coming back weird but this was a huge relief. We were supposed to wait on a call for other biopsy info. Our orders were to keep Lanie pretty calm for two weeks. Ummm, I had to ask for clarification there. She's a seven year old female. Apparently keeping her calm meant no running, playing, swimming, lifting, jumping, dancing, or exercising. So I guess I'll cancel her boot camp class for tomorrow. I actually laughed when the doctor gave us this list thinking she was kidding. I asked her 'well what can she do'. The doctor looked at me and said she can walk around. Hahahahaha...ok. Noted. I can already tell her we are gonna fail at making that a reality.

Anyway...Outpatient! We packed up the room as quickly as we could (which was 5125, our room during the biggest part of our transplant stay...it felt a little too much like home. And yes, I might actually pick that exact color of green for some accent or orange couch for fun) and got out of the hospital as soon as we were given the ok. Luke was with us, but no Jackson, so it felt a little weird with the 3 of us to go outpatient together, but outpatient is outpatient. Luke is so sweet and amazing and decided to take his girls out for dinner before we met friends for a parade and bonfire later. Why hello there Outback Steakhouse. I sure have missed you and your fire grilled steaks and veggies. A shout out to some amazing Hettingers for that gift card date!! Thankfully we missed the crazy amounts of traffic heading north out of the cities (Does every single person in the state of Minnesota have a cabin up north?!) and made it to Coon Rapids in decent time. Lanie wasn't feeling amazing in general. She didn't eat much at Outback (no worries, I'll teach her what's up) and she fell asleep on the way to friends. When we woke up her up, she was...grumpy. And that's putting it lightly. She didn't want sunscreen. She didn't want to go in the street for the parade. She didn't want it to be sunny. She didn't want her hair up. She lost at all of those things by the way - just don't want you to forget how stubborn I am. She did start to come around at the parade though and soon was out with her friends waving and holding her bag out for candy. Side note here. Sometimes I can't tell if Lanie's actually hurting or milking a situation. During the parade she didn't fight for candy (we're very competitive people, I'm sorry) but instead just held her bag open. Sweet little Josephine and Clara, who were at the parade with us, picked up candy from the street and put it in her bag. Now...maybe her side was hurting from the biopsy, or maybe she just wasn't feeling so great, but the girl also knows how to get her way. Jo and Clara...you guys are awesome. But if Lanie pulls this with you again...just say no. Outpatient. Outback. Parade. Bonfire......awesome.

Thursday --> Happy 4th of July! We let Lanie sleep in. Best start to the day ever. This also meant that Luke and I just got to sit in bed for a while and chat. It's been a long time since that has happened. And I love it. Funny how sweet little things like that are such big blessings. We let Lanie relax in the room after she woke up (she wanted to watch Charlie and the Chocolate Factory) because we knew it would be a really long night for her. Luke made us breakfast (AND COFFEE) and brought it up to us in the room. You guys. This man is pretty amazing, is he not? We took showers (I straightened my hair...which I'm almost positive I haven't done since our anniversary) and headed downtown for some 4th of July action. Which was actually kind of lame. Because it was 1:00 in the afternoon mostly. Our fault Minneapolis. Luke found a party in the park thing in Roseville and we decided to do that instead. And it was fun. They had climbing walls, and bouncy houses, and blow up slides and snow cones, along with a million other kid like activities (of which Lanie might or might not have participated in. I'm not at leisure to say). We made sure she was drinking constantly, though. After Roseville, we headed back out to Coon Rapids for a BBQ and then fireworks. Such a fun night. Lanie was a champ all day. A completely different child then she was the day before. She played (and by that I mean walked around slowly?) so well and was for the most part sweet and just had fun. And Luke and I were just really blessed to have such an awesome family take us in, not one, but two days in a row.

Friday --> Labs. Usually this is a quick process. Today...not so much. It was still fine though, and no one was hurt in the end (besides a routine poke which Lanie is an all star at) so...that's always good. Our friends, Zach and Calie (both from Iowa City) met us for breakfast in Uptown at this hipster coffee shop that supposedly has like the best coffee and pastries in the whole state of Minnesota. I tried to order a sugar free drink and they laughed at me, telling me how they melt their chocolate and use almond paste...what? Fancy. I ordered what the guy told me to order. He was right. It was amazing. When Zach got there I ordered just straight up Ethiopian coffee (as my second drink...I shared with Luke so it's fine). First time in my life I haven't put cream in my coffee. Mostly because Zach said no way to it. And he was right. I officially don't know anything about coffee. It was so fun to hang out with those guys. Calie gets to stay until Sunday, but Zach had to leave so we hugged him goodbye and then tried to figure out what to do with the rest of our day. I had a Groupon (yep...I'm that girl) for this Amazing Mirror Maze (it should actually be called "the pretty cool, but also a little lame mirror maze) so we decided on that. I was actually surprised. I thought maybe it would be really lame, which it kinda was, but we had fun anyway. I almost give that credit to us though, because we can be ridiculous. After that we met friends to go see Monsters U (Lanie giggled so much...LOVE) and then all went out to dinner. Another side note - I can talk forever. I just really love hearing about people and their stories. To everyone I've spent any time with at all here...sorry I'm not sorry. You're interesting to me and I want to hear about you. Today was a little rougher for Lanie then yesterday was. She slept all morning at the coffee shop, fell asleep on the way to the mirror thing, struggled being happy with random choices, and had a decent sized melt down when we got back to the house because we couldn't find a movie she wanted to see. On that note, I headed outside to meet Calie for some Cross Fit while Luke got to be the responsible parent. Please and thank you. Great way to end the night.

Today! Saturday! --> I'm sitting in bed and everyone around me is sleeping. Ummm it's almost 9am and I've been up since 645. Luke and I did stay up late hanging out so I'll let his sleepiness slide I guess. Luke's parents are bringing Jackson back today so I'm pumped for that but Luke will have to leave this afternoon. Bittersweet news. But until then, I'll hang out and play and enjoy my little bit of family time while I can get it.

Chapter 19: AUGUST 1

Jul 6, 2013 9:58pm

Asking God to be home by August 1!!

Want to ask God with us?! Sometimes I forget that God wants us to ask specifically!

Jul 10, 2013 11:46am

Do you ever have those days when the sun is shining, it's gorgeous out, there is nothing in the world to be down about...yet you still are? Um, yeah, me neither. Except for that I do. These last couple days have been like that for me. I can't really put my finger on it as to why, mostly because I think it's really a combination of things. A little having to do with Lanie, but mostly having to do with my own heart ... But because I don't want this update to be about why I'm discouraged, I'll instead tell you all about what I'm learning.

1. 7:45 am is a silly time for labs. I feel like we're having a good morning if we make it there by 8:30 am three times a week. And if we get there at 9 am ... so be it. Lanie's still rocking them out and she hardly even flinches. She gets to decide if she would rather have paper tape or koband. And little decisions like that are huge blessings because she gets to feel like she has a say in her own care. Every Monday, Wednesday, and Friday after labs we usually have a little breakfast date outside where I have an Americano and she'll have whatever suits her fancy (which is whatever we grabbed in a hurry from Ronald McDonald before we left). I love these dates. We solve all of the world's problems in those half hour/hour blocks of time.

2. Waiting on lab results three times a week is hard work. There is always this inpatient idea hanging around like a small gray cloud on the sunniest of days. I know the cloud probably won't produce rain and more than anything it's just annoying but it's still there and I catch myself thinking about it more often than I need to.

3. Lanie is just going to be emotional for a while. She can flip from being the sweetest little doll one moment and then, the very next moment have a severe meltdown because she had one too many tomatoes on her plate (of course it's a big deal! She asked for three cherry tomatoes. Why on earth would someone give her four? I mean, what are they even thinking? And no she can't just throw it away, her plate is now somehow tainted and she'd die before she ate another bite of anything). This is real life.

4. I love the Ronald McDonald house and everything it has and does for people: they have outings and free dinners, a gym, arcades, a movie theater, outdoor play areas, a fitness center, our own little space, and super great people, Yet I can't figure out why I'm so lonely here. Lanie loves being here and runs around like she owns every single square inch of this house. And so we will stay. For now. And besides. We're praying for August 1 as our home date and I believe that God will do it. It's only a few more weeks.

5. I need people. I'm not really learning this (people who don't know me know this about me), but I'm learning more about myself in this. Luke left Saturday. Jackson and Luke's family left Sunday night. And Rachel's gone for the week. I've been trying to keep us busy for the most part during the day, but I realize I'm just wearing Lanie out because I selfishly need to be going and going to stay busy. I don't feel like it's a problem to need and love to be around people. I do feel like it's a problem if I'm sad because I'm not. This is the first week that I've felt really distant from things and I'm not sure if it's just being homesick, or lonely, or just pouting. And God's been reminding me a lot lately to learn contentment in being alone. And you guys, this honestly has been like the loneliest week ever since we've been in the Cities, and I don't feel like I'm getting better at it yet. I guess it's only Wednesday though...a few more days to learn me some amazing lessons (Hurry up weekend!!). Ps - you might not want to invite me anywhere this week...I haven't spent much time taking to adults and there's a solid chance you'll want me to leave long before I'm going to. It's a fair warning, and I'm huggy sooooooo...

6. Lanie is so tired. All the time. The plan Monday was to take her out to lunch and then wash the car together and play in the water. I wanted to grab a couple things from the store while I was out and had some stuff to return as well so the plan was to spend our afternoon filled with those things. But what really happened was Lanie not eating her lunch because her tummy hurt and then me pushing her in a stroller for about 4 hours all around Arbor Lakes while she slept. On a bright note I got to try on lots of fun clothes because I had nothing else to do, which is so fun to me. Luke will be thankful too because I only let myself spend $20. You're welcome. It was nearly impossible. Lanie woke up fully when the clock hit about 8p. Awesome. I kept her somewhat entertained until about 10p and then let her watch TV til midnight until I finally made her turn it off. I make silly choices when I'm tired.

7. Mealtimes are not fun. I actually dread them. Lanie cries almost every time she eats real food. We have a GI appointment on Monday so hopefully we'll see what that's all about.

8. Home does not mean soon (depending on your definition of soon). Yesterday was the 1st time that I heard the word home used in a real sentence. My heart leapt! No lie. Before home comes though, Lanie has a lot of stuff going on here that needs to happen. She has to be okayed by GI and her eating has to be solid. She has to have an MRI. She has to be okayed by the renal team. She has to be okayed by pain management. She has to be okayed by transplant. And a home plan has to be set up. A lot to do, but we have til August 1 so it seems pretty doable.

9. I hate fear! Fear doesn't come from God at all and my heart for some reason latches on to it when people aren't around to throw some truth in my direction or take my mind off it. Instead of talking to people I think about all of the different things I'm scared of and then the downward spiral of stupid begins. And somehow I go from thinking about the idea of going home and how fun it will be to see everyone to how I'm never going to be able to reach expectations I've set up, and about her next transplant in the fall or winter, and how I'm never going to be able to handle another round of this. There is a reason God says not to worry...it just makes you crazy with no real truth behind it. And takes my eyes of God's sovereignty and love and puts me in control (and EVERYONE knows what a disaster that is...). 'What ifs' are no friend of mine. If you happen to see or talk to me this week, make sure and tell me to not over think anything, and to stop believing lies. And tell me to stop wearing athletic shorts and tank tops every day.

133

10. When I'm alone a lot I spend my time on crazy and some not so crazy things. Since Sunday night I've gone on 4 runs, kettle belled my way to completely lower body domination, done Insanity twice, beat 30 levels of candy crush (Bruce Behrens...I blame you and letting Lanie play with your tablet), read almost an entire book (which has broken and lifted my heart at the same time), tried on every outfit at Arbor Lakes, spent time at Lake Calhoun, journaled all my thoughts and feelings into a book that I'll throw away on Friday because I'm a little bit dramatic this week, tried at least 4 different Pinterest hairstyles, cleaned our Ron Mcdon space, read through Exodus and the book of James (that book does not play around! Love the harsh honesty of it), cleaned my car inside and out, and made crowns with Lanie. And it's not even noon on Wednesday. No wonder Lanie is exhausted most of the time. If someone wants to come and save her, I completely understand.

And now I'm realizing it's almost 1 and I haven't even fed Lanie lunch so...I'm thinking that we'll do that. And maybe relax and learn some contentment and whatnot.

Jul 16, 2013 1:18am

Good evening (is that still what you say at 1am? I'm actually not sure what to say here...). Anyway, you'll be super excited to know that I just got back from a run and a workout in which I'll be plenty sore from tomorrow so I'm in quite a pleasant mood...no more downer messages, I somewhat promise.

I kept thinking that I should write again after the update last Wednesday, but the truth was, it took me a good long while to get out of my funk. And I didn't want to write the same thing over and over, so I just didn't write. But now, I've had some good long cries, some amazing people stepping in and getting me out and about, and some really long talks (my favorites!) and finally am determined to rise stronger and more grounded in God's love and faithfulness than ever. Plus I realized the more down and teary I get, the more emotional Lanie gets. And, like I said in my last update, God's teaching me more about contentment and thankfulness than ever before. Seeing that I made it through last week bare knuckled and begging for the weekend, I'm not sure if I've actually learned any lessons, but I am feeling more thankful and know myself a little better than I did before (and sheesh...how do I not know myself inside and out yet?!?!).

My thankfulness lessons...

Outpatient is still going really well for the most part. Lanie's is feeling...decent. It really depends on the day. She'll have an amazing day but then needs one or two days after to recover. That's maybe to be expected? I don't really know, but it seems like a fair call seeing that she did just have a crazy double transplant 3 short months ago. And her emotional meltdowns seem to be less and less but maybe that's because she's sleeping more these days. Either way, I'll take it.

The people in Minneapolis are amazing...and take such awesome care of us. When I wrote the 'most depressing ever' update last week, 2 guys called me at the exact same time to invite me to the exact same thing. Yep. You read that right. I probably wasn't the best company in any way that night but was incredibly blessed by the caring hearts of those people around me.

Thursday we got to play at Lake Calhoun with our buddies Natalie and Brittany. Man, you guys. Talk about blessings...these ladies are incredible. How in the world did we get to have the best nurses in the world on unit 5? I'm honored to know every single one of those ladies, and yes you boys on 5...I'm quite honored to know you as well!

Also Thursday...pain management appointment. Without any argument whatsoever, they gave us the green light from their end to go home. I was elated. Lanie could care less. One down, 5 to go (when I say it like that, it doesn't sound as exciting). Lanie was pretty wiped from the last couple days so after her pain appointment we literally stayed in the room the rest of the night. By now you guys know me a little too well so when I tell you that we spent from 4pm until Friday morning in our room, I don't really need to tell you the feelings that flooded me that night.

Remember - left alone... think too much... downward spiral... frustrated... believe lies. You get the point. It isn't pretty. I prayed that the night would just be over, and then morning came. And with the Friday morning sun, came joy and excitement for the day. Thank you God, for not letting me wallow in self pity, and for bringing newness and life.

Friday was really great. I woke up so happy. I worked out. I showered. Lanie showered. Lanie had labs. And a Starbucks date sitting in the gorgeous sun. And then the boys got here about lunch time. We picnicked it up at a local park and let the kids swim and play at the pool. We got cleaned up and went out to dinner (loving the gift cards you guys. Honestly, such a sweet, sweet blessing to us. Thank you), and we just spent time together as a family. It was fun and playful and mostly normal. And I loved every single second of it. That night after we laid the kids down, Luke and I went for a really long walk outside, under the stars. And we talked. And laughed. And played. And it felt a little like we were dating again. The part of me that loves girl movies, and wearing dresses, and candles, and who is trying to understand what romance really means was elated.

Lanie felt pretty amazing Saturday...for her. I maybe fill these kinds of days with more than she can handle unfortunately because I get so excited and then we both pay for it the next couple of days. Luke and I let the kids sleep in a little on Saturday before we met some folks for brunch, where Lanie didn't even cry when she ate!! We had gotten an invite to try climbing in a gym, and Lanie was pretty pumped about it. We had a harness that didn't press against her tummy so that was perfect, and oh my sweet word, she rocked! She climbed like a little beast, especially toward the end of our time there, and I had to keep telling her "Okay, but just one more climb." Little rock star. And Jackson, that kid is awesome! I think that this is something they are going to beg to do often. And of course Luke did amazing. That guy frustrates me with how well he does things without trying. It's like "hmmmm I've never done this before but let me warm up with 15 pull-ups and then beast my way up the wall and turn a corner and then just hang there for a while cuz I'm awesome." As for me, I'll just say that I'm a bit sucky at the whole climbing thing and if I worked really hard, I'm sure I'd be nothing short of mediocre.

Saturday night we had dinner with friends (THANK YOU GUYS!) and then got to watch the Minneapolis River Rats waterskiing team do their thing on the Mississippi River. I'm not gonna lie. I was impressed. And then I wanted to go waterskiing like crazy. It was so fun. Plus, anytime I just get to sit on a blanket in the grass during the summer, I'm a happy, happy girl.

Saturday also brought an unexpected visitor from Oklahoma. Our buddy Chris was traveling through Minneapolis and was able to get his flight changed to spend time with us. Although we were all excited, Lanie and Jackson were beyond thrilled. Lanie kissed him goodbye at least 20 times Sunday morning when we had to leave.

Sunday brought meltdowns. Lanie was so sad that Chris left and said over and over that morning "I don't want to talk about it." Alrighty, I can respect that. And then a meltdown at church because the "gun" she had made on her arm was coming undone and, "she had just worked so hard on it." Then a meltdown after Luke and Jackson left because she wanted them to stay, then a meltdown in Target because she was just too tired, then a meltdown at Ron McDon's because she couldn't find her stuffed black dog and she wanted to rest cuddling him and she was "Just so excited to sleep with him." And then, of course a meltdown at the lake because there were too many people. Luckily our day brightened when my friend Sam came to hang out with us and help entertain Lanie for a bit. It worked and we made it through the day. Barely.

Today was a bit crazy as well. It looked a little like this:
Labs at 8; doctor appointment with GI at 9; sedation at 10; MRI/MRCP at 11; Lanie came back to the room about 12:30; She slept until 3pm where We waited and waited and waited for results and at 4 they let us leave because they still didn't have any. Upside? We're outpatient tonight! No news is good news? We haven't been okayed by GI or the MRI but maybe tomorrow. Rachel picked us up at 430 and it was a glorious reunion. Haven't seen that little ray of sunshine in 2 weeks, and a "little bit" of hugging definitely happened.

Lanie has been saying all day she hasn't felt great and that she's tired so I was really surprised tonight when she ate a little for dinner (who wouldn't eat tacos?!) and then played in the water fight that took place outside. That took pretty much everything out of her though and she cuddled up between Rachel and me to watch a movie, and lay down for the rest of the evening.

I'm excited to see what tomorrow brings. And to hear the news from GI. And the MRI. And I guess I'm just thankful that even though I don't always learn the lessons right away that God gives me, he offers me more and more chances. So tonight I choose hope and joy and thankfulness and freedom. And I pray that God gives me that same resolve no matter the circumstances that surround me tomorrow.

Have a sweet night friends. I am just in awe that you have stuck with us this long and my heart overflows with gratitude when I really think about how amazing you all are. Thank you for your continued encouragement and support. You guys rock.

Chapter 20: Crazy

Jul 18, 2013 11:19pm

So I realized tonight when I was laying down that I told you guys all about the MRI and whatnot on Monday and then never filled people in! Part of that is because we don't have a lot of answers. Another part is that we didn't find anything out until yesterday afternoon. And the last part is mostly pure and simple forgetfulness on my end. So, there you have it.

This week has been crazy, and by crazy I mean "what in the world is going on right now crazy." You already heard about Monday, Dr. appointments, MRI's, labs, yada yada yada, so I won't rehash all of that. After being stuck in the hospital all day Monday, I must admit I was pumped about Tuesday. Although I really should have skipped Tuesday all together...hindsight).

Tuesday morning I waited and waited for Lanie to wake up. I thought about waking her up numerous times but if you've ever seen a bear attack (thank you Discovery Channel) you understand my fear there. That child does not do mornings. Finally at 11a I couldn't wait anymore and ever so sweetly woke her up. First mistake. She cried. I brushed her off like any good mother would do, got her dressed, grabbed our bag that was packed for the lake, headed to Rachel's for lunch (which btw was awesome...I can eat homemade guacamole every single day of the week and when it's on top of a burger, there are no words). Lanie wanted Lucky Charms. We obliged. She started complaining of tummy pain almost instantly. Again, I somewhat blew it off knowing the mood she was in, which might or might not have made matters worse. We got outside to get in the car and Lanie started crying. And I mean CRYING, saying that she didn't want to go to the lake. And she didn't want to learn to paddle board. And all she wanted to do was go back to bed. Say what?! Whose child is this? Surely not mine.

After trying to talk sense into her, and clearly not being able to (yep, she might be mine after all) I just said fine. We would go back and let her sleep. You would have thought I took away her best friend. She started that thing where it's like crying and screaming in one sound (hopefully you guys know what I'm talking about. Nope? Just me? Okay then) saying the she wanted to go to the beach. Ummm. I was confused here. And I'm a little stubborn as well. Shocking I know. I told her no to the beach. We were going home, i.e. Ronald's place, so she could lie down. More scream/crying. All the way to the car, down Hennepin, onto highway 94, off Huron, and into the parking lot. She calmed for a second when we got inside but only because she was running ahead of me to beat me to the room (we're a competitive family) and all her energy was being expended on that. Once in the room, she could turn her full attention back to the crying. This lasted close to 4 hours. I'm not even kidding. I was so close to smashing my head into the wall, but chickened out right at the last second. I could tell you stories from all that happened in that four hours and your jaws would drop. We'll save that for another time, though.

After those 4 hours were over, I fed her dinner, put her in the stroller, and headed out for a run, which is really the only way I could think of to legally let out aggression. Those 4 and a half miles were bliss. I wasn't tired even in the 500 degree weather. Every drop of sweat (which was a lot! Gross) was like a solid detox from the day. Thank you Jesus, for giving me legs that can run, a stroller, and some sweet Minneapolis paths along the river. Just exactly what I needed. We got back to the house and Lanie went straight to bed. We did get to have some sweet convos through all of this about what it means to love people and on emotions and family. So...maybe good came out of it? Anyway, thus ends Tuesday.

Wednesday, yesterday, was decent. Lanie was super lovey because she felt so bad about Tuesday. Bless. We played around the first part of the day doing nothing important but just having fun. We had labs too, but skipped the Starbucks. Her decision, and I just went with it. Pick your battles, right? My headache didn't agree yesterday afternoon, but I can roll with it. We met with our transplant doctor (Dr. C) early afternoon. Lanie loves him. I mean she adores that guy. And he did help save her life and all so I kind of have a soft spot for him too.

His report? MRI looked good. There was no blockage anywhere that they could see. Good news! But also...what about all that pesky tummy pain after she eats? No one knows and more tests are ordered. Lab results also came with mixed news. Finally her creatinine (kidney function) was coming down (and that's a very, very good thing). Her pancreatic levels were fairly good too. Her white blood cell count...super low. Uhhhhhh. This is a first. Possible causes could be a virus, meds, or just plain some sort of crazy. Her labs are all over the place in general, so in true 'me' fashion, I've started somewhat ignoring them. We'll see how that plays out.

Last night was quiet. Lanie watched a movie in the theater here while I cleaned up the room (there's a chance the room got somewhat 'disheveled' during our 4 hour ordeal on Tuesday). I've been getting really close to Saudi family here and brought Lanie down after the movie to breakfast with them for Ramadan. The mom (Suhar) can cook like no one's business and the other night she made us Arabic coffee. Divine. I don't know if it was the fact that the dish was mostly noodles and I haven't eaten noodles in forever or if it was something else, but about 20 minutes after I ate I threw up (or tried to when nothing came out anymore) for a solid 2 hours and then fell asleep on the floor with a blanket over my face.

Today Lanie woke up around 630a. She can be just ridiculous. At home this is totally acceptable and I'm usually up then anyway. Outpatient, however, is late nights and sleeping in. I unashamedly let her watch the Disney channel while I crawled back into bed and slept another blessed hour. I sluggishly got up, packed our bag again for the lake, and was pumped to finally get out on a paddle board. Lanie was much more willing today so we went to get Rachel and then were off to Calhoun. Did y'all know that they don't rent paddle boards when it's windy? Yeah. Me neither. Foiled again. The wind surfers kept catching my eye and I so wanted to try my luck with that little adventure but couldn't see Lanie being on board. Literally. Haha okay, I think I'm funnier than I really am.

We still had a great day. Our friends from Iowa were in town and came to play at the beach with us. Well they played. I played for like an hour and then thought I was going to pass out from last night's little incident + not eating breakfast + not getting enough water. Lanie was still content. There was a boy now with us to chase her around and throw her in the air and tackle everyone into the water. Perfect. 4 hours playing on the beach is hard work and she was pretty exhausted after our day. We played the calm card tonight and showered, ate dinner (Famous Dave's...you Rock for serving up some free delicious food) played Bingo (which we happen to be amazing at...okay everyone pretty much wins, but still) made a Target run, did meds, and laid down.

Normally I would go to bed excited. I love Thursday nights because it means that I get to wake up and it will be Friday. Ok well that will still happen. But no boys are coming this weekend. Luke's away at a camp and Jackson's with him. I'm more than glad that they get to go and share God's heart with young adults, but they will be very, very missed here in the north.

Tomorrow equals more labs, hopefully highly caffeinated coffee, a possible ultrasound (darn blood clots), and some other fun things I'm sure. I can feel the idea of home getting closer and it's hard for me to not think about it fairly often. And finally that makes me more excited than fearful...

Jul 24, 2013 5:01pm

Wow...you guys. Lanie has had such a great few days. Less meltdowns, less emotional outbursts, less tired, and almost back to her old self! And because of that we have been pretty busy just living in Minneapolis (which is what I'll say is the excuse for not updating, when in reality it's because I forget or don't think people really want to be updated on every day of our crazy outpatient life). Plus there's really nothing medical to tell...labs are still fluctuating a lot between just barely okay and bad. There's still tummy pain when Lanie eats, although I feel like that's getting better, but she's lost some weight, and that's not what they want. Mostly she's just being monitored closely. And I'd rather stay up here than go home just to come back, right? Right. That's what I keep reminding myself anyway.

Anyway, I feel like there are a million things to be thanking God for this last week. Literally, I am just so full of thankfulness tonight and continue to be humbled and amazed at what it feels like to be so incredibly taken care of. I just can't get over it.

So...just a few things that I'm amazed by...

- God's timing and faithfulness. Yeah. This is a big one and I feel like I could write pages on this alone. But specifically in regards to my sweet friend Rachel. You guys all probably feel like you know Rachel because she has been around pretty much every single day of our journey here, laughing when I laugh and crying when I cry (bless her little heart!) She's spoken truth and joy into situations when I couldn't find any, and asked tough questions when they needed to be asked. She has literally been such a gift during this insane and beautiful season. I won't tell you all of her story through this (she's a much better storyteller than I am) but I will say that God has used her in the craziest ways to show me more about who He is, and I am beyond thankful for the role that God has allowed her play in our Minneapolis summer. All good things must come to an end though and our play dates with Rachel are now limited to nights and weekends. Yep...Rachel got a JOB!! She started today and we got to celebrate with her tonight (in true Rachel/Ali form...adventures, getting lost, talking to lots of strangers, buying some ice cream for some sweet cops, and Lanie being somewhat annoyed)! And right as we are about to go home. Wow God...you're timing really is beautiful! And yet there are still times I doubt that timing. And worry. And get stressed because I think things should go a certain way. So tonight I was reminded that I don't want to hold my future. Not in the slightest. I actually suck at trying to figure things out on my own and don't want the responsibility of trying to plan for things that might or might not happen. Instead, I want to be content where I am. And put my trust in a perfect God that will do it for me.

- I'm thankful for this awesome city. And the people who live here. I am so humbled by the community of people who have taken care of us while we have been here. Like gone out of their way, taken care of us. They've taken us out to eat and to family events. Met us at pools. Gone on ice cream and Calhoun dates. Taken us climbing. Invited us over. Watched fireworks with us. Called and texted to check in. Watched movies and eaten popcorn (except for me. I dislike the stuff). Seriously. I'm overwhelmed you guys. And you're making it hard to say goodbye. I literally got teary last night telling some of you goodbye...I think it was because of the goodbye and not out of jealousy of your cabin 10 day vacation, anyway. Either way. Please start being big jerks to me. That would make things a lot easier. Plus Minneapolis...I'm impressed. You provide amazing entertainment. I am in love with you. Sorry for all those times I made fun of my Minnesota friends.

Yes, you guys talk funny (its caddy corner) and play ridiculous sounding games (ummm duck, duck, grey duck?) but I'm starting to finally understand your love for this state. If I was promised that my O's wouldn't start growing longer and longer, I might contemplate living here at some point.

- I'm thankful for people...and their patience with me. I can be a slow learner. And I genuinely love when people take time to teach me something or listen to me talk for hours and hours about whatever I'm excited about or love me even when I constantly run about 10 minutes late or am just in a complaining or poor me mood. You guys are so full of mercy and love.

- And for Lanie feeling better. Finally her moods have started to stabilize and I can reason with her. Maybe the horribleness of last week had to happen for breakthrough. But maybe she's just actually starting to feel better. Oh she can still throw a fit. And still get upset because people are standing directly in front of her and she's distraught thinking about not being able to see the fireworks that will be directly over her head in clear view for the whole city of Minneapolis. But they are getting fewer and further apart. Indeed. Light at the end of a 3 month tunnel.

- And thankful for the Ronald McDonald. I know I'd rather be with friends but we are so blessed and loved and taken care of here. If you ever find yourself in McDonald's (which I'm not advocating by any means) and see the Ronald McDonald house change boxes, I can say with complete certainty that your money is going to good use...taking beautiful care of broken families, hurting people, sick little kids, and people trying to make the best of pretty despicable situations. McDonald's...even though your food is horrible and gives me an instant stomach ache that makes me wish I could just rewind time and choose not to eat it...I will never say another negative thing about you again. Your heart is good. And generous. And I have been so blessed by your love. On behalf of all of us here sleeping in free rooms and somewhat cozy beds in Minneapolis tonight...thank you. Your love for others astounds me.

- And for the nurses on unit 5. We got to hang out with them today and their love and beauty are evident to everyone that meets them. I know that you guys believe that your patients are the brave ones, and you're right...they are all so brave...but so are you. Every day you go into work to serve children and their moms. You get yelled at sometimes. You take the brunt of the emotions that come from having a sick child. And yet you serve, with smiles on your faces and love in your heart. You guys are brave. And I admire you with everything I have inside of me. You guys are my heroes. And I'm not just saying that. When I ask Lanie who her best friends are, she gives me your names...you're pretty special.

- And even though I haven't gotten to see my boys in forever, I'm so thankful that they got to go to camp and love on young adults. Luke is amazing at sharing God's heart and leading people into worship. I'm not bragging on him (okay maybe I am) but that guy has a way with people. And he honors God. And takes such great care of us, even though we're not together most of the time. There have been nights when I just cry on the phone with him (which is hardly ever because it's downright painful for me to actually talk on the phone) and he encourages and fills me with truth...and love. Or he does a really good job of listening to me go on and on when I get really excited. And even though I don't always like to share him (greedy right?!?) I'm so excited that he gets the opportunities that he does to impact others with the gifts God has given him.

- And then for sunshine, warm days, lakes (sooooo many lakes), grassy areas, laughter, picnics, fruit and meat and veggies, distractions, sweet friends, cold water, grown up boys that will play with and love on Lanie, Jimmy Johns unwiches, arbor lakes, big rocks to climb (and people that I love and trust belaying me - learned some new words this week too), Target, having a car, windows down and radio up, pistachios, sunsets (I'm a sucker for them you guys!), big tight hugs, orange beach towels and bear bells, non dairy piña colada smoothies, fireworks, borrowed strollers, late night runs, my iPad, strong coffee, adventures, fro-yo, getting lost, smart phones, snap chat, food gift cards, and dollar theaters.

And also, I think that even after we are done with all this transplant stuff, I'm still going to make frequent lists like this, because after I write just some of the millions of things I'm thankful for, I am able to see situations in a new and brilliant light. And circumstances aren't really as bad as I first thought.

Goodnight y'all. Falling asleep in thankfulness is just what this heart needed. Thanks for being the sounding board...

Jul 28, 2013 11:38pm

I have no real reason to update, but here it is anyway...

I kept trying to decide whether or not to write tonight because I don't have any new or exciting news for you guys. I don't have any bad news either though, so I guess that's cool, too. I just feel like I have a lot on my mind tonight, so obviously, I chose to share it with all of you amazing people. Plus I went on a run and that wakes me right up like nothing else on this planet. Which is why I should start running in the mornings again.

Anyway. The 3 top things on my mind...in no particular order.

1. August 1st is Thursday. I feel like this date is burned into my mind as the day we get released because it's the day we've been asking God for. But the doctors aren't exactly on board with this yet. It's not that they're against it...they just haven't made any solid decisions and are nervous to promise us anything. Every time Lanie has labs (Monday, Wednesday, and Friday) we get a phone call telling us how her labs look and what the med changes are to try and stabilize them. Three times a week I anxiously await that call, waiting for the transplant nurses to tell me good news and that labs are moved to twice a week instead of three times and that we are on our way out the door. Three times a week, the call goes a little differently then I plan, and labs stay annoyingly blah. Labs really need to go to twice a week before we can go home. So here's the deal. Tomorrow is Monday. Lab day. Tomorrow will have to be the day they call us and tell us labs go to twice a week (Monday and Thursday) for us to be actually discharged out of the cities. Which would be perfect, seeing that we have a wedding that 3 of the 4 of us are in on Saturday and we leave for Florida on Sunday. One week from today. And in all honesty, I'm not worried. I'm not even a little stressed about it. I don't feel the need to change our plans or get worked up. I mean, what would that help anyway? In my experience...nothing. So instead, I'm going to keep asking God for Thursday. And trust that His timing is perfect. (Btw I'll try to remember to update tomorrow. Otherwise, this update is just mean. If I forget, feel free to call and text the heck out of me. I give you my full permission).

2. It's honestly an incredibly strange thought that I'll be leaving this city that I've been living in for the last 3 months. Like I mentioned last week, I really do love this amazing city. And to think that tomorrow will be my last Monday. And then Tuesday will be my last Tuesday. And then Wednesday.

145

And Thursday. I can't wrap my head around it (I'm pretty sure that's from God because I tend to get sappy and nostalgic). And I actually had to write a 'to do' list for the week to make sure I get everything done. Which, by the way, Wednesday is night-out-with-Rachel-because-we-only-do-things-with-children-EVER, so if there are any takers on watching two adorable kiddos, there is no application needed. I will pay you in whatever currency you request. And I'm not beneath begging.

3. And lastly, today has been a weird day. It's been a good day, but also kind of a weird day. First of all, Luke left. That's always pretty sucky. Today was a little different though, because I know we'll be together soon, livin it up family style again. And that makes these few days without him seem like they'll be somewhat easier. Second, I'm keeping Jackson with me this week. Which is awesome. I miss that kid a ton. And Lanie has someone else to play with other than me or Rachel so that's pretty perfect too, because I can only play pretend for so long before I get insanely bored (the 'real' world has officially killed any spark of imagination I had). And third, it's my dad's birthday. And I have not been able to get that off my mind all day and am really overwhelmed by how much I miss him. And when my mind wandered today, it went to him and all the sweet memories that I had with him. And also made me realize that I need to start writing them down because I'm scared that one day I won't remember anymore. And in the midst of processing throughout the day, God just continued to fill me with thankfulness and sweet reminders of who He is and how He loves. My friend Mo talked to me once about the kinds of questions we ask God. And in my experience, the 'why' question isn't really the most helpful question to ask because a lot of times we don't really understand the answer. Oh, sure. I could've asked God today why my dad is gone. And why things happened in life the way that they did. Or even why with Lanie. But I can't figure out how that question really solves anything in my heart. So instead today, as I was thinking about my dad, and celebrating his life, God was reminding me of all of the ways He takes care of us. Like how He provides for me places to stay and amazing food that I can eat (my stomach is getting pickier by the minute). And how He sends money to cover bills and expenses. And how He provides people in my life that love on me and take care of me. And teach me all the things my dad would've loved to have taught me, but never could. And are patient with me...and my kids. And my brief bit of mourning turned to praise. And overwhelming thankfulness. For my dad. For my father-in-law. For Luke. For men that love and adore their children and grandchildren. And for all the guys that God has placed in my life that have just shown me so much love for no reason at all. Wow, you

guys. I'm so teary tonight knowing that God is so incredibly good in the way He cares for His children. And how He gives us gifts we did nothing to deserve. I could go on and on and on praising God for the men in my life, and celebrating my dad, but I think you guys get the point. Besides, this whole paragraph was like a jumbled mess of rambling. And my head is spinning a little still thinking through all of this, so yeah. I'll end it there.

And now that I've written this out while I laid in bed for a solid hour, the run is wearing off and I'm finally sleepy.

And I am once again blessed to fall asleep with a thankful heart and a humbled spirit.

Chapter 21: August 1?

Jul 30, 2013 12:10pm

Sorry I didn't write last night. I thought about it and had planned to, but just didn't.

We finally heard from our sweet transplant coordinator a little before 5:00p last night. She was telling me about Lanie's different labs and how we needed to make some more med changes in order to try and fix some of the issues with her labs...the biggest being her white blood cell count (WBC). A 'normal' WBC lies somewhere between 4,000 and 11,000. A higher count usually means that the body is fighting off infection of some kind. A lower count usually means that the body might not be able to fight off infection like it should if it is exposed (and this is the extent of my knowledge on white blood cell count). Lanie's has been sitting around 2,000 for the last couple weeks. And for someone who needs to be able to fight off infection, that's too low of a number.

At the end of the phone conversation with Marci (transplant guru), I asked if labs were switching to twice a week. She could tell I was hopeful, and sighed as she said no, and that we needed to stay on top of her WBC for now. I didn't ask about Florida. I didn't even really say anything other than 'oh ok...totally understand'. Which I did.

I was thankful that my friends Branden and Bethany were hanging out with us, so that I didn't burst into tears. Instead, I just shrugged and shook my head no to them. And in true awesome friend fashion, they gave me huge hugs and encouraged me a lot. After they left to go home, Rachel met us. And her first question, of course, was about labs. And then she asked about Florida. And all I could do was shrug. And ask her what I should do...how could I update people? And then I had to come to a few realizations. And here they are...

- It's still not August 1st. And really, anything can happen in 2 days.

- one of my first thoughts when I heard that we still have to do labs 3 times this week was that I somehow made God look really bad. I made Him seem not powerful. Or not loving. Or both. And I had this fear that when I updated people, that's what they would see...an unloving God, who has no power whatsoever. Or maybe they wouldn't see that but they would see this girl...who doesn't have enough faith. Or trust. And they would shake their heads in pity. And as I was saying all of this out loud to Rachel, I realized...I don't have to prove God. I don't have to prove His power...or His mercy...or even His love. And even though I don't understand everything, nothing has changed. God's timing is still perfect. And I still want to be in the center of it more than I want August 1st. No matter what that looks like.

- you don't know if you don't ask (We all know what assuming does). I emailed a note to Marci last night explaining the Florida trip even more and asked for her input. She called me this morning at about 10:30. Her answer? We'll see how labs are tomorrow. If WBC count has come up, we can do labs and some other things on Friday and are free to go to Florida. And can just do labs next Friday when we get back to see if she needs to stay here in Minneapolis or can go home after that. If WBC stays low, it's a no-go. So...we wait for tomorrow. By the end of this Minneapolis summer...I'm going to be the queen of patience (Brent...be thankful. I'll be ready to go hunting with you this fall without driving you completely crazy).

149

And that, friends, is where we are today.

Ps...If my kids tell you I don't feed them dinner, be sure and tell them fro-yo is dinner and to stop the whining.

Aug 1, 2013 12:55pm

Day 96

So it's August 1st. Which seems really weird because this date has been in my head for what seems like forever now (or like 3 weeks, whatever). And I can already tell you it's gonna be hard for me to write this update.

Yesterday was Wednesday, as you know. We had labs. We had Starbucks. We went for a short walk around the front of the hospital. And then Lanie fell asleep on me on the shuttle back to Ron Mcdon. Well that was weird. She's usually sleepy in the mornings but not that sleepy. She started complaining of a headache and then laid down as soon as we got back to the house. And we waited on a call from Marci - our transplant extraordinaire. And I checked Lanie's temperature. I had already checked it before labs like always and it was 99.1. I wasn't worried about it at all, so I was definitely more than a little shocked when it showed a temp of 102.6. What the heck?!? I let her sleep for a while and waited on Marci to call, curious about how her labs looked. When she did call, Florida no longer sounded like an option. Her WBC was up, but when I told Marci about the fever, we understood why. And it wasn't because she was doing better. Marci told us we needed to bring her in to the ED to get her assessed, and that she would probably go inpatient. Yep. Florida is definitely out.

I had Jackson with me this week, so I called Luke, knowing that I can't keep Jackson in the hospital. Like the amazing husband he is, he drove up right away and decided to stay the night, before having to leave this morning. Which also meant that Rachel and I still went to the Twins game while Luke stayed with the kids. We cut our night out short, of course, but it was brief and fun while it lasted. Luke, you're awesome. And I miss you dearly.

I slept here with Lanie and Luke took Jackson back to the house for the night. Not gonna lie, I had remembered these unit 5 couches to be much more comfortable. Hmmmm, that's odd. And our amazing nurses hooked us up with a sunset room, because they honestly are the best nurses in the world. Other things I forget about being inpatient...you get woken up a lot. And your neck is sore for a solid morning no matter how much you try to move it. Oh and you're constantly cold. And how in the world did I pull a muscle in my chest overnight?! - Thankfully the amazing staff here outweighs all of that...

Anyway...this morning brought labs. An ultrasound. IV fluids. And antibiotics. The rest of the day we'll just hang out. Which is a little bit of a task because Lanie's feeling a lot better. And being up on 5 is like caffeine to her. She suddenly has all the energy in the world and starts telling everyone what to do. Meanwhile, I'm still sitting in frustration and discouragement because I feel like I've taken a blow to the stomach. And I know it's not the end of the world. And I'm probably (ok, definitely) being a little dramatic in being so sad about this. I just had my heart set on something...which is part of the reason I think I'm such a bad planner (I'm trying to find a good balance in setting expectations and being ok if they don't happen. This is something I've been HORRIBLE at for a long time, which is no excuse, I know). And this weekend still has the possibility of being pretty awesome. We have the Twins meet and greet tomorrow. A wedding on Saturday. And Lanie throws the 1st pitch at the Twins game on Sunday. The doctors say that we'll make Sunday happen (even if she gets a pass to leave for a bit), but the other two are still up in the air.

I want to be cheery and joyful (well, most of me does, anyway. A part of me really wants to throw a big fit). I want to tell you guys that even though things don't look like we thought, I have peace and joy and rainbows and gold dust flowing out of me. But that's just not the case. And if I was honest with you guys, and had my way, I'd be sitting on the floor...knees to my chest...head in my arms trying to ignore that today is happening around me. But I'm not 5. And even I can admit that coping method would pretty ridiculous and not helpful at all. And then I look over at Lanie and Jackson. At how content they are. They aren't throwing fits. They aren't letting the fact that even though we've been planning something for a while, and now are not doing it get to them at all. They're happy and sweet and just shrug their shoulders at our change of plans. And they're putting this girl to shame. Kids have such a way of reminding us of how to behave, no? So instead of letting my poutiness rule me, I'm pulling up my big girl panties and am going to approach these next couple of days with my game face on (my stubbornness should come in very handy here). And remind myself that joy is a choice.

Aug 2, 2013 11:14pm

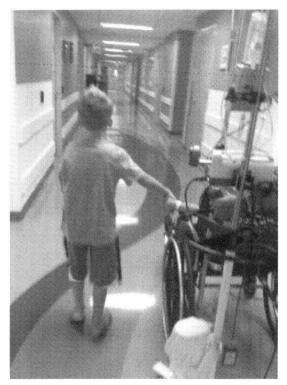

We went outpatient! I'll update soon, but I'm so sleepy tonight. And if this picture of Jackson walking Lanie to get her PICC line doesn't completely melt your heart, I'm also going to believe that you are not a fan of puppies, rainbows, or warm freshly baked cookies. Goodnight!

Chapter 22: So that's what 100 days looks like in real life

Aug 5, 2013 9:24pm

Hey guys. Sorry I haven't updated yet. This weekend was all sorts of crazy. The really good kind of crazy. And today just got away from me, mostly because I was still trying to distract myself from the fact that we aren't in Florida (and I promise that's the last I'll say about that).

FRIDAY

- I woke up Friday in a much better mood than Thursday. Thursday was hard. And I just want to be done with hard days for a while. So I'm going to (I guess I'm believing that my attitude will finally change for the better). Rachel and I decided to still take Jackson to the meet and greet with the Twins to pick up whatever we were supposed to go and pick up. I know I know...I'm now that mom that leaves her daughter in the hospital while I live the Hollywood life and schmooze with the all star athletes. Judge if you will (I know you won't) but I okayed it with Lanie and then headed out the door with Jackson and Rachel just in time for the limo to pick us up from Ron McDon's. And no...I didn't leave Lanie alone. Sweet Nancy came and hung out for the few hours we were gone (you've got to love her for braving the hospital side of Lanie).

- Meet and Greet was awesome. It included a sweet limo ride which dropped us off at Starbucks (we totally looked like movie stars I'm sure) and then took us the rest of the way to our destination, an awesome company that blesses its employees with fun picnics like this one, a huge bear (TC), two incredibly sweet pitchers from the Twins that stood 6'7 and 6'5, signed

Twins jerseys for the whole family, a Joe Mauer cape, and a stuffed TC bear. Wow you guys. What a humbling experience. There is no way we deserve to do anything like this...let alone go to the game on Sunday.

- we left the Meet and Greet a little early because I was nervous about the time and knew Lanie had her sedation scheduled at 2:30 to put in a PICC line. We made it back by 1:30 just in case. The nurses came in to tell me that sedation was running about an hour behind. No problem. Lanie had been NPO since 8:30 that morning so that was my main concern. The time kept getting later and things kept being pushed back. There were problems getting the meds released from Iowa City (don't get me started on that topic and insurance. It won't be pretty). Lanie was now going on 9 hours without eating or drinking and I was getting more and more frustrated. I kept trying to remind myself that there are still some people on my list that I haven't found to apologize to during transplant, and I didn't want to add to that, but it didn't really help. 3 names are now added to that list.

- Long story short, we FINALLY went outpatient at about 9:00p Friday night. And then I realized I didn't have my car with me. And the shuttle stopped transporting at 8:00p. Luckily people just take care of us so lovingly and someone was there to get us within 15 minutes to drive us to the house. What would I do without you people? And that's not a rhetorical question.

SATURDAY

- I can't sleep without a body next to me. That's just the way it is. And it's awful because I feel tired about 80% of the time because of it. Most nights I fall asleep around 1 or 2 am and then wake up around 6 or so. So it was with Friday night. In bed by 2am, and my alarm harshly waking me up at 5. And I would love to be a morning person. I like to wake up early...go for a run and then sit and drink my coffee for a bit. I like mornings okay, but only when I'm not here. Here...I like the idea of hiding under my blankets at even the mere thought of getting up in the morning. Anyway, I got up, gathered the things we would need for the day (packing up Lanie's meds are no joke. Some need a cooler, some don't. All different doses...and times...and colors...and headaches), and got the kids up to be out the door at 5:45. Rachel was already out front waiting for us and we hopped in her car to drive the 5 hours (when Rachel or Luke drives) to Iowa City for a wedding for some sweet friends. Rachel worked until midnight on Friday and had been up til about 1 and I was up til 2. We were very interesting company to each other to say the least. I giggle so much when I'm tired. And I talk and talk and talk. You gotta love sweet Rachel. She does neither one of these things.

- we got to Iowa City and pulled into our drive way. You guys. There are absolutely no words to describe what I felt. Like I can't honestly tell you because my emotions were all over the place. I haven't even seen anywhere close to home (besides the benefit in Sumner) in over 3 months. It was surreal. My goal was to get in, get my bridesmaid dress and Lanie's flower girl dress and get out as fast as humanly possible. And then just pretend it didn't happen. It sort of worked. I stayed out in the driveway forever hanging out with sweet friends that I haven't been able to hug in forever. That was awesome. And then I went inside. Oh my goodness, it smelled like home! And I didn't know home had a smell! And it was clean. I walked upstairs and Luke had painted Lanie's room exactly how she wanted it and organized it for her. And he painted an amazing tree along one of the walls in our room. Ad it was all so clean and perfect and beautiful and homey. And I made him lay on our bed with me for just a minute before I forced myself to get up, grab the things I needed, and get out of there ASAP. Oh, life. You trickster you.

- I love getting dolled up. Weddings are perfect for this. Lanie and I got to spend a few hours playing and getting all dressed up in a hotel room with some of the sweetest girls I know. Catching up while getting your makeup and hair done? What more can a girl ask for?! Plus, you guys, what an honor it was to be a part of a wedding of two people I adore so much. The pictures went smoothly and the wedding was beautiful. I had so much fun catching up with people I hadn't seen in ages (okay okay 3 months) and being silly with friends. Lanie kind of adores being a flower girl also. She is definitely not one to shy away from being in the spot light for a minute. I wonder where she gets that from...

- Luke and I had planned to leave the wedding at about 8:00 so that we could get a decent start back on the road to Minneapolis. Yeah. That didn't happen. But 9:30 works too. I tried very, very hard to stay awake and keep Luke company. That lasted all of an hour (maybe) and then he was on his own. Poor guy. What a trooper. We pulled into the house in Minneapolis a little after 2am. But I slept like a baby that night.

SUNDAY

- We all slept in. And it was amazing. I'm too embarrassed to even tell you what time I finally got out of bed. I knew some guys were coming at about 10 to hang out, so it's not as bad as you're thinking. Jackson had lots of fun showing the guys around the house before we all had some breakfast and waited for the limo to pick us up. Oh my word. Lanie was pumped. She missed the limo ride on Friday, and actually took it like a champ. I mean, of course she did...little rocker. And when she finally saw it pulling up I almost had to grab her because she started running for it. Stardom makes us insane apparently and the girl forgot it was a car moving toward her. After I yelled both kids stopped, gaining their sense of reality again. Oh my heavens.

- The limo ride was fun. Lanie just kept talking nonstop. Yet another thing we have in common when we're excited. When we got to Target Field, we met with Richard (the awesome guy who put on the meet and greet). He hung out with us for a bit and treated the kids like super stars. 'Oh, you want some eye black? Let's go find some. Lanie you want some bows for your hair? What about this? Would you guys like bracelets and lanyards? How about 2 of everything?' Richard. You are awesome. And if you keep spoiling my children, you are going to have to take them home. Or deprogram them so that they realize this is a special treat and normally we wouldn't be driving to a Twins game in a limo and buying awesome souvenirs. What an amazing start to the day though. The kids were wide eyed and pumped the whole time. As were their parents.

- Richard walked us to our seat for the game. Right off of third base...first row. Are you kidding me?!? And they were playing the Astros. And for those of you that don't know...I'm from the Houston area. I was just standing in awe most of the time. A few minutes before the game, the girls who were with us explained to Lanie what to do. Take the ball and chalk, run it out to the pitcher's mound, where Pelfrey would get it, and run back to TC. She was pumped. Until it was time to go. Then she froze up. Luckily they had Jackson go out with her and it was the cutest thing I have ever seen in my whole entire life. I could have died right there.

- After the kids got back from the millions of pictures they grinned for, we headed back to our seats (which I still couldn't get over!!) and sat down to watch the game. I tell you what. Not a second of that game was uninteresting to me. When you are that close, the game for real comes alive. The time we spent sitting there felt like minutes. I'm really not kidding

156

when I say humbled. And the thought occurred to me. God already knew that we weren't going to Disney this week. And that I would be a discouraged mess because of it and probably pout like a baby. And so maybe he planned this game for us. For Lanie. We thought we would miss it because our flight was supposed to leave Sunday morning, but something (duh, God) kept telling me not to cancel the game just yet. Even though I felt pretty dumb not canceling. And it hit me like a ton of bricks. God, being the amazing Father that He is, maybe gave us the Twins game, instead. Wow! Right?!? Are you guys with me? How cool is that? We don't deserve to be at that game, sitting where we're sitting, in the spotlight here and there. We didn't deserve Disney, either. Actually I can't think of a darn thing that I do deserve. But God, the God that created us and knows us, is so incredibly loving that he pours gifts down every day of things we don't deserve. Otherwise they wouldn't be gifts. And it blows my mind you guys. And how can I not be in awe of that?

- We met some friends toward the end of the game (our guys that came early, our friends who made a sign for Lanie and cheered like crazy, and one of our sweet nurses) and then after the game was over went back out for the last ride in the limo. The kids were exhausted. And so were we. Luke had to leave right after we got back and I was bummed. Less than 24 hours together. Take what we can get though, right? The kids and I headed over to Brooklyn Park to drown our night in ice cream (well sorbet for me...darn lactose intolerance) and just relax. And that was awesome and much needed.

MONDAY

- Labs. Like always. Except now, Lanie minds even less because they can draw out of her PICC. After labs we skipped Starbucks (GASP) at the request of the kids who apparently don't know what's good for them. And really just spent today hanging out, getting them a couple new shirts and whatnot for school, having a frozen yogurt date (again...not me) and wandering around stores looking at whatever they wanted without rushing them. They loved that. Marci from transplant called me sometime in the afternoon to let me know that Lanie's WBC are still too low and we'd do labs again on Wednesday and Friday. Darn labs 3 times a week. I am completely over you. So for at least another full week we live here.

And now that I've tasted home, I think it about it more often than I should, which makes the days seem long (and by days I mostly mean today, I guess).

I keep thinking about how much I miss having distractions that keep my mind off of being here. And how much I already miss the idea of heading out to Calhoun or a pool to pass the time (stinkin PICC line). But I'm walking in joy knowing that we've made it 100 days. And God has brought us through a lot in only a fairly short amount of time. And I can be completely thankful for that.

I am so blown away tonight by God's love and the way that He cares for us. And it's not just the Twins game. Or Florida. Or any of the awesome things like that. These last 100 days have been a privilege to walk. They've been hard. And good. A little bitter. But overall amazing. And what a sweet way to close out tonight. Resting in thankfulness...once again.

Aug 12, 2013 3:48pm

Seriously...where does the time go? I cannot believe that it's been a week since I've updated. Remember when we were inpatient and I would update twice a day? Yeah, me neither. And wasn't that like a year ago???

Well, outpatient life has been kind of the same thing over and over, but not really at all. Therefore, even though I find life fun, exciting, and interesting, there's not really much in me that believes you feel the same way about it. Because its life.

Things that are pretty much exactly the same week to week...

1. We have labs 3 times a week. Monday, Wednesday, and Friday. And then we drink Starbucks on Riverside Avenue (where I now have a drink named after me...I'm not kidding) and chat and hang out with some sweet Somali friends that now know us by name and occasionally text me to check on Lanie. ~ By the way, we have used Starbucks gift cards the entire time we've been here thanks you amazing people! I know we're going home soon because I only have a $15 card left in my purse, and we all know how far that gets you in Starbucks world.

2. We go to Target. Because we always seem to need something, even when we don't. And when we have nothing else to do, Lanie and I try on clothes that we wouldn't normally wear and spend way too much time wandering around looking at nothing in particular. Because we're girls and it's just in our DNA apparently. We have had Jackson with us more as of lately and he

doesn't love this as much as we do. Or at all. He left with Luke again this last weekend, so let the summer of Target continue.

3. We watch Disney while Lanie does her IV antibiotics twice a day. And I'm not gonna lie...I'm so over it. If I don't have to see another Disney show for the rest of my crazy little life, I would in no way be devastated.

4. We play bingo on Thursday nights at Ron McDon's, because let's face it...it's legit.

5. We wait on phone calls telling us we can move labs to twice a week and go home soon. It's got to happen sometime, so until it does...we become masters of waiting and hopers of distraction (is hoper a real word? These days I'm just making up stuff, I realize).

Things that are new to this last week...

1. We had Jackson with us last week. He is the best entertainment for Lanie so it's safe to say we are in big trouble this week without him.

2. Lanie ended up in the ED Wednesday night, which was a huge bummer. For one, when you get called into an emergency room, you better pack snacks because you'll be there for hours. For two, we were living it up at an outdoor picnic on the most gorgeous day ever. And we didn't want to leave to go sit in a hospital room. Lanie's sweet transplant coordinator had called us to tell us about her labs, which had gone from blah to bad...again...especially her potassium. A few fluids and a med to help her block some of the potassium she eats in food and we were out of that place in no less than 3 hours. Speedy in the ED world.

3. Thursday was fun. It included pomegranate and mango sorbet with a gluten free cone for me, (the kids got homemade ice cream, which I didn't cry about...did I mention the sorbet???) Starbucks (which never happens on a Thursday), reading books at some local bookstores, Luke surprising us by coming a day early, and winning at bingo. Outpatient life isn't so bad at all, really.

4. We got to go to the 1st preseason football game in the Metrodome, which just happened to be Vikings vs. Texans. Have I mentioned I'm from Texas, and I grew up with all things football? So being able to go to this game was such an awesome experience. I almost didn't know who to cheer

for, but at the last minute I remembered how awesome the Vikings are to the children's hospitals around here and how I've experienced their generosity first hand, and the choice was no longer hard. Texas, if you guys want our allegiance back, send some sweet gear and tickets to the Ronald McDonald house, Twin Cities, and I'll think it over. Until then, Go Vikes!

5. The weekend was chill...and therefore awesome. It included a little Como Zoo, some amazing food, a bonfire, some REI goodness, a couple trips to some nearby parks, and a visit from some adorable Iowa City friends. Just the way a weekend should be.

And then there's today. Labs (again). Starbucks (again). Mall of America Sea Life (that was new). And letting Lanie get some rest before we have dinner and some fun with a friend tonight and then a slumber party with Rachel. All while we wait on a phone call (again) to hear about labs. Because its Monday. And as you know, that's what we do.

Chapter 23: Hard to believe, I know

Aug 13, 2013 4:49pm

Hey guys! Shorter distance between updates means shorter updates. You are welcome.

We waited almost all day yesterday to hear back from labs and at approximately 4:30, the phone rang. And I knew the number. Transplant. I was excited so instead of letting it play through half of my ringtone like normal (what can I say...it's Mumford and it never gets old!) I answered it right away. Verdict? Labs were inconclusive. Something happened and they weren't able to process any of her labs. Man, waiting all day for that was kind of a bummer. Good news is that Lanie was scheduled to her PICC line out today because her risk of infection is high (but yay!!) and not-as-good-news-but-still-good-news was that we would need to redo labs today, with the PICC line still in (no poke required).

We getting used to all the waiting, so this was just another thing to wait on...which actually feels fine. I honestly just feel like we're going home soon anyway, so what's a day or 2 more??

Today, a Tuesday, was labs. Starbucks (the cards are officially completely gone friends, of course we're going home soon). The park. Resting, which unfortunately included a little Disney (Dog with a Blog wasn't on, Shannon. Otherwise I really, really would've tried to appreciate it. And failed). 2 hours spent in clinic for a 10 minute procedure to pull the PICC. And now a nice hot bath for the girl (because that's what you do when you can finally use both arms in the water). I still haven't heard any results for the labs today. But it's ok. It's still only 4:30 and the day is young. Or so it seems.

One victory at a time, and today's was getting that PICC line out.

So tonight we'll celebrate that. With free Crave being catered into the hospital (we're freeloaders and not at all ashamed of it) and then with some cheering on a friend at a slow pitch later tonight. And maybe a sunset glass of wine with Rachel after we get home (i.e. Ron Mcdon).

Thanking God for so many sweet little things tonight. And I love that even the small victories make my heart happy these days. And home is just over the horizon.

Aug 15, 2013 10:26am

It's Thursday. Which is weird because we just got back from labs. And Starbucks (don't judge...I know I know, I PAID for coffee. I have got to learn how to make coffee...these days it's just getting embarrassing). It feels like a Friday, which is a little disappointing because then it's really just a tease all day long...thankfully I have plans pretty much all day and evening, which makes the day fly by!

So I'm updating today because I honestly thought I would be packing up our room today, ready to hit the road tomorrow morning. Home. After the craziness of labs this week, and then redoing labs this week, I was positive that the results would be good and we would be spending our first weekend in over 3 months on Iowa soil. The labs from Tuesday came back...decent. Not great, but decent. We heard the news Tuesday that if labs were good Thursday (today) we would be home tomorrow. No problem.

And then there was yesterday. A phone call from our Minneapolis hospital. Awwww, congratulating us on hanging in there this long and sending us home with a smile and 'good work team'. If only. The actual phone call was to make an appointment with infectious disease on Monday. What?? They found something 'weird' in her blood and want to look at labs today and Monday and then see us Monday afternoon. 'Weird'?? Is that an actual medical term? Coming from infectious disease...I'm not comforted. So apparently 'weird' means that it's not bad enough or infectious enough to come in today or tomorrow and get it taken care of, but just annoying

162

enough to mean that we will spend the weekend here. And then wait on Monday to find out more. And if and when we can leave.

Weird is now my least favorite word ever.

And God's timing is still perfect, even if I don't in any way understand it.

Aug 18, 2013 4:28pm

Hey everyone! We had such a great weekend with the boys here. Lanie wanted to send you all a little message (okay okay, it was my idea, but she was so, so excited about it, as you can tell. Okay, okay maybe she just did it because I told her to, but we can all agree it was a brilliant idea) to let you know that we all appreciate you guys so incredibly much.

Lanie has been feeling pretty awesome for the most part. Sure, she has had some rough patches, but all in all, I'm pretty amazed with what she can do with her body. And how she doesn't let anything get in her way. And that she's stubborn and strong when it comes to recovery.

I mean, only 113 days after transplant (but who's really counting) and she can run, play, tackle, and swim. She can do cartwheels, head stands, and roll down hills. She is a beast (in such a sweet and girly way of course).

Today, on the other hand has been rough. I haven't been able to keep her awake or get her to eat. When she is awake, she cries that her tummy and head hurts. She doesn't have a fever and I can't figure out anything else going on. Her pain seems pretty hardcore though. She's not being dramatic or playing the system. She just feels terrible. And I don't know why. The plan has been somewhat that we would go home soon...and after our appointments tomorrow we would know more. But this has me a little worried.

Maybe she just overdid things this weekend. Maybe she just is having an off day. And maybe we will go tomorrow and they will go on and on about how great she's doing and I'm just being over cautious.

So again, we wait. I'll still pack up our room this evening, letting her sleep off whatever this is. In hopes that our maybes will all come true and my next update will be to tell you guys we are out of here and on to the next adventure that awaits us at home.

We love you guys. And are constantly encouraged by you. Peace out til tomorrow...

Ps. If I don't update you by midnight tomorrow, feel free to call, text, and harass me like crazy. Hopefully I'll be on the road or packing, but if not, there's a chance that I'll be the one hiding under the covers, and will need someone to slap me out of my funk.

PSS...I couldn't get the video to upload on this. It's on the living thru Lanie Facebook page for those of you that have access to that.

Chapter 24: Joy is a choice

Aug 19, 2013 11:11pm

Here is my honest post...

I wanted to be driving home right this minute.

I don't have a lot of words to describe how heavy my heart feels. Or how frustrated I am. Or even my understanding of circumstance.

And I don't like to talk a ton when I'm full of emotion because feelings are relative. Truth, however, is not. Joy is a choice, not a feeling. And even though this situation full out sucks, I will ask God every minute to fill me with hope. And truth. And kindness. And patience. And joy. Because there is no way I can muster any of that on my own. Not tonight. Actually, not even on my best day.

I'll update tomorrow when I know more about what's actually going on. Until then, I'll be here. Unit 5. Room 38. Laying on the couch, or perhaps in Lanie's bed. Covered in blankets. Asking God for new strength to come with the blaring sunrise that will be pouring in our window.

And for the courage to choose joy.

Aug 20, 2013 10:47pm

Isaiah 40:28-31- The Message (MSG)

'Why would you ever complain O Jacob, or whine, Israel, saying, "God has lost track of me. He doesn't care what happens to me". Don't you know anything? Haven't you been listening? God doesn't come and go. God lasts. He's Creator of all you can see or imagine. He doesn't get tired out, doesn't pause to catch his breath. And he knows everything, inside and out. He energizes those who get tired, gives fresh strength to dropouts. For even young people tire and drop out, young folk in their prime stumble and fall. But those who wait upon God get fresh strength. They spread their wings and soar like eagles, They run and don't get tired, they walk and don't lag behind.'

Dang it. Ok. So I totally know God hasn't lost track of me. And I fully believe with every single ounce of my soul that God is a good Father that cares about what happens to me...and to Lanie. But even with that knowledge, my attitude whole heartedly stinks. I told Rachel today that I am really struggling with the thought of choosing joy. That I feel so over all of this and because of it, I'm letting little things get to me and feel teary at the drop of a hat. She looked over at me and asked 'why?'. Why?!? Oh sweet little Rachel. I thought my hand might reach out and smack her right then and there (out of love of course). Why?!? What kind of question was that? Because this situation is pretty high on my suck list. Because although I love the nurses and doctors in this hospital, I would much rather meet them for picnics in the park then sit in this room. And also because home was so close, I could almost see it, and now the tunnel just got dark again. It seemed like the why question was taken off the table a while ago.

And yet, there it was. 'Why?' So instead of losing the craziness I felt in that second, I took a few minutes to think it through (plus Rachel and I are both pretty scrappy, so it would have been a toss up what the outcome of that would have been and I like the odds to be a lot more in my favor). Why did I feel so...frustrated/annoyed/lost/alone/worried/and dare I say, angry?

I mean, yeah, the circumstances are hard. Yesterday they were concerned about rejection and scared the living day lights out of me even mentioning it as a possibility. Today they decided that it isn't. It's probably a virus + dehydration. And with a kidney that still struggles some, that's not a good combo. Lanie's actually been feeling better today. She's gotten out of bed.

166

Played. Eaten. Watched Disney. And taking selfies with various objects and people around the hospital. They unconnected her from her IV today to see if she can maintain on her own. Tomorrow will tell. I've seen worse circumstances and didn't struggle this much.

And, yeah, I'm tired. I'm really tired actually. This weekday single parenting stuff is tough. Even with the amazing support system I have. And I miss my bed. The one piece of furniture (mattress) that Luke and I paid completely full price for because we saw it as an investment in our sanity. We were so right on. Nice work Luke and Ali from 5 years ago. I am so proud of both of you. It is like sleeping on a cloud. And I'm regressing...and being tired is just an excuse. Not a source of whatever this is that I'm struggling with.

I kept thinking, but everything I came up to answer the 'why?' question just seemed like another lame excuse. And then it hit me. I know why I'm struggling so hard. It's because it's easier this way. It's easier to lay on the couch today and remain frustrated. And it's easier to complain and get teary and take offense to stupid little things.

Choosing joy is hard, you guys. But hard things are almost always the things that are worth something. And it's not like I have to do it alone. Or in my own strength. "God energizes those who get tired and gives fresh strength to dropouts. For even young people tire and drop out, young folk in their prime stumble and fall. But those who wait upon God get fresh strength. They spread their wings and soar like eagles. They run and don't get tired, they walk and don't lag behind." Yeah. This sounds better than what I've been doing when left to my own devices. (The idea of running and not getting tired pulls me right in. I run. And I get very, very tired. This seems like an easier choice now by the way).

So I think it's time to let go of this situation and continuously make the decision to choose hard over easy. Joy over anger and frustration. And hope over lost and alone.

Thank you, God for allowing me a day to whine and hide under my covers in what seemed like defeat. But thank you even more for the question of why and for not letting me stay in my place of comfortable frustration. And the encouragement that you send through amazing people that come to visit bearing sweet words and strong hugs.

ALSO!!! Pretty big side note!! Tomorrow is the first day of school in Iowa City. My tough little Jackson will be going into 3rd grade with no parents there to take his picture or pray with him or tell him how awesome he is (Luke is at a training and I'm, of course, here). We have amazing friends taking care of him, but still...pray for his heart to be protected and that he would know how incredibly much we love him! (I can't think about this for too long or I'll immediately fall back into hide under the covers knowing I'm the worst parent that ever lived mode). My sweet Lanie Lou is pretty disappointed that she's missing this day too. Please pray against discouragement and the feeling that she's always missing out.

Thanks you guys. One day I hope to give each of you a solid 5 minute hug.

Here's to tomorrow...and whatever adventure it holds.

Aug 21, 2013 9:12pm

Today was a better day. Partly because my attitude was better, but mostly because it was just a better day.

Labs woke us up bright and early (not early enough to see the beauty of the sunrise, but perfectly on time for the sun to be blazing through our fifth floor window). Lanie usually goes back to sleep after labs, which was my hope, but not today. Once she was awake, she was ready to rock...and by rocking, I mean watching Disney and eating breakfast. While she was content, I called Jackson to talk to him before school. I almost teared up once, but sucked it back in. So proud of that awesome little guy.

Mornings drag on a bit at the hospital, mostly because I'm usually waiting on rounds to see what the plan is for the day. And today was no different. I was curious to hear about labs and what the doctors are thinking in terms of care...and in going home. If you want to see doctors get uncomfortable, ask them about specifics in regards to a home plan. They are so funny. I don't think that they want to be the one to say when home is happening and then have to take it back (understandably). I asked anyway. Which brought about a long answer talking about white blood counts, and antibiotics, and viruses, and my comfort level. Hmmmm. I understood everything the doctor said, but still didn't know the answer to my question. Next best thing, ask the resident (who is this case is an awesome girl that we've been with in one way or another throughout all of transplant, and knows us).

168

The verdict? We could leave the hospital today and go outpatient. My heart jumped. Man, in 2 days I went from holding my breath scared to breathing huge sighs of relief. Thank you God for being there during both of those times. I asked what she thought about home and she said that our transplant doctor wanted us here while Lanie was on the heavy hitting antibiotic so that we knew she was actually getting better. And to make sure that she would be fine to go home. Roughly 10 more days. Aye aye aye. But ok.

It's hard to be upset about being outpatient when we were just inpatient. And I'm content with the plan. Lanie and I celebrated our freedom today by staying out of the heat (no more dehydration!!!) and going to the movies for a matinee showing of Planes.

We have a completely free day tomorrow before labs and appointments on Friday. And I'm kind of excited about that.

Thanks for sticking with me you guys! I feel like there are times when I go from one extreme to the other, and you guys are just there. Encouraging me. And humbling me. And praying for us. And loving us.

God's family is a beautiful thing.

Chapter 24: Sigh

Aug 26, 2013 10:05pm

Hey guys. I'm not going to update much tonight (you know, the whole bad attitude thing) but I brought Lanie to the ER around 4:00 with 105.1 fever. Apparently that's a real temperature again. I vaguely remember when she was inpatient after transplant and for two weeks straight we saw temps like that, but I had no idea they existed in outpatient world.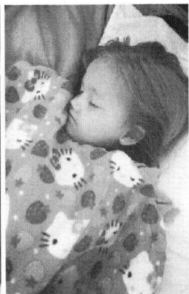

Needless to say, I'm writing this from the 5th floor of Amplatz Children's Hospital...downtown Minneapolis. And you guys, I'm not gonna lie, it's been a rough day and I don't know the word for the emotion that lies past discouragement, but that's where I am (sorry Brittany for totally breaking down in the hallway on you!)

I'll update again in the morning. Or afternoon. Or for sure by tomorrow night.

Aug 27, 2013 11:52am

Man, it's a beautiful day in Minneapolis. It's hot...like stepping into a bright, glorious sauna...but still beautiful. I woke up (is it still called waking up if you didn't really sleep during the night? No matter...) feeling way less emotional and clear headed than I was last night. Last night was...well...a mess. Seriously, poor Brittany. Can I just say that the nurses here are way more than just nurses. I'm wholeheartedly blessed by their strength, love, high spirits, resilience, and empathy. I wish I could take you all on a sweet vacation with beaches and sun and rest (as if that would even be enough to say thank you, my daughter says your names when people ask who her best friends are for pete's sake).

So I wish I could give you a good update with lots of answers. I have none to share with you. Lanie's still getting Tylenol every 4 hours to try and keep her fevers down.

That was written about 9:30 this morning, when I still had high hopes for today.

At 11 or so our transplant doctor came in to talk to me. Lanie's blood pressures were low and her fevers were high. On top of all of that when she wasn't sleeping, she would talk about things that didn't make any sense. She would ask why the kitten was on the ceiling or how many dollars it took to pay for a mint. Every now and then she would say something to me that was legit and make me smile.

Honestly everything that happened next was kind of a blur. And I praise God because I know he'll wipe most of it from my memory just like he did after transplant (oh Lanie's transplant? It was totally fine. No, no real bumps in the road or huge unexpected things crashing around--> a real conversation I had with someone a couple weeks ago until Rachel stepped in and was like whaaaaaaat?!?)

A little after 1:00, Lanie's nurse and team came in the room and told me that Lanie was really sick and needed to head down to PICU. And within minutes (not exaggerating) our things were loaded up and carried downstairs to a room that I remember all too well. You guys...I freaking hate the PICU. And it usually brings either bad or very bad news that I don't want to be a part of.

Lanie and I were down here a solid 2 hours, most of which she was awake for (not a good thing...labs, finger pokes, respiratory tests, holding her down, plus the fact that she still isn't making sense when she talks but still trying to reason with her (I'm sorry I can't find your magic wand Lanie, I'm looking everywhere. Oh wait here it is! *she throws it off the bed yelling that wasn't it*). God must have given me some super strength through that because only a couple tears were shed trying to get through the nonsense of my life til 3pm.

Everything changed at 3. Doctors were more hurried and there were a lot more of them around. And I saw one push in the intubation cart. Wait. Instant tears. Doctors explained that they needed to figure out what is going on and they need to hurry and in order to do that intubating her was the safest thing to do. More tears. They went on to explain that she is very sick and they needed to get a CT of her head, stomach, and pelvis (her belly and head pain are pretty out of control), put in a central line, maybe get an MRI, put in more IV access lines, and do a lumbar puncture (spinal tap). All incredibly scary words.

It took them a while to intubate her, but once they did I just sat in a familiar green chair in the back of the PICU not wanting to see her sedated looking like that. At about 5 though I heard her moving. And things escalated quickly. She was wide awake. Probably one of my worst nightmares. Fear in your child's eyes is the worst thing ever and I couldn't control the tears even if I wanted to. To make matters worse, she started throwing up...while intubated. So while I held her hand and talked to her using my strongest mom voice possible (which honestly sucked) 5 or 6 nurses held her and took care of her before they finally got her back to sleep so they could take her to run all of the tests.

Luke and Jackson are on their way up, which is amazing because the longer I sit in this PICU room, the less I feel in control of my responses. (I might or might not have texted Rachel that if another doctor or nurse that I have never met tried to touch me she would have to come and bust me out of jail). But for real.

You guys. I don't understand any of this. And I'm completely broken down...begging for God to pick up the pieces to create something more beautiful out of this situation. Which he always does. Somehow.

I'm kicked out of the PICU room for a couple hours so that they can put in the central line and spinal tap. Sitting in this waiting room on the end of unit 3 that I actually dislike more than any other place in this whole hospital. This waiting room holds little to no positive memories and sitting here tonight is as about as high as it gets on my life-why-are-you-so-stupid list.

Thanks for standing with me friends. Asking God for big things tonight...

PS: I couldn't bear to put a picture up from today. I haven't even taken any. So instead I'm putting one up from yesterday morning, when she wasn't feeling amazing and wanted to rest and just play her harmonica. Because she's awesome like that...

Chapter 25: Four months to the day

Aug 28, 2013 3:26pm

Wow, you guys. It's already been a long day and its only 3:00. And we don't have a lot to update. There's a lot that has happened, we just don't have a lot of results.

WHAT WE DO KNOW/WHAT HAS HAPPENED...

- Lanie went into septic shock yesterday, which is why we were brought down to PICU so quickly and why things happened so fast.

- the spinal tap results look fine, no signs of anything abnormal there.

- CT of head looked great (the sepsis explains the disorientation)

- CT of belly and pelvis showed a tiny amount of fluid by the liver, which has been there a long time. It also showed that her bladder was holding over 800 ml of urine. That's a huge amount.

- the central line was placed last night, but was not working this morning. It will be pulled and a PICC will be placed sometime tonight.

- this morning she had a bronchoscopy to understand a little more about fluid found in her lungs.

- last night was a little rough. She woke up around 4:30, thrashing around trying to pull her breathing tube out. You guys...that was awful. She was so scared (I would have been too waking up to all of that!!) It took almost half an hour to get her calmed down and somewhat sedated. A half an hour in

174

that situation is like 10 years. So awful. Thankfully she responded to Luke's voice really well and started to calm down.

- she woke up 3 more times since fighting her little heart out to pull those tubes out of her throat. And man is she strong. I cry every single time.

- her team has added numerous antibiotics to cover just about anything. Knowing the source is important but not as important as getting her stabilized.

WHAT WE DON'T REALLY KNOW... (the big question)

- what the infection is or where it's coming from. It's probably bacterial because she's responding well to treatments. Which is good (good is a relative term) but the fact that's she responding makes me breathe a little easier.

THE PLAN...

- PICC placed at some point tonight...it was supposed to happen around noon

- so many labs are being done to find source of infection and to see if anything grows

- if the source of infection isn't found today, the doctors will take some of Lanie's white blood cells and tag them (I don't know exactly any medical terms, but you guys get the idea) before placing them back into her body to see where they go to fight off infection. Seems pretty legit though.

- extubate her tonight if she is able to breathe on her own

It was exactly four months ago we got the call. We were still in church and I can see Luke - clear as day - answering the phone and telling me it was transplant. I can see the kids jumping up and down with excitement and Lanie saying she was so excited to not be sick anymore. I can also remember the drive to Minneapolis and so many of our friends and family sitting in these rooms trying to keep ourselves entertained. Wow. I am so humbled at this journey. It's not at all where I want to be right now. And I still don't understand a darn thing about what's going on and have honestly spent a good part of the last couple days crying...but I am still humbled.

I can see the billions of ways God has provided and it calms my heart in the midst of this hurricane of a storm to know that He has this too. Don't worry friends, we're not losing hope in the outcome...we're just hurting and broken within this circumstance.

We love you guys and are BLOWN AWAY by your continued love and generosity. I'll hopefully update again tonight.

PS this picture shows you the reality of the situation without showing you the REALITY of the situation. Please pray against fear for our little Lanie Lou. Pray that as she sleeps so soundly she sees Jesus.

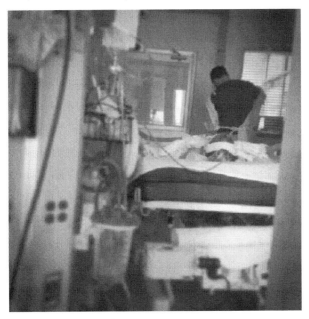

From the bottom of our hearts...thank you

Aug 29, 2013 11:07am

Hey guys. So I actually updated last night, but somehow lost it at the last minute and then instead of redoing it, I chose to pout. So there's that.

I think it was a little after 6:00 when the nurses started turning off all of her sedation meds so that she would wake up and prove that she could breathe really well on her own. And then we would be able to take out the breathing tube. Once the medication was turned off, it took her about an hour or so to actually wake up, little sleepyhead. All it took was a cough and then within seconds we were holding her arms and head so she didn't pull the tube out. We only had to wait 5 or so minutes after for the tube to come out. And then...

Coughing. Lots of coughing.

And tears. From more than just Lanie.

It took her a while to calm down. And every now then we could hear her whisper things. One whisper was for the oxygen to be gone. Another was for letting us know her throat really hurt. And then she asked for grandma. And then Jackson. And they both separately came and held her hand and talked to her which calmed her more than anything else. Melted my heart so completely.

Finally she calmed enough to ask for a popsicle. Yes! Of course she could have a popsicle! Her perception was a little off and her body is so swollen from all the fluids, but she managed to get it to her mouth with only a few misses. Because of course she wanted to do it by herself. She fell asleep with her popsicle in hand.

She woke back up around 9:45pm pretty happy. She was smiling and wanting to eat more popsicles and asked to see one of her nurses from 5 (who of course obliged and came down for a short time to see her). She was so comfortable, so I came back to lie down while Lanie and Luke cuddled in her bed and watched cartoons. I had just fallen asleep when I heard her yelling and screaming. She was fighting the nurse about her PICC line. And yelling about her tummy. And just so worked up. It took forever to get her calmed down and then she would just get super upset about something else. Finally she calmed enough for me to come lay back down around 12:30am. Luke decided to lay with her until she fell asleep (he told me this morning that she seemed like she was dozing off finally a little after 3:00am so he came back to lay down). A nurse came over and woke me up somewhere around 3:30am because Lanie would not let them touch her to fix some of the tubes she has. I went up and talked to her and calmed her down again. At 4am she was finally calm enough for me to crawl in bed and cuddle with her. She tries so hard to cuddle but both of her arms are attached to tubes and are held straight making it difficult for her to turn on either side. I just held her close and she held my arm. Her breathing was still so raspy and she is nervous that she won't be able to breathe.

Needless to say, she did not fall asleep. I did let her start watching some TV at about 5:00am because I was just so tired and when Luke woke up a little after 7, I happily switched places with him, and was able to sleep from about 7:30 to 9. Lanie slept from 8 to 9. Luke got it easy.

Since 9, there are times when she's somewhat content and times when she's crying that her tummy and head hurt. And sometimes just crying because she's mad or annoyed. We rounded with the doctors this morning, and they actually are really happy with her progress and say they feel as though she is out of the danger zone. Never been more thankful for words like that. She still has quite a few things to get done today...ultrasound, more labs, scans, getting her foley out, removing her ART line, getting her to eat, and figuring out more ways to find the source of infection, and hopefully moving back up to the 5th floor now that she's more stable.

I could not be more thankful for the fact that Luke is here to help me. I'm so tired and he is just incredible. And for Joyce (Luke's mom) being here and keeping Jackson last night. And for Leah hooking us up with food and support. And for all of the people who came yesterday (and didn't judge or comment on the fact that I look like I've been living alone in the woods for weeks). You guys are all direct blessings from God.

Hoping for some more positives today. And ready to have my spunky, little lovely back.

Chapter 26: First day of many

Aug 29, 2013 10:54pm

Well hello there from Unit 5!!!! That, my friends, means that although some of the scariest days of my life just happened and more tears have been shed than I can even count, we are out of treacherous waters. Praise God!!

A brief update on today...brief because I've slept less than 6 hours in 3 days and my eyes are burning to go to sleep.

We still haven't completely narrowed down an exact source from where the bacteria started, but we do know that the 5 antibiotics Lanie is on are working. The game will be taking one away at a time to see how she does. Lanie has had a much better afternoon then she did night and morning. She was able to talk more this afternoon and constantly wanted Jackson by her. The video that I put up on the Facebook page was a brief window of good. She is still struggling a lot with pain and breathing. She takes pretty shallow breaths that are super raspy...which I'm sure is to be expected after having a breathing tube and then adding in a bronchoscopy. Her oxygen levels are stable.

We don't really have a plan as of now and are still waiting to see what all of the cultures are going to bring back. And then I'm sure we'll find out more in rounds sometime in the morning.

One thing is for sure...when I'm told she has a compromised immune system, that is no joke, my friends. And there is a tension inside of me that I didn't have before. And suddenly I'm realizing that everything we do matters. And that I'm somehow in charge of it all. And I just don't feel like a responsible enough person for that kind of task. And in all honesty, I feel really afraid that I'm going to make mistakes. From my track record...probably lots of them. And I know God has this, and I need to let go of all of these control issues I'm feeling tonight as I lay down. But I haven't been able to do that yet. Praying that God will take all of that fear out of me or help me to see His hand through it.

I'm thankful for the sweet little moments today and praying for a lot more tomorrow, when the sun rises, along with the promises of a new day.

Aug 30, 2013 3:18pm

Last night was somewhat uneventful. Just the way we like it actually. Joyce and Jackson left around 7:30 to head over to Ronald MacDonald and Lanie fell asleep around 8:00. Usually it's just me here, so I read or watch a movie or write or go for a run. Last night, Luke stayed up on 5 with us though. A sweet change. Hanging out and having a little movie date was a perfect night-in activity. Sometimes it's the little things...

Lanie slept really well most of the night (her parents however were another story, that little green couch with 2 people on it can only feel comfy for so long). Her breathing remained pretty raspy throughout the night, but not terrible, and her stats still stayed fairly good.

She woke up at 6:30, though, sounding terrible. And she was scared, which made things worse. At 7:00am the pulmonary team was in with an albuterol nebulizer. Lanie screamed and fought. This is the girl who gives out her arms for labs, lays perfect for chest X-rays, ultrasounds, MRI's and the like, takes a million meds a day even though she hates most of them, but this...this she has a problem with. Bummer. The albuterol did nothing for her. Directly following albuterol, she got epinephrine, and that helped...for like 20 minutes. Before no time she was stridorous again and getting another blow by of epi. After 5 visits from pulmonary, she was started on an IV steroid, which has definitely been the most helpful.

In between all of the pulmonary doctors, kidney doctors, GI doctors, transplant doctors, and infectious disease people she slept like a rock, but is still struggling with her breathing. A chest X-ray was ordered as well to make sure we weren't missing anything. And somewhere in the craziness of the morning one of the doctors heard a 'rub' around her heart. I still don't know what that means exactly and they've used the word numerous times now. Something about inflammation, I think. So then we had an echo and an EKG...results are still pending. Cultures are still pending on the source of infection also. So much pending!

I guess I assumed that being on unit 5 again would mean that Lanie would start feeling better really soon. Our sweet nurse was telling us though, that it would probably take Lanie a while to bounce back from this. And that somehow, was a really encouraging statement to me (I know it sounds crazy, but to hear that it's not the end of the world that she's still struggling so much, and that it will just take some time, helped me to see this as a longer process and not get impatient with her progress...or lack thereof). One doctor mentioned the possibility of heading back down to PICU and I almost pulled my big soft blanket over my head and pretended that he wasn't there. Like that would've worked. I'm an avoider.

Otherwise, for today, Lanie has slept like crazy. And I wish I knew more about anything...but I don't. So we'll wait and wait and wait and keep asking God for big things.

UPDATE ON our sweet little friend with the Berlin heart in the PICU. I talked to her dad for a while the other morning to see how things were going. He told me that they had to move to a new room just that day because it was their 1 year anniversary of being at the hospital and you can only stay in one room for a year before it needs deep cleaned. He told me that he hoped that the new room would bring them better luck for receiving a heart my little friend. He also said that this last month has been really hard for her health wise and their family was very tired. You guys. Please pray for this amazing and strong Saudi family! I am so blessed by them, and I know others are too.

Thanks friends. And sorry this update is all over the place. I'm being distracted by all kinds of craziness happening in this room around me.

Aug 31, 2013 1:49pm

"Faith is deliberate confidence in the character of God whose ways you may not understand at the time." Oswald Chambers

That Oswald Chambers...he was brilliant.

This last week was no fun. And we can all agree that this is an understatement. And I don't for the life of me understand anything about what happened. Cultures have come back---UTI. Are you kidding?! A UTI?!? Apparently when someone is extremely immune suppressed a common little thing like a UTI can throw some bacteria into the blood and cause an all out raging war that turns an easily fixable problem into a pretty serious, fear causing incident. Who knew ...

My feelings are mixed. I'm having a pretty intense party that Lanie is doing better today than any other time this week and that once we got her stable, this is a fairly normal antibiotic fix. On the other hand, this is a common thing. And within the smallest time frame ever she went from awesome to PICU. To a mom...that's pretty scary. And I'm learning more and more about letting go of control, but there is still this piece of me that's fighting to figure out all the ways I can protect Lanie from, well, I don't know...THE WORLD?! And we all can agree that is a ridiculous thought. And when I say it out loud, I know it is too. But where's the balance? What can I let her do? What should we avoid? All the answers are pretty subjective, I think.

But enough about things I have no way of controlling...let's move on to today. Yesterday was still so rough, so my hopes for today were just that it would be a little better. Thankfully God works bigger than my hopes! Today we woke up to a day of firsts (since Monday anyway).

Today was the 1st day...

She got out of bed
She walked
She got dressed
She peed on her own
She fixed her hair
She belly laughed

182

She read a book
She sat in a chair
She sat on the floor
She left the room
She went outside
She rode a trike
And she ate a full meal

And it's only 1:30 in the afternoon! This girl is gonna sleep well tonight, friends.

I'm so thankful that circumstances are just what they are...just circumstances. And trying to remember that my little sense of control that I feel the need to try and keep is holding me back from experiencing the fullness of God. And all that He is.

Today I'm thankful that God allows me to appreciate the light even more because of the brief instance of darkness I got to experience. Just another testament to the goodness and grace we're all learning more about through our experiences. Thank you God, for all of that...

Sep 2, 2013 11:08am

So I realized today that I haven't update since Saturday. Shame on me. The good news is that we were super busy yesterday with people here and Lanie was feeling pretty good! Not as good as she did on Saturday, but still pretty darn good! So I'm trying to think of what all even happened yesterday...BBQ happened, so of course I remember that! But I'll try to fill you in on the rest as well...even though we can all say there's not a lot that can compare BBQ (I'm still from Texas after all!!)

Yesterday morning was pretty chill. Lanie had struggled again with breathing throughout the night and had received 2 more epi-nebs to get things under control. I've had my share of epinephrine. That stuff's a beast. Chills, shaking, and fast heart beat all come out of it. Because of all of that, Lanie slept in (which meant Luke and I got to have ourselves a little coffee hangout date). Don't mind if I do. Doctors rounded at a decent time, partly because it was a Sunday and partly because we are like 1 of 8 patients on this floor. Yay for all the kids and families getting to go home on a holiday weekend!

The first thing they told us was that they were going to let us go home (as in Ron Mcdon) until they found out that Lanie was still struggling with her breathing. Darn it! I told them they could have kept that little bit of information just between them and we all laughed, well, because I was right. They also said that Lanie was doing really well from their perspective and that she should be ready to go soon. No real plans for the day medical wise with the exception of her IV antibiotics and fluids. Easy enough.

We had some friends from Sumner come late morning to hang out and that was awesome. Man, I love our family in that small town. No matter what anyone says, God put us in that town for our benefit more than theirs. Those people are the most loving, forgiving, generous people ever and it is such a privilege to be a part of that family. Part of my heart is always there. Sorry guys, you're still stuck with us. Get used to it.

Also...every one of our friends overlapped today. Worlds colliding!!!!

While Sumner folks were still here, our new superintendent from the conference came and they all got to meet and then our sweet friends who do every single part of life with in Iowa City came (which includes Lanie's future husband...although we're not telling the kids yet because we all know that if the idea comes from mom, it's discounted immediately). And once Rachel and her new roomie Amber got there, it was time to take the party outside to the park. The rooms on 5 are big and awesome, but when you get my family, the Dekkers, plus 3 more adults, you're looking at 7 adults and 6 kids. That kind of party cannot be contained.

Thankfully there's a park outside (again, John Sullivan, you are awesome). And although Lanie pouted a little at first that she couldn't do everything the other kids (and let's be honest, adults) could do and play with, soon she realized the error of her ways and joined in where she could, IV pole in tow. She's somewhat a go with the flow kind of girl and I tell God thank you pretty often for that.

More Iowa City friends came as well as my sweet little friend Leah, and the fun (which included interactive story time, trike racing, and a piñata) was moved back upstairs. In the midst of all of this, all I could think was outpatient has to happen soon, we are all certainly out of control once again. A tale tell sign, if you ask me.

The night started calming down some around 6 or 7 (which is when more BBQ happened...that's right I said MORE. This girl, right here, is loving it!) Lanie and Jackson ate a little and then laid down to rest and watch a little TV while the adults got to hang out. Fabulous.

Lanie finally fell asleep around 10 and slept all night. ALL NIGHT. For the first time in over a week. There are still 2 of us grown adults on this little green couch so not a huge amount of sleeping happening there, but that's beside the point. The girl slept! No breathing problems. No tummy pain. No headache. Just quiet, blissful sleep. FINALLY.

She woke up well rested and in a decent mood. No coffee date this morning. Doctors rounded and the plan is to be discharged today...on a holiday (that never happens, not to us anyway!). Which is awesome, because the boys are still here for a little bit and they can move us back over to Ronald McDonald before they leave this afternoon. Not thrilled about the latter. Because we had no idea we would ever be here this long, it's getting much harder for the boys to come up, even on the weekends. So I know when they leave today it will be at least 2 more weeks until we see them again. You would think that part would get easier. Friends...it does not. It still sucks. Trying to remember that it's just the way it is right now. And it certainly won't be like this forever.

And until that happens, to remember to enjoy the days we're here.

Chapter 27: Outpatient life: Wait. Didn't this already happen?

Sep 4, 2013 9:39pm

Is it really September 4th?!? I just can't believe it.

The last few days have been...weird. It's not like anything bad has happened, especially compared to the horribleness of last week, but there's something in me that's frustrated...and down...and just having a really hard time. Like I'm fighting myself to not be sad and nostalgic. Sometimes I just honestly don't understand the way my own head operates (my guy friends are out there cheering right now because they've been saying this about girls for years).

Lanie's been doing really well outpatient, for the most part. She's cheery and insanely talkative. We went out to dinner at Chili's last night (thank you sweet friends for that gift!!) and she chatted the whole entire hour we sat there. I had no idea so much is on her mind. And, you guys, she is so funny. She has the best sense of humor and is a bit sarcastic and is genuine and loving. She really cares about people and their needs. And last night, spending that hour understanding more about the world as she understands it, was beautiful. I'm literally crying as I write this because I am just blown away. And I pray that she always wants to talk to me like this, candid and open. I am turned to mush at the mere thought of it.

That was definitely the highlight of yesterday. It was a fairly rough day, which is maybe another reason I could just sit in the moment last night and take in everything about it. The day started promising...meet the teacher day at the Ronald MacDonald School. Lanie was beyond excited. She missed the first and last day of kindergarten and the first and last day of first grade. And now also the first day of second grade. She's missed a lot. And she completely realizes it...and it bothers her. She gets so discouraged by it actually. So, knowing that she would be at the first day of school, enrolled in the Minneapolis district with the Ronald MacDonald house was nothing short of awesome for her (and probably one of the reasons she couldn't stop talking last night). After visiting the school and meeting her teacher for the next couple of weeks, Lanie was pumped. I fed her a small lunch because she wasn't very hungry and headed over to the hospital for her IV antibiotic. I'm not going to rant on insurance here, even though I'd really like to. Some things are just the way they are and rants don't really solve anything. I was told these things usually took a little over an hour. Fabulous. Except it didn't. It took over four hours. At no fault to anyone. There was just a lot of trouble caused by her PICC line not wanting to work and TPA not wanting to help. That session ended with me feeling incredibly frustrated and Lanie having an insane headache. She claimed when we were done with outpatient she still wanted to go out to eat so we did. After some pain meds and a cool wash rag an hour of crying and prayers asking God to take her pain, she was completely headache free. And then Chili's happened. I got her to bed at a decent time for the first time all summer, I think, telling her she needed to sleep so she'd be ready for school. No argument. She was too excited. Another smooth night if sleeping for her.

SIDE NOTE: Lanie's been getting pretty severe headaches every 2 to 3 days that complete debilitate her. We're still looking for the cause. High blood pressure? Migraines? Something else? I wish we knew...

Today Lanie woke up (on her own, which is a miracle in and of itself) bouncing off the walls. I told her we needed to do labs before her first day of school. Man, was she bummed, but was dressed and out the door within minutes. All the way to labs and back she talked about how she would just be so embarrassed to be late on the first day of school and that she just wanted to get there and that labs are making her so crazy and annoyed (her words. Because she's what, 15 now?). Labs were somewhat smooth. Still having problems with that darn PICC. We got back to the house 2 minutes before she needed to be in her room. Perfect. I walked her to the room and she assured me I could leave anytime and she was fine and excited. So I took a nice long breath and left. As the door closed behind me, I walked down the hall of the house and became instantly teary. Not because it's her first day of school (sort of) but because it hit me that this girl, who I've spent practically every waking moment with since April 28th was going to be doing things without me for 3 hours today (because today is a half day) and then 6 and a half hours tomorrow and the next day and so on. And I'm just here. Alone. Being completely unneeded and unproductive. I realized I don't know how to live in Minneapolis without Lanie. And I don't even think I like the idea of it. And during those 3 hours today I missed her so much. I ran to Target to get some groceries for a dinner I was cooking tonight for some sweet folks. I sipped on a pumpkin latte while I strolled the isles knowing that even in an alternate universe I can't fill my hours at target every day, but today I would. I prayed for friends and let my mind wander. And watched the clock, ready to head back to Oak Street as soon as the clock on my phone said I could.

I picked up Lanie from school a little early because she had another IV antibiotic appointment today. This one was scaled down to an hour and a half. Much better. And then we headed to our cooking destination and worked on making dinner together (which we haven't done in forever). It was such a blessing to have people let us use their kitchen to make dinner. Felt almost like we were home.

And now Lanie's asleep, so ready for her first full day of school, and I'm feeling all of these weird things, not understanding myself at all. Tomorrow Lanie will go to school from 8:45 to 3:15 and then I'll take her to the hospital to get her antibiotic and then we'll meet friends for dinner. I feel like I should be so excited, like she is. But the truth is, I'm a little bit sad. Okay a lot of bit sad. The end of an era I guess. Which means the beginning of a new adventure. And that, that sparks a little excitement within me.

PS...If anyone wants to hire a girl from 9 to 3 to do whatever the heck you want her to do, I might know someone who would be quite interested.

Sep 9, 2013 7:41pm

Day 130

I've been staring at this blank screen for a while now (we won't say how long) completely unsure of what to write. Sometimes I would love to just throw caution to the wind and say whatever I'm feeling, which I actually do more than I maybe should. But then there are other times when I stay a little more conservative in my writing and save how I really feel about things for my notebook that I will throw away at the end of this Minneapolis summer because it has nothing really to do with Lanie and everything to do with the crazy happening inside my head - let's please not forget that I'm a girl and even though I like to think that I'm fairly tough and unemotional, it's just not always true.

Maybe this update will be a mix of both.

As for my little Lanie Lou...if it weren't for those darn headaches she would be loving life (mostly) right now. She is so happy everyday to go to school and I think it brings in a sense of normalcy for her. She's made friends really easily (social butterfly maybe?) and has already progressed some with her reading. We're still working on writing, although I feel like that's getting better too, and she enjoys practicing more. She told me on Friday 'mom, I'm gonna try so hard this year it will blow your mind!'. You can't blame a girl for that! She's pumped. And even though I'm still pretty pouty about being alone here in the cities somewhat, someone reminded me last week that this is a really good transition for her and that probably exactly what she needs. A true statement for sure.

Really, not a lot has happened since I last posted. Lanie goes to school and I find ways to occupy my time (sort of). And then I pull her out of school an hour early to take her to clinic to get antibiotics which takes a couple hours. We eat dinner, play, take showers, brush teeth, and go to bed (well she does...I sometimes run and then stay up way too late, because even after 130 days I still haven't learned the art of going to bed alone). We wake up and do it again. Monday, Wednesday, and Friday are still lab days, minus the Starbucks dates. I usually have those alone now while I'm getting other things done throughout the day. Can I just say another HUGE thank you for all of the gift cards you've given to us lately?!? Food and Coffee are such amazing gifts and we are so blessed by your generosity. Seriously. You guys... Thank you.

189

We kept up her antibiotics over the weekend as well. The clinic wasn't open, so once a day we settled into room 25 on unit 5 for a couple hours to be taken care of by our sweet nurse friends. Lanie was pretty excited about that. Any chance she has to go to 5 is glorious for her. Both days we were there she said she didn't want to leave. Now that says something about this hospital. And the team of people that work there.

So now we're at today. First of all, last night was horrible. Lanie didn't feel great going to sleep, but I took her temperature and it was fine. She finally fell asleep around 10, but every now and then would cry a little in her sleep. I couldn't sleep last night either, mostly because there is so much on my mind and night is prime thinking time...or so it seems. And when i do sleep, I have been having the craziest dreams. And when I wake up, I can't even believe they weren't real. Anyway...I regress. The point is Lanie fell asleep at 10:00pm and I fell asleep sometime after 1:00am. Around 4:00am I woke up to Lanie crying. She said that her tummy and her head were hurting 'just so much'. I gave her some pain meds and snuggled her up with me. She laid there and cried for a while but never fell back asleep. She finally started feeling better at about 730a. We hopped on the shuttle and headed over for labs at 8a and then were back in time for her to go to school at 8:45a. I was so tired, but I got dressed to run before we left for labs, knowing that I needed to just get out there and do it, no matter what I was feeling. And I did. It was a lame run by everyone's standards, but it was a run nonetheless. I showered, grabbed coffee, and then headed out to a park to read and gather some of my thoughts (have you guys ever tried to do that? Gather your thoughts? Sometimes it feels like an impossible task without people asking me the right questions, and this was one of those times. Most of the time, I just sat there distracted).

I picked her up from school at 12:30p today because we had appointments with infectious disease and in clinic to get her antibiotic. The ID appointment went fine. Same ole same ole, really. Then we headed over to clinic to get her antibiotics. Today was the last day of those, thank you so much Jesus! Because she runs a high risk for infection, they pulled her PICC line out immediately after she was done today. She was pretty excited about that as well. It was a little short lived, however, and once we were on the shuttle to come back, her headache reared its stupid, ugly head again. Once she gets those, there is not a lot that makes her feel better and she usually just cries about them until she falls asleep or throws up. Hopefully we'll find some answers soon on those beasts.

Tomorrow I'll have to pull her out of school again at 12:45p for afternoon appointments. 1 with her kidney doctor and 1 with her transplant doctor. Honestly, I'm nervous and excited at the same time. Who knows what news these appointments will come with and I'm trying to prepare myself either way. I know that the transplant team had a big meeting today where they talked about her, so I'm a little anxious to hear more about thoughts on how she's doing.

Now...for my crazy head part of this post. And I'll keep it short. Okay...so I'm still really struggling with this school thing. And I think every day it will get easier, but actually, it doesn't. It's not like it even has anything to do with the school or with being in Minneapolis, but more to do with the fact that I had no idea I had so much stuff going on in my head. I've had a few people ask how I am or how things are going these last few days and I realized every time someone asked me, I would give them a somewhat surface answer. 'Oh, I'm fine...I'm lonely and I suck at being a single mom in a new city with no job, but I'm fine'. And people usually accept that answer pretty

well, which is good, because if anyone ever pressed me for a more real answer, they would have to hug me while I fell apart. And it might take awhile. And I fully realize that by saying this I'm gonna have to become a recluse for a bit so that people will forget that I actually said that and not ask me questions that are hard.

Eeeeeek...moving on. Tomorrow we will hopefully find out more about headaches and fevers and liver/kidney function, and labs, and a home plan. Like always, text or harass me if you haven't heard anything. I'll try to remember to update, although we all know most of my updates happen at ridiculous times at night when I can't sleep.

I really do just appreciate you guys so much. You continue to blow me away with your support and encouragement. Thank you...

ALSO! Complete SIDENOTE but I never proofread these updates at all (please try to hold your shock) so the mere fact that you are sticking with me through all of the misspelled words, run on sentences, and incomplete thoughts says a lot about you. You guys are my heroes.

Chapter 28: UPDATE! And also...I'm sorry

Sep 14, 2013 9:02am

Ok guys. I'm sorry. This update is long overdue and I have a list of really good excuses...but I'm not going to rattle them off to you (an excuse is an excuse after all). Thank you guys for calling, texting, and messaging me. I'm serious. Even when I'm being kind of baby about things, you guys keep letting me know how awesome you are.

So Tuesday. I feel like here is one of the only places that you can meet with the kidney doctor, the transplant doctor, and the transplant coordinators all at once (the only people we were missing were the GI and the ID). I love that. We've never had that experience at any other place and it honestly just feels amazing to know that the team of doctors here care so much that they are willing to all meet together! I'll sum up the meeting briefly. Lanie's immune system cannot be trusted. It does what it wants, and apparently what it wants is to not protect her from infection. We talked a lot about this actually. Everyone is in agreement that we should go home...except for that darn immune system. I mean, seriously. When she went to the PICU with septic shock, she had less than 10,000 little bacterial colonies in her urine. 10,000 seems like a pretty big number to me, so I asked the doctors how many of those little colonies a person would need to call it a UTI. The answer...over 100,000. That's what they said. OVER 100,000! That means Lanie got super sick, sending her body into shock, with something that doesn't even count as an infection. Aye aye aye. No wonder they're nervous to send her on her way. I have to admit. I'm a little nervous about it too. They very briefly talked about a home plan, which included the words 'air lift' and my brain shut down. I'm not comforted.

I talked to them more about her headaches too and some med changes were tossed around and it was pretty agreed upon that we should see a neurologist. It sure couldn't hurt, right? Those headaches are just pretty out of control and if we could find something...anything that would help them, I'm on board. The main plan then was to do some med changes, schedule appointments this next week with GI, ultrasound, neurology, and transplant. And see how she does.

I have to admit, at no surprise to you guys I'm sure, I had a hard time processing the appointments on Tuesday. So as soon as Lanie went to sleep, I laced up my shoes and busted out of the Ron Mcdon for the type of run I usually only do when I'm frustrated or angry...or just at a loss and can't understand my own girly feelings. I ran fast (well for me). I blasted music through my headphones so I didn't have to think anymore and just took off running down East River Road. And then Mumford came on. Which is actually completely normal. I always have Mumford on my running list. That underlying beat is awesome you guys and they always pick up my pace in runs. Well, they're kind of just awesome in general. This isn't the Mumford fan page so I'll stop. Anyway, my favorite Mumford song came on. I sang in my head while I ran. And when I got to the chorus, I just started to bawl. Like crying so hard that I had to stop running. It goes a little something like this...

'There will come a day, you'll see, with no more tears.
And love will not break your heart, but dismiss your fears.
Get over your hill and see what you find there
With grace in your heart and flowers in your hair'.

So I sat in the grass at 10:00 at night and cried. And hit replay on the song so that it was all I could hear. I didn't even know why I was crying. I just was. And after maybe hearing the song a full 10 times in the grass, I looked around and realized that I didn't even know where I was. I'd never ran this far south before and there wasn't a street light in sight (which is actually a blessing because how embarrassing would that have been...some other runner out on the path thinking they have absolutely no idea what to do with this disaster of a girl they just so happened to see, thinking they should stop to see what's going on, when all they really wanted to do was go for a simple run).

Anyway, after that little episode, I left the song on repeat and ran back, following the river home. And I felt better. So much better, actually. I guess sometimes all you need is a fast and reckless run and a sobfest. It works for me. I came back to the room feeling empowered that night. Because Mumford is right. There will come a day that I'll see with no more tears (I mean, not in this world, but still). And this is just a hill. It's a beast of a hill sometimes, but it's still just a hill. And the imagery of God bringing us to the other side with grace in my heart and flowers in my hair is one of the most beautiful images I can think of. I have at least 2 dreams using that image recently, which I completely believe are God's reminders to me.

Wow...sorry you guys. That was a lot.

Anyway, the rest of this week has been good. Lanie had her first full day of school without me pulling her out early on Wednesday. She loved it. We celebrated by using a gift card and going out to eat. She was so incredibly talkative and I love those times when she just chats it up about anything and everything. I got her to bed at a decent time and sent her off to school again on Thursday. Thursday was so fun. This house that I live in, they do not mess around when it comes to taking care of the people that stay here, and not just with dinner and rooms and play areas and crafts. I continue to realize by living here that there is not a darn thing that I deserve. Nothing. And yet God still gives. And I don't understand it. I honestly don't. It's a struggle I deal with a lot actually (why do I get to do/have this or that and others don't. I don't deserve it. I don't even ask for it, necessarily, but yet it is given. And I promise I won't go into this in full out detail because you would be able to see the craziness of the inside of my head and no one should have to do that, but I struggle with it way more often than I would ever like to admit). If you see me in person, feel free to ask more about it, but only if you're willing to REALLY get to know me and talk through things that just don't really make sense. This subject will keep me talking for hours.

And wow...I need to wrap this up. The boys came yesterday, which is completely awesome. They'll have to wave tomorrow morning, but I am not complaining. A tiny amount of time is better than nothing and I'll take what I can get. Poor Luke. I have not stopped holding his hand or hugging him since he's been here. I had a Groupon for the MOA Sea Life aquarium so we did that yesterday and then just hung out last night. Awesome.

SIDENOTE: bad news alert - we got a call from transplant last night while we were out having dinner and Lanie's labs came back not fabulous. Her urine showed bacteria again and we all know how that story turns out. We are taking her in this morning to get another UA and blood work to see what's going on. I'm not gonna lie. I feel nervous.

I'll honestly try and remember to update again when we know some details. This next week we have more appointments and labs and then we'll just wait and see...which is actually something I'm getting a little better at. Thank you Jesus for making my heart more flexible to a 'wait and see' lifestyle. Funny how he transforms, huh?

Sep 17, 2013 10:22pm

Well hello everybody. It's been a good day. It's actually been a good few days. And I am soaking in all kinds of thankfulness. Let me tell you why (in list form of course, otherwise I get super distracted and this update will end up taking a good portion of my night).

1. The boys were here this weekend. They came on Friday afternoon and were able to stay until late Sunday morning. Not a huge amount of time, but worth it nonetheless. I already filled you in on Friday and then Saturday morning so I'll leave out the details of those days.

2. Saturday after labs, we drove down to Shakopee to go to Valley Fair --> an amusement park. Ronald McDonald had given Lanie and me 2 tickets and the boys were given 2 tickets as well. We were excited. First I have to say that I am incredibly thankful for people and how giving they are. Wow you guys! I am continuously floored by your generosity. And second, I have to admit, I almost ruined the day (bad attitude alert). Here's the story...

- I looked at the time that Valley Fair opened wrong and we were 2 hours early. There's not a lot happening in Shakopee but we kept ourselves entertained.

- Once we left and came back at noon, the real opening time, we walked to the ticket window and they told us the tickets from Ron Mcdon were expired (one place on the tickets said that they had to be used by a group

196

date in August and another spot said that the tickets were valid until Sunday, September 15...and it was Saturday). The ticket window said sorry. And I started to cry (because I cry when I get frustrated...you know...like any normal person) which actually didn't help at all. And then I immediately felt guilty for spending so much money on the day, because there was no way that I could tell the kids we weren't going. We paid a fee and in we went.

- Luke started feeling pretty sick not long after we went into the park. And it really only got worse. He was a trooper of course and still rode rides and walked every inch of that park.

- Lanie is short. I mean, so little that there were kid rides she was too small for. Most things were out for her. But she didn't complain. Not once.

- All the kids wanted to do before we left was go on a water ride. It started raining and the rides started shutting down. We made it over to the only water ride left open (the one they had been waiting for all day) and Lanie couldn't go. She cried. And we talked her into standing on the bridge while Jackson went and she was content with that. And through all of this, besides the little cry at the end from Lanie, the kids had so much fun. This was their day. And we did what they wanted. And at one point during the day, I looked over at Luke and just started laughing. Because in all honesty, the day was hilarious. It was one crazy thing after another...a snowball of insanity. And it was so funny. And he put his arm around me and hugged me and we watched the kids spin and twist and turn and I was overcome with sincere thankfulness. A kind of thankfulness that doesn't come from a situation or circumstance, but from something deeper that I don't always understand. Plus who doesn't like a story that starts with 'remember that one time at Valley Fair'...I know I do.

3. Saturday night was chill. Mostly because Luke was sick (with something he had eaten the day before? that was our best guess). At 8:30p, I looked around in the room and EVERY SINGLE PERSON other than me was asleep. At 8:30! My initial thought was frustration (yikes...I'm seeing a trend with myself). It went something like 'oh my goodness I miss my husband so much and he's asleep. He's here, lying in bed...asleep. What on earth am I going to do tonight by myself??' Completely rational, right? But actually, it turned out okay. I kept myself entertained until I fell asleep at about 11p, thankful for the day and the stories that were made.

4. Sunday morning was pretty relaxing as well. Our thought was that we would go to church, but when I realized that the boys had to leave late morning, that wouldn't really work. Instead we stayed in and just hung out as a family. Luke was feeling better and made us breakfast (the kids love when dad's around...I'm not allowed to offer the kids a cup of coffee, so usually breakfast is whatever is laying around that they can eat as we're on our way to something. Also, please feel free to judge here. Lanie once asked me if I even knew how to make toast. This is for real).

5. After the boys left, the plan was for Lanie and I to go to the zoo, which we were pretty excited about. Not 5 minutes down the road, though, Lanie started crying that she was getting a bad headache. We don't mess around when those beasts show up, so I turned the car around and had her lay down for a while at the house. She fell asleep. And I watched the Vikings (along with a few other friends via snap chat and text. Almost the same as watching it all together. Minus the food. And collective yelling at the TV. And the actual friends. Okay, it's not at all the same). Lanie woke up a couple hours later feeling so much better. Excited to get out for a bit, we headed to a bonfire and then got back to the house in time to see the beginning of the Miss America contest (is that what it's called, I'm not sure). 20 minutes in and Lanie was fast asleep. And I went for a run. And no lie, it was a really good run (ummm I did just watch the beginning of miss America after all). Another good day overall.

6. Monday = labs, school, GI appointment, school, and ultrasound. All went well. The house was having pizza for dinner (which I can't have) so we went out to eat. I was just going to grab something quick, but Lanie wanted to go OUT to eat. We still have some gift cards so I said no problem. We never go out to eat at home. Like never. So being able to do this with her here has been a sweet little blessing. And by little, I mean ginormous. Thank you guys. I learned last night that I really like wood-grilled tilapia, especially with a side of green beans and broccoli. Oh my goodness, that week in the Upper Peninsula last summer changed my life forever in regards to fish. Joel and Sarah...you win. Monday was the first day in a while that Lanie was completely pain free, tummy and head. Also Lanie and I were wrestling around last night and she laughed really hard and said 'you hit me right in the transplant!' and continued to laugh and giggle. And then all I could do was laugh too...really hard actually. Because only high spirited tough girls get to say things like that.

7. A piggyback on #6. About a month or so ago, I was diagnosed with having celiac disease. Which was actually a really good thing. I've been sick for a while and it's kind of nice to have a name and do not eat list. And I can't really eat dairy either, so...yeah...I'm pretty awesome and not high maintenance at all. So in between eating the food served at Ron Mcdon that I can have, eating with gift cards, and my fairly decent cooking skills, I have been eating super clean (and by that I mean mostly meat, veggies, fruits, coconut milk and some nuts...annnnnnd of course coffee) for the last week and a half - better to start late than never, right? And I have been feeling amazing. Like amazing! And my clothes fitting looser isn't a bad side effect either. And tonight, even as I'm thinking about it, I'm just amazed at how God provides reminders to me to not eat stuff that will make me feel horrible (even though all I want is just a piece of cheesecake!) and then even provides means to eat food that makes my body work like it should. Wow, you guys. And now I will stop talking about me.

8. Lanie had an appointment today with our transplant doctor. I'll admit it. I was anxious to see what he would say. Turns out he had good news, which is this...... A best case scenario. I love a good best case scenario. This is what he said. IF all of Lanie's doctors (GI, ID, kidney, transplant, and neurology) are on the same page about getting to go home soon AND they can all come up with an agreed upon, written out plan of action AND can set up appointments to see some just in case Iowa City doctors, we can think about going home this Friday or Saturday. You guys!!! I cannot even tell you about the amount of excitement that explodes out of me at even the possibility (there's a good chance some of it is nerves, but we'll let that go). And I know we've heard similar things like this before, and there's a tiny piece of me screaming 'what are you doing?? Stop getting excited. This is the very BEST case scenario and that means that all the other scenarios are just not as good, which means they are bad!!' But the rest of me is ignoring that and just gonna let myself be really excited. Because why not. I love being excited. Especially when I'm ignoring the idea of overhanging disappointment.

9. We had dinner tonight with friends. And it was fun. And I laughed a lot. And Lanie played hard. And I don't have to pull her out of school for the rest of the week for appointments. That makes her very happy. And me too actually.

10. Lanie has had 2 pain free days. No headaches. No tummy pain. Nothing. And labs were moved to twice this week. TWICE! Yesssssssssss! That is awesome news my friends.

I'm excited about this week. I'm excited to spend part of my next few days helping out people and working some. I'm excited to get a phone call Thursday after labs telling us everything looks good and we have a home plan in place. I'm excited to have lunch with my friends on Friday to celebrate the amazingness of everything that happened this summer. And I'm excited to pack up our little room, drive the 4 hours home, and fall asleep in my amazing bed.

Yeah...excitement isn't overrated.

Chapter 29: Waiting

Sep 19, 2013 2:30pm

I thought I had gotten a lot better at waiting. Waiting for phone calls. Waiting on labs. Waiting for the boys to come. Turns out, after almost 5 months of practice, I have not.

Ever since Lanie had labs this morning, I have been waiting on that phone call and it finally just came. Not with the exact news I wanted, but at least the waiting for today is over.

The news? Lanie's WBC has dropped even more. And last night she was running a fairly low grade temp and didn't sleep at all.

The plan? Labs and urine culture again tomorrow morning. If she still has the temp and WBC is still low or if anything shows up...we stay. If she snaps out of whatever this is and labs come back awesome (or even mediocre) we go on Saturday or Sunday.

It's a strange feeling to live a life of wait and see. Not necessarily bad, but really strange. No plans (I kinda love that part actually, finally I have a legit excuse to not plan anything) and no obligations per se. Just wait and see.

And so I guess we will. After all, I trust the plan more than I hate the waiting.

Here's to more practice ... And maybe I'll learn a little something in the process.

Chapter 30: Bad is relative, I'm sure of it

Sep 20, 2013 10:09pm

I haven't really slept the last 2 nights, so I was waiting to update until I felt a little more clear headed today. Well that has never happened, so I'm just going to update and then apologize tomorrow for anything I might say in my altered sleepy state.

I've actually learned a lot of lessons today, you guys. Which is crazy. It's only been a day. But it's true.

#1. Lanie is pretty proud of how strong she is. This morning during labs, Luke's parents were with us and Lanie was quick to show them how well she would sit, and hold out her arm, and pick her prize. She really loves being fearless. And I realized that I love that about her too. I love that she is the first to try something new or to show her strength. I pray that God will continue to teach me how encourage that strength that she has within her while also helping her to realize that it's ok to show weakness. And to cry. And to be angry. And to also show compassion on those that don't see strength the same way she does. I am beyond amazed sometimes at how similar we are...this girl and I.

#2. I can order whatever I want at a restaurant. It doesn't have to be on the menu. And for some really insane reason, I love that.

#3. People are the biggest blessing. I have been with people all day today. It's been somewhat lonely since Lanie went to school. You guys know that. And thankfully, some amazing people have allowed me to keep somewhat busy (btw I am absolutely horrible at staining windows. I hope that I didn't mess up anything that can't be fixed. I totally realize that it's only considered helping out if I 'help' out).

#4. We hardly ever hear about labs from the day until late afternoon. Today we heard at about 11am. Home probably isn't gonna happen this weekend. And we'll do labs again on Monday to see how things look. I'll be honest. It felt like a blow. But in another way it didn't. I don't want to take Lanie home if she isn't 100%. What's another weekend when we've already been here nearly 5 months, anyway? I want to go home with a confidence that she is feeling great...fever free and stronger than ever.

#5. I was talking to my in-laws this morning over breakfast and I said something out loud that I didn't even know I believed until I said it. I said that I would rather get really excited about something and then have the possibility of disappointment than to just live protecting my heart. I am positive I never used to believe this. I can remember a conversation a few years ago with someone about hating the idea of planning because I was scared of dealing with the disappointment if something didn't turn out. Today, I realized I don't believe that at all anymore (I mean, I still don't like to plan, but now it's mostly because I'm lazy and it's overwhelming). I have a friend from Iowa City who always says 'live hard'. I love that. I was missing out when I wouldn't let myself get excited in fear of disappointment. I want to experience all of those 'live hard' moments. I'm perfectly and finally okay with living a life of valleys and mountains and streams and deserts and oceans in lieu of miles and miles of plains.

#6. I was a little relieved to not be going home this weekend (in a whoa kind of moment way). Oh sure, I was incredibly disappointed and discouraged. I miss home so much that there are times I can't even function just thinking about it. And I'm sure the boys are tired of seeing me cry a little on FaceTime when I have days where I miss them so much I can't even express myself in words...only tears. But today, when I heard the words 'you better hang tight here this weekend' there was a tiny sigh of relief...in other words, fear starting to raise its ugly stupid head.

#7. I racked my brain today thinking of different things that Lanie and I could do together tonight so that she wouldn't be so incredibly bummed about not going home. All I could think of was getting her a pony, or at the very least a puppy. I was nervous. But man, you guys, kids are resilient. And they know how to live hard (right, Zach?). Here was a girl who thought that today at school would only be about her (i.e. an all day Lanie party complete with balloons, cake, and grilled cheese) because she was sure it would be the last day to attend here at the house. Now that was excitement. So then I had to tell her that we had to stay this weekend...armed with a list of amazing and fun things we could do together tonight. She was sad. But then, in true sweet, childlike form, she looked up at me and asked if we could go to Disney tonight instead. I said probably not and she shrugged and said 'okay, I kind of just want to stay in and snuggle and watch a movie'. Really? No fit? No crying? Just straight up acceptance and contentment. I have a lot to learn, you guys.

#8. I don't really know what's best for me...or for Lanie, really. And I kinda thought I did. I asked God for this weekend to be the one where we go home. I thought that was what was best. For me. For us. And then I remembered. I can make poor choices. I can be selfish. And incredibly near sighted in my thinking. Man, that can get depressing if you think about it too long......except it's not depressing. It's undeniably freeing! I don't have to trust in myself. Lanie doesn't have to trust in me either. Our trust is in the very same God that created this whole entire world...with WORDS! I don't have to know what's best. I just get to trust in Someone that does. Freedom!!

#9. We have too much stuff. I'm overwhelmed. And a drive a Hyundai. Packing up is about to get very, very interesting. All of those years of Tetris is about to finally pay off.

#10. The Life of Pi. Lanie summed it up pretty well tonight - 'wow. That was too sad. Did you see how skinny that tiger was? He should've just eaten the boy'. Hmmm good point. Where was Hollywood on that one?

Praying that God is teaching you guys new things every day too. Live hard, friends. I honestly believe it's worth it.

Sep 23, 2013 11:06pm

Okay. I've been thinking about updating all day. And then I thought, I should run to target first. Oh and maybe I should clean our room next. Oh and then laundry. And then maybe watch The Voice. And now, well now I've completely run out of excuses. The truth is I don't know if I should give a - real, all out this is what I'm thinking - update or just a - this is what's going on - update. I still haven't decided. This should be interesting.

So today's Monday. Lab day. We've been waiting on this day since Friday (honestly this is probably the ONLY time I can think of that I've been waiting on Monday since Friday. Something is so wrong about this statement). We went in for labs this morning and they went great. Like always. Our shuttle driver today was new...and amazing. He kept me captivated the whole 30 minutes I rode with him by telling me stories from Desert Storm and then becoming a police officer and Blaine and transitioning into a non adrenaline led life. Wow. I didn't want to get off the bus, and instead just ride around all day listening and asking him questions. I'm getting side tracked.

I took Lanie to school and then went for a short run (fall hates me. Hates me!) Before running some errands (which we all know means downing an Americano while wandering around target). I didn't want to even think about packing up the room until I heard from transplant. Around noon, I saw the familiar number and answered it before Mumford even had a chance to try to get out the first words of 'Hold on to what you believe'. Transplant. Marci told me that Lanie's liver levels were up just a bit and that they were going to have a meeting on her this afternoon and she would call back after it was over to tell me about it. Perfect.

I picked up Lanie at 3:15 and the first thing she asked was about home. I told her I still didn't know. At 4:00 Marci called me back. Everyone was in agreement. We could go home on Wednesday! I don't know how to bold my lettering on here or I would. So Lanie will go to school tomorrow and maybe Wednesday. And then we will leave sometime Wednesday afternoon. How crazy is that?!? Wow. I have been literally dreaming about this for 5 months. And it doesn't seem real yet that it's actually happening. You guys, God is amazing, is He not? For 5 solid months He has more than provided, cared for, and lavished us with His love while living here in the cities. He has put in me a deep love for this city and its people. I'm overwhelmed by the beauty of it all. And I should probably stop the update here. But I feel like I wouldn't be true to myself at all if I did. Like I would be lying because of omission. Feel free to stop reading here ...

The last couple of days have been really hard. I mean really hard. I'm kind of freaking out, y'all. I was lying in my bed the other night and I started thinking - that is dangerous territory, laying in bed alone and letting your mind wander...and wander........and wander. No good comes from it. I need to process with people and talk through things. And have people challenge me and question me and tell me I'm being dumb. I tried praying about it and I honestly somehow freaked out even more, maybe because I was saying things out loud? I'm not sure. This is how my thoughts went...

- I haven't driven 4 hours in a really, really long time. I should get some good music together for the way.

- packing my car should be interesting. And is it normal for that little engine light to be on? I'm sure it's fine.

- I wonder if I should wash the windows in our room. And wow...this little room isn't going to be our home anymore

- this city isn't going to be our home any more

- wow, I'm really going to miss all my buddies here

- I'm really going home

- I'm really going home!! *a little fear*

- its fine...Luke will be there and all my friends are there

- wait. Luke is leaving this weekend. He has an all new job too...and is friends with people I've never even met. Oh my goodness I have to meet his friends. This is just like when he would take me to his hometown after we were dating and I would awkwardly meet his friends (not because the situation is awkward but mostly because I'M awkward). I'm sorry in advance.

- and this weekend is Luke's birthday. And I won't see him. And that makes me pretty bummed

- but I can just hang with my friends. Wait. My friends have new friends and are knee deep in the program that they work with. And I don't work with that program anymore *insert small amounts of panic*

- and I don't have a job. I need a job. I need a job for real. The job hunt starts the day I get home. Or maybe the day after I get home

- and I have been gone for 5 months. 5 MONTHS! And everything has changed. Life happened. Kids grew. Summer came and went and school started. Luke is now apparently driving a motorcycle everywhere. And started watching football.

AND THEN THE BIG PANIC HIT...

- I haven't been a wife in a long time. Or a mom to more than one kid. Or a counselor. Or gone grocery shopping. Or had responsibilities other than Lanie...and showering. I don't know where I fit into people's lives anymore...including Luke or my friends.

- and if I were to be completely honest I'm a little scared that you guys think I'm someone else. Someone who is witty and graceful and strong. And in reality you are going to see that I'm awkward and I laugh at really dumb things, and I make stupid mistakes and use bad judgment sometimes (I mean this one time I bought a set of pans that was $1200. Thankfully God saved me from regret and the wrath of my husband and got me out of the deal. I cannot even begin to watch infomercials...oy).

Rachel asked me how I was doing on Sunday and this madness that you just read exploded out complete with lots of tears and snot...in a very public place...that was a completely different culture than mine. Awesome. People in every single culture are so full of grace, you guys.

And Rachel sat there while I made a gigantic list of why I was whole heartedly freaking out. And she smiled. And when I was done she talked for a couple minutes and then she said 'you aren't going to fail at this Ali'. THAT WAS IT! I hadn't said it. I hadn't even necessarily thought those words, but that was it! The fear that's rearing its ugly stupid head goes by the name of failure. My expectations for myself are high. And the idea of failing or not meeting those expectations makes me not even want to try. Which just causes more fear.

C.S. Lewis said 'I pray because the need flows out of me all the time, waking and sleeping. It doesn't change God, it changes me'. I believe this to be true. I prayed about this a ton last night. And today. And this is what I keep hearing...

Was it scary when your dad died?

How about when you picked up and moved to college far away from everyone you knew and loved?

Or when you graduated college and still didn't know what you wanted to do with your life?

Or when you had Jackson? And you thought Luke broke his head?

Or how about when you had Lanie? And she got sick? Like really sick?

And do you remember when you heard the words CF? And liver disease? And FSGS? And everything else that doesn't need mentioned?

And how about switching to Minneapolis doctors from Iowa City? Remember how nervous you were?

And do you remember the move to Iowa City? Away from a family of people that loved you like you were their own?

Or how about the first time you heard the word transplant?

And when you got the first call on Christmas night when you were 7 hours away from the hospital still?

And then there was the day in April when the second call came. And all of the time that you have been up in Minneapolis.

Wasn't that all 'unknown'?

'But now, this is what the Lord says—
he who created you, Jacob,
he who formed you, Israel:
"Do not fear, for I have redeemed you;
I have summoned you by name; you are mine.

2 When you pass through the waters,
I will be with you;
and when you pass through the rivers,
they will not sweep over you.
When you walk through the fire,
you will not be burned;
the flames will not set you ablaze'. Isaiah 43:1-2

God keeps reminding me that I can't fail, because this is not mine to fail at.
And that, you guys, oh my goodness, that is freeing.

Chapter 31: Home sweet home

Sep 30, 2013 12:09pm

So, we're home. That's crazy, right? I sure think so. Wednesday was like the best send off day ever. I don't know why I was worried. We met our sweet nurse/sister/friends (I don't know what to call them) and Rachel for breakfast. Lanie was out of her mind excited. So many people she loves in one place equals best morning ever. Seriously. Amazing. I didn't cry at all through the whole breakfast...it was a serious celebration. And then after we walked outside, Rachel gave me the longest hug ever, like only she can do and I bawled. And we hugged and waved goodbye to the nurses...and to Lanie's bear Ginger. And I bawled some more. Happy/we feel the love tears. And then we finished packing up our little 121 room at the house and headed to grab some coffee with our friend Leah, which was awesome. Send off complete.

I could update everything else from Wednesday until today, but you guys would be reading a book and we can't have that. Instead, I'll tell you about the things I've learned since leaving our Minneapolis home away from home.

1. Highway 35 is so incredibly boring. I don't know how Luke did it over and over again. Thankfully I'm decent at entertaining myself. And no matter what anyone else tells you, that drive only takes around 4 hours. Not 5. And that's with stopping for a bathroom break.

2. I love SnapChat (I hate when you're right Rachel!!). Perfect way to entertain myself and keep Luke updated all the way home.

3. Signs and people welcoming us home were awesome. God reigned down the love, you guys! Lanie was screaming in the car! I absolutely hate screaming, but I allowed it this one time.

4. My husband is amazing. He hates cooking but made steak and veggies so that we could eat when we got home. I didn't just learn this by the way. Just reminded again and again.

5. I have too much stuff. I'm overwhelmed you guys. In Minneapolis we lived in a little room. It was perfect. We had what we needed plus some. At home...oh my goodness. This is how Thursday morning went --> I should start putting things away. "Where did all of these clothes come from? I don't need all of these clothes" *start pulling clothes off the hangers and throwing them into a pile. And then walk down to the living room to put some blankets away* "what the heck?!? Why do we already have 20 thousand blankets?? We need 4. At the most! And that is if everyone just happens to be cold at the same time and doesn't want to share *I start throwing all of our living room blankets into bags for the homeless or cold of Iowa city* and walk out of the living room and into the kitchen where I decide it will be safe to put some Tupperware away. I open the cabinet and it's bursting with containers. That all fall out. "Why on earth do we need this many storage containers. In no world will all of these be full of leftover food in our fridge. And if it ever was, so help me, I'd be ticked. *I sit on the kitchen floor exasperated and determined to do something about this*. The goodwill frenzy begins and nothing is safe. This is still happening by the way. I don't want to spend my life cleaning/organizing/managing things instead of experiencing life. Plus I'm lazy...so there's that. GOODBYE STUFF!!

6. Again. My husband. I decided on Thursday to make dinner. I knew that full out grocery shopping would be overwhelming. So, along with Luke and the kids, I ventured to the grocery store to get only the couple of things I needed to make dinner...curry (something I used to make all the time). I

wandered the store for a couple minutes grabbing a couple things. And then I just wandered. And wandered. And Luke and the kids wandered with me. And the kids asked for every single thing on the shelf. And I finally stopped walking and started to cry. Poor Luke. He had no idea what to do. So he asked what was wrong. And the only answer I had was that I couldn't remember how to make curry. First trip out and I have a mental and physical little breakdown. Oh my word. Someone do something before my husband sends me back to Minneapolis. He won't do that...I think.

7. I feel like I'm just visiting. It's weird. And unexpected. I thought my house would feel like home. It in fact does not. Not yet anyway. I feel like I'm visiting family and at some point, sometime soon, I'm going to have to go home...to Minneapolis. And I hate that.

8. The idea of being in my house alone is terrible. Or terrifying. I'm not sure which word is more accurate. Luke was gone this weekend for a retreat. And so was Jordan. And Lauren left. And Jennifer. And then there were 3. Me and the kids. (For those of you that don't know, we have roommates. Most of them college students). So thankful that my friend Lilli started hanging out with me Friday afternoon and then I didn't let her out of my sight until like 9 that night. Poor sweet Lilli. She had no idea what she had gotten herself into.

9. This is the first time in 5 months that I haven't slept in the same room as Lanie. Wow. That scared me a little. How would I know if she was crying in the night? Or sleepwalking? Or needed to go to the bathroom? I'm still a little nervous in regards to this. I've got some work to do, I know.

10. Labs here are much different. They don't know Lanie and It takes a solid hour if not longer to get through the process. This will get easier. It's just a bit of a headache here at the beginning.

11. The transplant call after labs still comes. Last week it didn't come with good news, however. Lanie's WBC is super low. Again. Except this time, I'm 4 hours away. This is where I keep reminding myself that there's only so much I can do to keep her healthy. Everything else is in God's hands. And when I keep that perspective I'm okay. When I don't, I freak out. Option 1 is clearly better.

12. The people here in Iowa City have a lot of grace for me. They've let me vent and cry and laugh all within 10 minutes of time.

13. People everywhere actually have a lot of grace for me. You guys. I can't get over the fact that you read this. And care so much. And love Lanie like she's your little sister/daughter/niece. I'm completely blown away. And so is my family. I might or might not be sitting in a coffee house with tears while people stare at me right this moment thinking about you and your grace and love and kindness and generosity.

God's love is flowing you guys...thank you for being one of the vessels.

ALSO!!! My updates will be less but they'll still come! Lanie has Minneapolis appointments next week and lots more to follow. And, let's face it. I'm addicted to

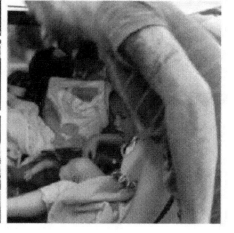

writing. Darn it! Never would I have thought that would happen, but alas. David and Meggan. I'm coming to you guys for some tips on how not to make myself sound like a 4th grader in the writing department. Be warned.

And LASTLY! If you guys want to follow on Instagram, I put a lot of pictures up and you can keep a little more updated. I think I'm under alberteingayle. Shows how much I know. If you do, prepare to be assaulted with pictures and nonsense however. I love you guys! For real.

Chapter 32: Highlight Reel

Oct 15, 2013 4:20pm

Hi everyone!!!! I feel like I've put this off for a while because I tend to be long winded (wipe that shocked look off your face). But today, I'm in a short and sweet sort of mood. Let's see if it actually happens.

HIGHLIGHT REEL (chronological order)

- Lanie hasn't had to miss a day of school from being sick (this doesn't count appointments). LOVE having a healthy girl!! Headaches have practically disappeared also. Amazing. God heals, even when we don't understand.

- my beautiful sister came to visit. She flew into Minneapolis from Colorado, thinking when we booked the tickets we would still be there. We weren't. So, her good natured self rented a car and made the trek to Iowa city. I don't ever really get to. Spend any time with her so this was seriously a sweet time...even if I did put her to work goodwilling my house.

- I went skydiving. Yep. I solo jumped out of a perfect fine airplane. Well, I didn't jump. I fell. That wasn't good. But other than that...amazing. What a sweet birthday present to me from my amazing friends.

- we got to visit our home church in Sumner, which is sweet because...well, we love those people. It was like an awesome family reunion.

- Lanie had appointments in Minneapolis last week. We were fairly concerned because the transplant team had told us the week before that her labs were bad and that there was a good chance she would be hospitalized. She wasn't. Thank you, God.

- Lanie's pancreas (we think) is part of the problem with her labs. It has to do with her pancreas digesting the anti rejection meds slowly and then dumping them all at once into her system, which causes a lot of problems. We're working on med changes to fix this.

- the appointments went well. Lanie was crazy active and all over the place, which made the doctors pretty happy. Next appointments are in the beginning of November.

- We got to stay with sweet friends and hang out with Rachel. Oh, and eat fresh walleye. Enough said.

- We had a welcome home tea party extravaganza for Lanie on Saturday. Ok, you guys (that's for you McGowen), I am absolutely NOT a tea party kind of person. I'm not fancy. I hate baking. Especially anything with 'petite' in the name. But it's the way Lanie wanted to celebrate being home. On with the party then! It ended up being really fun (thank you to all those that helped!! I couldn't have done it without you!).

- the last couple days have been normal (whatever that means). I honestly don't even know that word anymore. I think that's a good thing. I'm learning a lot about what it means to be a wife again. And a friend. And a mom. And even what it means to just be me in a completely different environment. I'm learning to let go of some of the high expectations I put on myself and instead try to rely on what God can do when I'm not standing in the way. I'm in the process of getting my counseling license renewed and still meeting with girls when I have free time.

Iowa City life is good. And hard. But hey, I've always loved a challenge. And an adventure. And that's exactly what this is.

I am truly thankful for every single one of you. And for my Minneapolis family, who I miss so incredibly much. And for my Iowa City folks who have been incredible in helping with this transition and for being the most loving people ever.

AND!!!! I'm not gonna lie...I actually did a decent job keeping this short. You are very welcome. And yes, I just gave myself a pat on the back

Chapter 33: Only the Concreteness of Life

Nov 12, 2013 11:34pm

Wow...so it's been almost a month I guess. And I've been looking at this blank screen for a solid 45 minutes now trying to figure out how to tell you guys about everything that's happening in life...mostly because a lot of it is abstract. I feel like I've learned more about myself in this last month...my priorities, my self worth, understanding my own thoughts and feelings (somewhat...it still counts though), and the things that break my heart but in a really good way. My mind has really been blown by all of that, actually. And I feel like if I start talking about all of that, this update will literally never end...and it wouldn't really be an update then, anyway, but instead just a crazy monologue of the inside of my head. In general, the abstractness of our life right now is complicated...and so incredibly beautiful. And maybe one of these days I'll update a little on just that alone (if I find the courage to enter in to that world of vulnerability and transparency that is).

So for now, I'll update on the concreteness of our life.

Lanie. This girl keeps us on our toes. For the most part she is a loving, generous, hilarious girl who likes dressing up, dancing, gymnastics, and now all of the sudden practicing WWE moves. She loves getting everyone in the house involved in whatever she's doing (and it's usually very physical and someone almost always gets hurt...adults included). She's been getting along great with Jackson -mostly- and I really think they just love being together. She really loves school and is pretty excited to be home again with her friends, playing outside, and living a normal, healthy kid life. There is this small other side of her, though. The side that says that she gets to win...in every argument, every game, in decision making, and anything else she can think of. I'm sure that there is some elegant and graceful way to hone this skill that she has into leadership and strength, but as of right now, I haven't found it. Please...someone...anyone...teach me your ways.

About 3 weeks ago she started getting a cough and a low grade temp. We took her in to see the doctor and her chest sounded clear...plus there's just a million things going around right now. Every week she seemed to feel a little bit worse though. This last week I was in San Francisco with a friend and Luke told me that her cough was starting to keep her up at night and that he thought she was getting sicker. I prayed like crazy. This was the first time I was away from her in close to a year and the thought of her going to the hospital without me scared me some (insert abstract issues I'm dealing with here). I knew that we had doctor appointments in Minneapolis on Monday and Tuesday of this week, so I prayed that anything that was going on would hold off until then. And it did. There were no calls when I was gone about temps spiking, or worsening cough, or any other sickness related issues (although there were discussions regarding behavior and hour long fits being thrown - refer back to the last paragraph and the idea of Lanie winning).

I got home from California Saturday fairly early. Luke and the kids were able to go see Luke's family in Missouri last weekend and so they didn't get home until Saturday pretty late. Sunday we were able to go to our church - Veritas as a family before Lanie and I packed up a little (and by packed I mean grabbed the bag I took to San Francisco and threw some of Lanie's clothes on top of mine) and headed up to Minneapolis. Insert sigh of relief.

Monday: Monday started out great. I had planned to get up and run, but didn't realize that Lanie's cough was bad enough to keep her...and me up the whole entire night. That run went right out the window. On the way out the door to her appointments, Lanie started coughing so hard that she threw up. AMAZING SIDE NOTE: she caught it all in the sleeve of her coat. Ok, you guys, I was too impressed to be grossed out. There was zero vomit in my car, after all. Bummer for her coat though. I ran back into the house where we stayed and washed her coat out in the sink with soap and water while she cleaned up and borrowed a small adult sweatshirt to keep from freezing to death. What is up with this state and its Alaska-like temperatures?!? Then we headed to her GI appointment at 10am, which couldn't have gone more perfect...Lanie is growing like crazy (almost 3 inches since transplant!!) and has been fairly pain free in regards to her stomach. Seriously. It was like the best GI appointment we've ever had. With the exception of getting a flu shot. I thought the shot would be a piece of cake for Lanie. She is like a medical champ. Apparently she has a little rage in her still however and decided that she would fight that shot to the death. 30 minutes, 3 nurses, and a lot of 'discussing' later, and we were finally able to walk out of that room and get on with our day. I'm not kidding when I say the girl likes to win. Once we got out of there we had a long talk about respect and how it's ok to not like something and even say you don't like something...it's not ok to kick, spit, and flail about. Valuable life lessons, I know.

The rest of the day was spent trying on dresses for a fashion show that Lanie was asked to participate in as a fundraiser for Amplatz - www.mmf.umn.edu/events/wws/index.cfm (oh my heavens...I haven't seen her spin and twirl that much in a dress EVER. She had the time of her life. And Rachel and I had a blast watching her) and just having fun in this city we like to think of as our second home. Overall...awesome day.

Tuesday (today): Today started out similar to yesterday. I had no clue Lanie was having this much trouble with her cough until I slept with her the last 2 nights. I got absolutely no sleep. I have no clue how she managed to. That cough is bad. But I figured since we had discussed it some yesterday at her appointment, that there was really nothing we could do about it besides let it run it's long and annoying course. We started today with labs, which were amazing. The lab techs here are incredible. Lanie barely even flinches anymore. After labs we had an appointment with our renal doctor. Lanie didn't have labs yesterday, so there was nothing really to look at there in regards to her cough or inflammatory markers. Today she did. Her CRP was up some and her cough was awful. During the appointment, our renal team felt a little uneasy sending us back home. Only one other place to go, then.

Inpatient. Yep. We got admitted. Unit 5. Room 29. Sunset side (because we have the most amazing nurses on the planet).

Needless to say this was really unexpected. And I was shocked. Usually I can kind of tell when she's going to be admitted. Today was a complete surprise. I mean, I had plans. I was going to stop by the outlet mall and use my coupon at Gap that expired today. Also, it's my sweet friend's birthday and I was going to get home at a decent enough time to take her out and spend time spoiling her. I was going to cook an awesome dinner for the boys, and I was going to lay down beside my husband tonight, who I haven't really seen in over a week. And in all honesty, I was totally bummed.

But then there was Lanie.

Even though she was bummed at first, she genuinely and loudly cheered as we were heading up to unit 5. And with every nurse that walked in our room to hug and love on her, my heart softened. Even her past resident, Dr. Luke stopped by...the girl was floating on the clouds.

As I was walking back from Starbucks tonight (because God is STILL providing sweet little gifts of coffee through your generosity!) with 2 Americanos in my hands (one to put in the fridge for me to drink in the morning of course...yep, I'm that girl) I suddenly remembered it. Circumstance. This is just another circumstance. Not bad. Not good. Just a circumstance. It's my belief about it that adds meaning. And up until then my belief was that this day completely ruined my plans for tonight. And it wasn't really fair. And come to think of it...it ruined my plans for tomorrow also. And I was fairly annoyed. I don't make plans often, so when I do and they fall through, I am instantly frustrated. But walking back and seeing the hospital with the sun reflecting off the colored exterior walls, God reminded me. There is so much joy in this. Overwhelming joy actually. Lanie is at home here. She undeniably loves this hospital...these nurses and doctors...even her room. She knows her place here. And as weird as it seems, she's comfortable. She belongs. And she overflows with pure joy.

This circumstance isn't bad. It's not what I expected, or even necessarily wanted. But it's certainly not bad. It's actually kind of the opposite.

I couldn't stop listening to the song 'Something Beautiful' by NEEDTOBREATHE on the trip up here. And it instantly came back to me as I was walking back to the hospital tonight... The lyrics look kind of like this...

In your ocean, I'm ankle deep
I feel the waves crashin' on my feet
It's like I know where I need to be
But I can't figure out, yeah I can't figure out

Just how much air I will need to breathe
When your tide rushes over me
There's only one way to figure out
Will you let me drown, will you let me drown?

Hey now, this is my desire
Consume me like a fire, 'cause I just want something beautiful
To touch me, I know that I'm in reach
'Cause I am down on my knees.
I'm waiting for something beautiful
Oh, something beautiful

And the water is rising quick
And for years I was scared of it
We can't be sure when it will subside
So I won't leave your side, no I can't leave your side.

In a daydream, I couldn't live like this.
I wouldn't stop until I found something beautiful.
When I wake up, I know I will have
No, I still won't have what I need.
Something Beautiful...

And that's what this little stay on Riverside Avenue in Minneapolis Minnesota is turning into...something beautiful...

Chapter 34: Back Again

Nov 13, 2013 10:50pm

Hey everyone! Still here at Amplatz, 5th floor. I honestly thought that we would be on our way home today. Things don't always turn out like we think though, which isn't necessarily a bad thing. Lanie slept a little better last night than the previous 2. Still a lot of coughing, but it didn't wake up to it as much...wait...maybe I just was so tired I slept through it. I'm all the sudden rethinking her night...and my parenting skills.

Doctors rounded this morning and were waiting for the ok to leave after her antibiotic this afternoon. The doctors listened to her chest, a couple of times. Both agreed that she sounded worse. They also showed me some spots on her X-ray that showed that there was a very high possibility that she has atypical pneumonia (pneumonia that is all over and not just confined to one lobe). The treatment for that would be the same as the antibiotics that she is already getting so the plan didn't change at all. Oh...except for the part about going home. Our doctors thought that if they sent us home there would be a solid chance that she would get worse before she gets better and they would rather have that happen here at the hospital instead of somewhere so many hours away. Fair enough.

Other than that, today was uneventful medically. Lanie and nurse Natalie built an awesome fort which kept Lanie more than busy all morning and into the afternoon. By 3:00 we had a steady stream of visitors and friends who brought me some Starbucks, food, and shampoo. Side note here: you guys continue to blow my mind! Thanks for caring so incredibly well for us. It's so amazing. I feel like I have learned so much about the humility of receiving...and man is it hard.

Thank you so much for all of the prayers, texts, calls, and messages. You guys are truly the most encouraging people I know. And thanks for sticking through these last 6 and a half months with us. You're more of a blessing than you'll probably ever know...

Nov 14, 2013 1:22pm

Well it's Thursday. I really like Thursdays. The kids get out of school an hour early, we always do a kid date after school to a new place in Iowa city or just go to one that's already a favorite, and we get to see Luke for like an hour or two in the middle of the day (which makes me super happy because he never gets home on Thursdays before 11p). Today is obviously a little different (ok a lot different) from our *normal* Thursday routine, but it's still a day worth looking forward to...

In all honesty I woke up a little grumpy. And tired. And isn't it interesting that during transplant I could be here day after day after day and it would be okay but now only 3 days in and I'm going stir crazy?!? Home has made me soft I think.

It took a while for the doctors to round this morning (which reminded me how impatient I can get) so we kept ourselves entertained by playing in the sweet fort in Lanie's room and playing games, which mostly included tea parties and dance a thons. I felt like if the doctors could walk in and see how hard it is to keep her contained in this room, they would certainly set her free. Lanie wore out before they came, though and was lounging on her bed again when they walked through the door. I was a little disappointed. Both doctors listened to her back and asked each other what they thought. Still so much junk in her lungs. Shoot.

But then our main kidney doctor said this (paraphrased) ... Well, she's not getting better. She sounds just as bad if not worse as she did yesterday, but

224

look at her! She looks so good! I really think it's just a virus that has to go the course. And she might get worse before she gets better. And you may end up bringing her back in...But look at her!

It's true. Lanie looks great...I mean just look at her picture here...jumping on her bed like her old silly self. Yeah, she still has a cough and a runny nose, but she's getting more and more energetic and spirited. It's time to go and see what happens. I feel super confident about leaving too so I think that's a good sign! Lanie, of course would like to stay here forever. She told Dr. Luke this morning that she liked it here because she got to build forts and play all day. I told her she got to do those things at home too, and to that she rebutted that she doesn't have a TV in her fort at our house. Touché.

We'll spend tomorrow and this weekend at home, letting ... I mean, MAKING Lanie rest before she goes back to school on Monday. And I'm excited. Excited to be going home again. Excited to see the boys. Excited that we were able to connect with our sweet Amplatz family for a few days. Excited to hang out with Minneapolis friends that I wouldn't have seen otherwise. And excited to fall asleep in my own bed and have Lanie once again on the road to recovery.

After all, it's a beautiful day to drive home, is it not?

Nov 21, 2013 9:28pm

So every single day this week I've thought about updating. And then something random and crazy would happen. Man...Can I just say that I am super glad that this week is coming to an end?

Here is what I mean about crazy... In order, of course

- we get home a week ago today from the hospital, I don't know, maybe around 9:30 or 10:00. And I decided to have this be my starting day of a completely whole food, no sugar monthly challenge thing (Whole30). I had no idea the week that was I store for me...

- I kept Lanie home from school Friday, per doctor's orders, to give her the weekend to rest. She was feeling pretty darn fabulous though, and so I kicked myself all day for keeping her home

- Saturday morning was pretty lazy, which was actually awesome. I'm pretty sure I didn't change out of my sweats until around noon and then we had a little get together with friends on Saturday night, which was so fun. And full of Mediterranean food. So, I think that in and of itself is something amazing.

- I woke up Sunday morning to Lanie crying in our upstairs bathroom and saying she couldn't breathe. When I finally got her calmed down she started throwing up. Awesome. Except not. I am so thankful for my sweet husband. We said from the very beginning of our relationship that I would do all sorts of gross things that happen with kids but vomit is not one of them. He has handled that every time. Luckily she was already in the bathroom.

- Lanie finally fell asleep again downstairs in our family room snuggled next to a bowl. All day Lanie either slept or was awake crying that her tummy or head was hurting. I kept taking her temp and she was teetering right at 99.9 and so I waited. Around 4:00, her temp started going up. 100.2. 100.3. 100.4. I know those seem ok, but for Lanie they're not. The rule is that if she hits 100.4 we get labs.

- I called the local ER to let them know that I would be bringing her in. That was a mess. The plan didn't work out at all as I had thought it should and I hesitated on taking her in. I decided to not take her in. She had labs first thing in the morning anyway and we would see what transplant had to say and see how she was feeling. She slept all night.

- she woke up the next morning feeling a lot better. I took her in for labs and kept her home from school waiting on a call or email from transplant. She was seriously back to her normal self. Crazy. Labs came back decent except her kidney stuff was elevated a bit...probably because she was pretty dehydrated.

- Luke and Jordan (a college guy that lives with us) both started feeling pretty bad on Monday.

- Tuesday. Luke starts throwing up. Jordan's sick now too. And Jackson wakes me up (because I'm sleeping downstairs on our couch) telling me he's sick and crying about a tummy ache.

- Wednesday.. Jackson goes to school. I plan to get a lot done. Luke and Jordan are still sick. Lanie and I are perfect. 2 hours into the school day and

226

the school calls...please come get Jackson. I won't even comment on how different boys are to take care of when they're sick compared to girls. Let's just say it's very...uhhhh...different.

- SWEET SIDENOTE! Lanie started gymnastics on Wednesday night. Oh man. She was so nervous. She told me a million times. But let me just be a proud mom for a minute. She totally rocked it. That girl is built for gymnastics. She was just so in her element. She struggles with school, with being sick...just with all of these different things, but in that gym...she was confident. And strong. And she knew she belonged. And I watched her that whole hour, with teary eyes (no worries. I didn't let one tear fall...she would've been so embarrassed) tumble and play and run around. Thank you so much Coralville GymNest! Seriously...you guys are absolutely amazing.

- And then today. Today was the first semi-normal day of this whole crazy week. I got some things done. I met with some people. And I baked like crazy. Tomorrow's Jackson's birthday and his request was cake balls for school and pumpkin bars as his 'cake'. I really stink at baking. I mean I really do. I'm not one of those people that are like 'oh I only bake here or there, I'm really not good' and then bring some beautiful fondant cake thing that looks like it came straight from winning an award on some Hollywood reality show. That's not me. I actually ran out of lollipop sticks and tried to cut kabob skewers in half to use on the rest until my younger, but more levelheaded friend discouraged it because of the pointy piece in the cake ball and the jagged end that the kids would hold. Point taken. We used popsicle sticks on the rest. I should not be allowed to make decisions sometimes. Especially with anything that takes a little creativity.

And that was our week. Whew. So thankful that tomorrow is a new day. A fun day! Jackson's having a couple boys over for his birthday to have a boy night/slumber party...wait...do boys say slumber party? Probably not. Anyway. No girls allowed. And apparently mom's count as girls.

And Lanie, my friend Sam, and I are headed to Minneapolis for the evening. Lanie was asked, along with some of her favorite hospital friends, to help with a fundraising event for Amplatz Children's Hospital. In all honesty, I feel like we would just about do anything to help there. That place is embedded so deep in my heart, I will always think of it when people ask me about home. To help out with a fundraiser is definitely an honor. You can check out the event.

It's called Wine, Women, and Shoes:
http://www.mmf.umn.edu/forms/wws/index.cfm.

I pretty sure they have a Facebook page if you like to follow along with things like that.

She's pretty excited about being asked to help. After all, what little 7 year old girl doesn't like dressing up, walking a runway, and being treated like a movie star? Yep. Exactly. I'm actually pretty excited to get all dressed up too.

The event goes until 10:00 and so we'll find someone's floor to crash on and then leave first thing in the morning to head back to Iowa City to spend the majority of the day celebrating Jackson and the 9 sweet years I've gotten to be his mom.

I'll update again this weekend to let you know how everything goes. And to tell you about the amazing things that are coming up this next week. And some big things I'm struggling through as well. It's all connected. But isn't it always.

And wow...Thank you guys, again. I keep meeting more and more people that have followed this roller coaster of a story. And I recognize your names from the comments of encouragement and support you gave. And every single time I meet one of you, I am beyond humbled. And I just stand there and don't know how to tell you thank you. I'm just so in awe of you. To stand wholeheartedly alongside people you've never met. I'm amazed...and a little star struck when I get to put faces to names that have become close to my heart. So please ignore my awkwardness when you meet me in real life. I really do thank God for each and every one of you.

Chapter 35: Gratitude

Dec 9, 2013 10:57am

Hey there sweet family. Wow. So a lot has been going on here with us. And in all honesty it's been like a big beautiful blur and I'm still trying to make sense of it all. And God is teaching me immeasurable things about Himself that I never fully realized before. And just...wow. Disclaimer! I haven't proof read this. My apologies for the rambling, ahead of time.

Here goes...

I think the last time I updated I was taking Lanie to Minneapolis to be in the fashion show to help raise money for Amplatz. What an incredible night. First of all, you guys, I was so out of my league. I had to wear a cocktail dress (what is that even?!? My friend Sam vetoed most things I pulled out of my closet) and there were NFL players walking around holding silver trays with champagne on them and women boldly wearing Prada and Gucci. And it was amazing to be a part of. And to see the amazing amounts of generosity as people gave to a cause to incredibly close to my heart. I left that night blown away. By the experience. By the generosity. And just by the fact that God allowed us to take part.

That was on Friday night. We drove home again on Saturday morning and then spent the weekend getting ready for our next big adventure (and by getting ready I mean doing laundry, cleaning the house, hanging out with people, and running around crazy doing all of the things I meant to do in the last week or so leading up to this). And then Monday came. We sent the kids to school telling them we'd pick them up around lunchtime to head toward Minneapolis. Precursor: I'm not sure if you remember this, but back in May an amazing family who has extended their love and generosity to us in a way that I can't even express fully in words gave us a trip to Disney World to help us be able to reconnect as a family. We were supposed to be able to go in August and then Lanie got really sick and we stayed in Minneapolis for another 2 months. Crazy, right?!? That seems like a lifetime ago now. Because Luke works with college students, the best time for us to reschedule the trip was over Thanksgiving. Now, back to Monday. We pick up the kids from school and head to Minneapolis. On the way, we were able to make a stop in Decorah, Iowa to hang out with our sweet friends who gave us the trip. And I'm not just saying this...every single time I am with them I'm in awe of their love and kindness. They have completely shown me a side of giving that I haven't seen before. And it's challenging...and life giving.

After we left their home, we got to Minneapolis in time to hang out with Rachel and her twin sister Leah for their birthday. This could not have worked out more perfectly and I wouldn't have wanted to spend Monday night anywhere else. Birthdays are my favorite.

Tuesday. 4am. Get up to go to the airport. Rachel made us coffee, because she's awesome and then drove us to our terminal. The kids were crazy excited. Never mind the fact that it was the middle of the night by some peoples standards. They stayed awake the entire plane ride watching Monsters U. Lanie did finally fall asleep on the shuttle from the Orlando airport to the resort that we were staying. Of course. Once there, we were able to smoothly check in to our room and head to the first park. 5 days. 5 sweet days of reconnecting as a family. No stress. No responsibilities. No deadlines. Just being together and enjoying each other. That gift was so much more than a trip to Disney. It was a gift of time. And 5 days of carefree living. And lessons in God's grace and love in abundance.

I would love to talk more about Disney and tell you guys everything that we did and experienced, but this update alone would be a book. And oh my goodness, no. I'll give you some highlights of actual experiences there, though...

- our friends gave Jackson a camera for his birthday. The first day we were there we went to Animal Kingdom and he took picture after picture while on the safari. It was the sweetest thing ever.

- we hopped on the wrong bus at the end if the first night and finally ended up where we wanted to go an hour later with 2 exhausted kids and starving parents...and we ate the best food ever that night at an all you can eat African steak buffet.

- Epcot. Our kids loved it so much. And Jackson and I won on TestTrack, because yeah, we build the best cars.

- Lanie got to meet princess Jasmine while wearing her jasmine outfit. And she also got a lesson in belly dancing.

- Magic Kingdom. Lit up at night for Christmas. Oh my word. Also...space mountain, big thunder mountain, and splash mountain. Yes.

- My mom was able to meet us for half a day on Thursday and all day Friday. The kids were glued to her hip

- At Hollywood Studios, Jackson's favorite ride to go on over and over was Aerosmith's Rockin Roller Coaster and Lanie's favorite was the Tower of Terror. Yep. My kids have no fear.

- I got to see my amazing friend Holly and her beautiful family as well as Ken and Sue for dinner one night. Those people. I love them so much and to be able to spend some time with them during this trip was definitely a huge blessing.

We flew back in from Disney on Saturday and then were able to go to the Vikings game on Sunday. Where they won. In overtime. And it was glorious. Being a part of a huge cheering mob is awesome. I would do it every day if I could. And now we've been home for a week. And we'll be here for 4 more days, counting today, before Luke and I fly out of the Moline, Illinois airport headed to a beautiful resort in Playa Del Carmen, Mexico for a week. Just him and I. On vacation. Somewhere warm and amazing. Luke and I were just talking about how we have never done something like this. Take a vacation with just the 2 of us. Let alone to a beautiful resort on the Caribbean. It's another sweet an amazing gift that I can't even wrap my head around. Like at all.

And here is where I get really truthful and honest and raw with you guys. This is the part of the update I've been dreading because I don't quite understand this all myself. Ok...here goes. I have been struggling lately with these trips. Like a lot actually. Not with the trips themselves, but maybe with the way that I perceive them. These trips are beautiful and amazing and extravagant. They are literally once-in-a-lifetime things. And I'm excited beyond words about them. But there is something struggling in me. Like the fact that there is nothing that I did...or Luke did...or anyone COULD do to deserve something like this. Or repay it for that matter. I've had a couple conversations lately with my sweet friends who I just honestly love and trust so much to tell them all the crazy things in my head and I think it boils down to these 3 things...

1) I had a good friend tell me this summer that everything that has been given to me and Lanie isn't really fair. Now he was totally kidding and making a joke out of it, but he was so right. It isn't fair. People go through hard things all the time. There is nothing fair about us getting good gifts and others not. I think the reality of people saying "Life isn't fair" is hitting me hard lately. And usually people only use that phrase when something bad happens. But it's true in general. It's not fair that I get to live in a warm home while others are living on the streets. And it's not fair that some people will battle illness their whole life and others are in perfect condition, no matter how terrible they treat their bodies. Life really isn't about being fair, though is it? In reality, we don't really deserve anything. Not a good paying job. Not a week off. Not food, or new clothes, or a manicure, or even a warm place to sleep. And so everything that we have, everything that we get and are able to do is a gift.

2) Gifts aren't meant to be repaid. I know this seems like common knowledge, but I really struggle with this. I was talking to my friend Wendy the other day about this exact topic and how I'm struggling with these extravagant things because I have no way to repay them...or pay them forward to someone else. I honestly just don't have the means to send a sweet family to Disney or set up a couple in some amazing resort. I don't have any way to give in a way that I have received. And that really bothered me for some reason. I WANT to be able to give like that. And then I realized, through the words of my wise and annoyingly right friends...that this is a lot

like grace. Boom. They're right. There's nothing we can do to earn it or repay it. Even though we want to. And we REALLY want to be able to do those things...but we can't...uhhhh...because that's what grace is. Mind blown. In other words...stop trying. Give joyfully when God says to. No matter how little or how much. And receive joyfully in the same way (which is way harder in my opinion).

3) And lastly this. Thankfulness. I get stuck in my head sometimes. Ok. A lot of times. And I've been laying in bed sick for the last 2 and a half days, so I've had plenty of time to just think. I don't recommend it. And I've come to realize that I don't know how to show thankfulness well. I mean, how do you tell someone...

"Thank you for making the decision to donate your child's organs so that mine can live" OR

"Thank you for the amazing support you guys showed us these last 7 months...the gifts, and cards, and food, and texts" OR

"Thank you to the Amplatz doctors...and the nurses who not only saved Alaina's sweet life through their gifts of medicine and skill but also through their love and friendship" OR

"Thank you for giving a WHOLE YEAR of your life to put together a benefit for us" OR

"Thank you for the amazing trip to Disney World so that our family could reconnect in a way that we haven't in a really long time" OR

"Thank you for the trip to Mexico. I haven't had this much alone time with my husband ever and I'm excited to spend this week getting to know each other again apart from the craziness of the world"

You guys. You can't SAY thank you for that stuff. You can't SHOW people how thankful you are well enough. I don't think it can be done. My friend, Lindsay, told me the other day that I don't have to prove to anyone that I'm thankful. And I didn't think that was what I was doing...but it totally is. I was struggling so much because I couldn't figure out how to prove to everyone that their gifts to us were amazing and how grateful I was. Lindsay told me to that I don't have to show thankfulness in the way I was thinking; I can just live OUT OF thankfulness. I know...I'm still trying to wrap my head around it, too.

Man. It's humbling. To receive. And to feel overwhelming gratitude and let go of the need to repay everyone or prove myself. And I haven't come to a complete resting place on all of this yet. I still struggle with some of these ideas. And maybe I will for a while. I'm not really sure. But what I do know is that my heart literally overflows with thankfulness for all of you. And I am getting to experience a side of God that I maybe didn't fully understand before...and that is incredible.

Chapter 36: Happy New Year! And belated Merry Christmas

Jan 3, 2014 8:43am

Good morning from Minneapolis! I hope that this Christmas season was amazing for you guys. Full of love and laughter and family!

Ours was crazy busy, but in such a good sweet way. I think I can paraphrase our time, though, so you guys are reading pages and pages of craziness. If you just want a super short update on Lanie you should definitely just scroll to the bottom. My feelings won't be even a little hurt.

Last time I wrote I was pretty sick, but didn't know why. Well I found out why. It turns out that wisdom teeth are really supposed to come out whether or not you have insurance when you are younger. I obviously thought that they were in my mouth for a reason, even if they were all crooked and crazy. I might have been wrong. On December 11th I had emergency dental surgery. I want to love the dentist. I really do. But let's just say I could make a very, very, very long list of things I'd rather do with my 2 hours, and I'm pretty sure that falling out of a tree and breaking my arm would be on there, because at least climbing a tree is fun and it would make a good story.

The next night after surgery Luke and I headed to the Moline airport to hop on a plane to Mexico. The dentist told me that this was a no go. When he told me that I immediately, of course, started crying, but in my head thought 'yeah...I'm still definitely going'. When we got on that plane at 6am Friday morning and sat into our seats, I was too excited to care anymore about my somewhat swollen face and pain that accompanied...until we started the decent into Atlanta. Oh my word, you guys. The pressure from that plane in my jaw...I just cried. And I'm sure Luke was just thrilled about starting this amazing trip off with a girl whose face was swollen, sitting in the seat next to him crying. Poor guy.

We made it in to Mexico around 11am which was absolutely amazing. The resort, Playa Del Carmen, the people, the food (once I could eat again), it was all so beautiful and delicious and incredible. Of our 8 days there, we spent 2 and a half days hanging out at the resort and the rest of the time cliff jumping, zip lining, snorkeling, cave swimming, ATV-ing, rafting, and seeing the Mayan ruins. Oh man, you guys. It truly was awesome to get that time away with just Luke and I. I didn't even know that I had needed it so much (the alone time that is...the trip was just the icing on the being alone cake!) It was hard to leave the 85 degree weather to come home to the ice storms in Iowa, but we definitely missed the kids and were excited about being home for Christmas.

We spent one day home in Iowa city having Christmas with our kids before we headed to Kirksville, Missouri. Man. I hadn't been back there since last Christmas since we got Lanie's first transplant call on Christmas night and freaked out a little (fine, a lot) about being roughly 7 hours from the hospital when we were only supposed to be about 4 or 5. This trip was way less chaotic and really just sweet. We got to see a ton of people we hadn't seen in at least a year and also were just able to rest and have fun. Those few days went way too fast.

After getting home from Kirksville, the kids and I headed up to Sumner, Iowa (our home for 6 sweet years) for an impromptu overnight stay and church service. Can I brag a little on those people? They are truly amazing. They still do such an intense job of caring for me and my family and every single time we go back I am blown away by their genuine love for people. Their judgment might be off sometimes...I mean, Luke and I were only 24 when we moved to Sumner to pastor the church there, but they love people in a way I've rarely seen. The people there will always be family.

And then there was New Years Eve, which I was pretty excited about. We had friends over in the morning for coffee and just spent the day letting the kids play at home. Lanie woke up that morning with a low temp and headache. I gave her some Tylenol and within an hour she was feeling a lot better. The day went on fairly normal after that. I made snacks for the 2 places we were going that night and was starting on dinner when I saw Lanie laying on the couch wincing and holding her head. I asked what was wrong and she told me her headache was back. I took her temp. 101.8. No.

Just no. It's 530pm on New Year's Eve. Nothing is open. There's no one to call. Luke and I went back and forth on what to do for a solid 30 minutes and when I took her temp again it was 102.9. Stupid. I called the on call transplant doctor at our hospital in Minneapolis and he said we needed to get her up here as soon as we could. I'm not gonna lie here. I was so incredibly disappointed. This is not how I wanted to start off the New Year. I had such high hopes for this year, and starting it with making a middle of the night trip to Minneapolis was not how I saw this all happening.

We got to Minneapolis about 11:15p. The boys left us at the hospital so that Jackson could get to bed at a decent time and Lanie and I waited in the emergency department until 3am when a room up on unit 5 was ready. She finally fell asleep about 3:30. And the next day, New Year's Day, I sulked a little. And I slept a lot. And then I realized that just because we were here over New Years doesn't mean anything for this next year. At all. And the truth is I'm still pretty pumped about all of the things God will do throughout this next year. I love the idea of the unknown. And adventure.

I also haven't been outside in a few days but I am hearing enough complaints that I think I'm probably never going out again. 30 below wind chills?! Uhh no thanks. I choose sitting in the hospital over that nonsense. Luke and I were starving yesterday but when we weighed our hunger against walking outside 4 or 5 blocks to Jimmy Johns, we both decided that we could share the couple of tangerines we brought as a snack. Yep. I officially cannot stand this weather.

As with Lanie, we still don't really know what's going on. They started her on antibiotics when we came on New Year's Eve. The next day she was feeling so much better already. They doctors were sure that we would go home yesterday. But her darn Creatinine (kidney function) keeps going up and that has to be stable before we can leave. Her kidney team decided to stop antibiotics last night to see what happens with that. Will she spike a fever? Or get headaches? So far so good, but today is a bit of a waiting game.

The boys will be here soon this morning, which just reminds me of all the times that they haven't been able to come, and to look at this trip with thankful eyes. It's so different when they're here. Things just go smoother. I don't go as stir crazy in these walls. And Lanie and Jackson play together so well (mostly because Lanie becomes the boss and Jackson lets her because he's sweet and kind like that). I pray for both of their future spouses daily...but much differently.

Thank you guys for your unending support and encouragement. On days like today, your words from transplant and even after ring in my head and I am filled with awe in how God continues to move.

Cheers to the new year friends! May it be filled with love, trust, faith, and obedience...

Jan 4, 2014 9:22pm

Ooops. We're home!

Just wanted everyone to know (a little late) that we're home!!! We got in around 12:30am last night and slept in late, well, for us, this morning! We had breakfast and ran errands and played a little before I realized it had already been most of the day and I still hadn't updated to tell you guys we got released!! Sorry!!

Lanie didn't have any other fevers yesterday and had been off antibiotics for a full 24 hours so the only real option was to send us packing...and we obliged.

Thanks for the prayers! And the texts! And the calls! - Please always continue to do that when we don't update. I actually love it.

I'll try really hard to keep you guys updated on life and the randomness of my thoughts more frequently. Thanks again for everything! HAPPY NEW YEAR!!

Chapter 37: An update...on well, life

Feb 15, 2014 11:59am

Happy frozen Saturday morning! I hope you guys have enjoyed your morning cups of coffee, yes I said cups, of coffee and some sweet family time. Yeah, that's not usually what my Saturday mornings look like either, but today it is, so basking in the awesomeness of that.

The last couple weeks have been a little crazy. Good crazy, but also busy crazy. Lanie had appointments in Minneapolis with both her liver and kidney doctors. I love her doctors. Like honestly just so much. They have been with her since she was 3 and they know her. They know the difference in her stomach aches and something bigger. They know the way she talks about pain, and how she has to be really struggling with it to complain at all or stop what she's doing. They KNOW her. And I am always just thankful that God has allowed us to be able to take her to a place like that.

First Lanie had her liver appointment. Her liver is doing amazing by the way. For only having a part of a liver, that organ is being a serious rock star. We also talked a lot about Lanie's pancreas. For those of you that know a lot about what's going on, you know that Lanie still has a malformed pancreas that doesn't completely do the tasks assigned to it. It's rebellious. The doctors have talked about an auto eyelet transplant (taking out the pancreas, purifying the islet cells, and putting them into her new liver, leaving her without pancreas...I know...mind blown) for a really long time. They decided not to do all of the transplants at once, so this last transplant has been put off until her liver was in fairly amazing condition and the pancreas decided to cooperate less than it is now. In talking to her liver doctor, this is what was decided... Lanie's pancreas is still malformed and has abnormalities where the ducts are, causing it to be a serious annoyance on the road to not taking up residence at the hospital. Here's the funny part though... Even though her pancreas should be causing her lots of pain and should be acting out more than it is, it's not. It's just hanging out in there halfway doing its job. Why? Doctors aren't really sure. Probably because "the sick are healed, and the dead are raised, at the sound of HIS great name" is my guess. So even though we were thinking that the next

239

transplant would happen this spring or summer, that's not really the plan now. Doctors are saying that we'll just wait. They say her pancreas WILL stop working so when it starts to get worse, we'll take action. Lanie is her own donor in a sense so nothing needs to be planned too far in advance. I say, yeah, maybe the pancreas will stop working. But maybe it won't. Either way, no matter what though, it will be because God allowed it to happen and not because of 'medical certainty'.

Kidney appointment went awesome as well. I always feel a little more nervous before kidney appointments because when Lanie's been hospitalized in the last few months it's usually by the kidney team, and it's not always expected. Lanie's kidney has had a struggle from the beginning. It works hard to keep it, but it's doing the work all on its lonesome. This appointment finally showed signs of her kidney bursting to life. And that is exciting. A new kidney that is working properly also means that's it's releasing more growth hormones! You guys, I have been buying Lanie size 5/6 clothes!! Do you know how exciting that is?!? She's been in a size 4 for like, ever and now she's finally outgrowing clothes she's worn for a few years. And she loves to talk about how much she's grown. She's so proud of it and excited to start to look her age. She's feisty, that one, and I was starting to get a little worried about the next time someone asked her if she was 4. My mind pictured Lanie throwing a punch or trying to take someone down. Little doesn't mean timid. We're presently working through new ways of solving things because right now, well, she's a fighter.

Because her appointments went so well, Lanie has been moved to every other week labs (say whaaaaat?!?) and a month and a half in between her next appointments. Progress! Sweet, sweet progress!

Because her appointments are in Minneapolis, we usually get to see so many amazing folks when we make the trek up there. The Wilds (is that not the most awesome last name ever?) have been putting us up at nights when we come, which I can't believe, since Lanie has been known to sneak their ice cream and make them watch Disney for hours on end. They are beyond generous and completely encouraging...if you find people like this, don't ever take them for granted. It is a huge blessing to even know them. After the appointments, we headed over to unit 5 to hang out for just a bit with some of Lanie's best friends, who just so happen to also be nurses. I mean, they all have BFF necklaces so it's a real thing. That is ALWAYS a joy. Those girls are like my sweet sisters. I absolutely adore them. The unit 5 trip is always for me just as much as it's for Lanie. We also have just awesome friends that live in Minneapolis, so we usually try to see a few of those people every trip also. After the nurses, I met up with my friends Hiba and Rachel for dinner. Those girls can challenge me and make me belly laugh in the same breath. How in the world do I find all of these people?!? Such good gifts that I don't deserve.

(This next part of the update is going to be me babbling about the world and adventure and what not, so please feel free to skip over. My feelings will never be hurt...mostly because I won't know).

When I was with Rachel and Hiba, they asked me about life. About how things were going and whatever else that entailed. Now, there are some people that ask how things are going and they want a brief answer that doesn't really share large amounts of personal information. And I think that's ok. And sometimes time only allows for brief interactions. But when these girls ask...they lean forward and are ready for me to spend the next 10 to 15 minutes talking...the good, the bad, and the ugly. And the great. The great is always fun to share too...I'm just willing to share it with a lot more people. So when they asked, I told them. I told them how I thought I wanted to live a normal life, whatever that meant. I wanted to do day to day things and take my kids to school and make dinner for my family and hang out with girls and counsel a little and clean the house and walk the dog and workout and watch episodes of 24 or Breaking Bad because I was one of those people that never watched those shows when all the cool kids were doing it. And since January, my life has finally become that! And that was awesome. Except it wasn't. All of the sudden I craved adventure. And new things. And anything but ordinary. And how I have been desiring excitement and challenges and trying to do things I haven't done before. What in the world? How can I go from wanting one thing to immediately wanting its opposite? I know I'm maybe too young for a midlife crisis...but maybe that? I didn't know. And so I was telling the girls all of this. And how I couldn't understand my lack of contentment. I wanted to be content in anything, but I wasn't finding it. Now...disclaimer. I don't think there is anything wrong with living a life that is 'normal' (man, I honestly hate that word...like honestly...but I'm not so great with the English language and that's the best I can do right now). I also don't think there is anything wrong with living a life that is seemingly crazy. Honestly most people have a great mix of both, right? My frustration came from the fact that I wasn't finding contentment and desiring adventure. And I just couldn't figure out what was happening in my heart. So we talked and shared and laughed. And then, even though we didn't want to, we had to leave. I had to make the long drive home and the girls had other plans for later also.

This is God's sense of humor I think...Hiba rode with me and Rachel was behind us driving. We hadn't even left the parking lot yet and I started telling Hiba about my battery light that came on in my car and how that was weird and how it probably means nothing though. Just then, my cars lights started going dim...AS I WAS DRIVING...and then went off. I pulled over and my car proceeded to completely die. So apparently when the battery light comes on, that's important. Good to know for future reference. I did what any girl, with 3 other girls, would do. I called this guy that I know, named Bruce that I believe with all my heart can literally fix anything. And because he is amazing, he drove out to where we were (in the freezing, below zero temperatures) and fixed my car enough to get it into his garage. And while he was outside fixing my car, even though it was getting pretty late, his awesome wife, Nancy, took care of all of us inside by the fire. In the end, Bruce fixed my car THAT NIGHT so that Lanie and I could leave first thing in the morning to get home. Oh my word. These people that God has introduced me to...I can't even. From now on when I beg God for adventure, I will try to be more specific, and also try and leave others out of it. Unless, of course, Bruce and Nancy and Hiba and Rachel had all prayed for adventure that day too. In that case, you're welcome.

There actually is a point to all of this nonsense I'm sharing with you...I promise. That same weekend, I heard a song come on the radio from my iPod. It's not a 'Christian song' by any means, but man does it speak some truth. One line from the song says that people 'don't understand the power of significance'... Wait, what? The power of significance? God spoke to my heart so clearly, you guys. And what he told me was this...

My heart isn't craving noble adventure and excitement. It's craving significance. In what I do. In what I say. In where I am. All of it. For so long, I have been in a job that I felt good at, I have been in and out of the hospital with Lanie, or going through her little surgeries, I've been waiting for a transplant call, living in the unknown of transplant and all that brought along with it, and then in and out of the hospital since transplant has been done, and going to different places...I have felt like what I was doing was significant. I felt like it all meant something. Like it was important. And now? Not so much. I feel like what I do doesn't matter and doesn't make a difference. And God pulled something really ugly out of my heart. The need to feel significant. Ugh. Gross.

And then God changed my perspective. Significance doesn't come from what I think is important. It doesn't come from what other people think is important either. Shocking I know. You guys are probably stunned that I'm just now figuring this out. Significance does, however, come from walking in obedience. From sometimes doing things that people don't see or even care about. Sure...it's a little easier to trust God and obey when that's the only option. When things are crazy and chaotic and things don't make sense. When the only stability we know comes from God. When we feel like we are doing things that are important. But in all honesty, those things don't make us significant at all. We can't do those things without God, it's true. But we can't do day to day things without him either. We can't serve others or find contentment and joy or love our kids or friends or neighbors or any of these other things on our own.

God is what is significant. And it's a lonely and discontent world when we live life any other way. And so, friends, no more midlife crisis for me! Freedom from significance is amazing. And I'm totally not just saying that. It really is! It's super hard to try and be somebody all of the time. And it's ugly. So letting go of all of that feels like a massive weight has been lifted from my shoulders.

So, ok. I'm done with my rambling. Thank you guys for allowing me a space to talk and share. I didn't even know that this was a real thing until transplant.

I'm praying for you guys today. That you would find joy and contentment in doing the dishes and walking the dog and running your kids from place to place. And that you guys would rest in the fact that significance comes from obedience and not from accomplishment.

Chapter 38: Time flies when you're having fun

Apr 27, 2014 11:58pm

It honestly feels so weird to sit in my bed tonight with my iPad open to caring bridge. We've been so busy being semi normal here, that I forget what life was like just a few months ago.

You guys. This last week has been a mighty one in the overwhelming department. All week I was like "today is April 23rd. Do you guys remember what we were doing a year ago? We were living life. Waiting on a call." And then "hey guys. Do you remember April 26th last year? We were partying it up with our sweet friends at an indoor water park!".”And hey guys...do you know what we did a year ago today? We were at sweet Ramy's birthday party at the park. We had no clue what was going to happen in less than 24 hours!". The tears have been a bit uncontrollable this week.

And honestly, as I sit on my bed tonight and think about tomorrow, April 29th, and how our lives would change with one phone call on that day, I am overcome with so many emotions that it's hard to even name them all...let alone understand them. Thankfully Luke's not home to see this mess of a person sitting on the bed, typing on her screen, blowing her nose every 15 seconds, otherwise he would feel like he needed to ask me every so often if I'm okay and if he could get me anything, and I wouldn't even know what to tell him. Bless him

I totally want to share all that's on my heart tonight and this last week, but because I promised myself that I would keep this short, I'm going to resort to my fabulous list making skills in hopes that it will keep my mind focused and on topic...here goes nothing

- it really has only been a year. ONE YEAR. How can that even be?!? So much has happened! I've changed. My family has changed. Everything around me has changed. And it's insane. It honestly feels like years ago that this crazy thing happened and we are just using this time of year to remember it. But seriously, we left Minneapolis almost 7 months ago to the day. 7 MONTHS AGO! I know I'm using a lot of all caps but you guys, it's because my head is yelling it to make it sink in. Wow

- I'm not in control. Like at all. And the times I thought I had things under control was nothing but a mirage. I can't predict or plan or contain anything. And, surprisingly, that is a HUGE weight off my shoulders. It's one of the most freeing things I've ever felt. And God has taught me over and over and over and over this past year the freedom of letting go. And oh my goodness, the trust that has grown in my heart because of that is unbelievable. Luke was talking to a group of us tonight at the dinner table about prayer and what we've learned from it. I think that what I've learned the most is that it changes me, not necessarily my circumstances or situation. What's going on around me may never change, but my perspective does. And I honestly feel like God has been showing me that again and again this year. And it is so good! God has done things that year that I didn't even know we're possible. He's mended relationships, showed me things in myself and in my past that I didn't even realize we're still there, and showed me every single minute of the day my desperate need for Him. And that, in and of itself, overwhelms me with joy and gratitude

- Lanie is celebrating her one year transplant anniversary tomorrow and Tuesday IN Minneapolis. And oh my goodness! Is that not the most fitting and perfect thing EVER?!? I'm sorry to all the sweet people I am going to see while there...I have absolutely no control over my emotional state lately and my goal is to keep it together and pretend to be a reasonable and well mannered adult. I make no promises. This could be somewhat ugly...but also in a beautiful-smeary makeup-tangled hair-snot drippy way, I think. We are rejoicing y'all! This is a big deal. The idea is to leave here tomorrow after I drop Jackson off at school and get to Minneapolis around 1ish. My girl, Rachel took the day off so I'm just gonna say I am so beyond excited for that, I can't even handle it. I'm hoping we'll get to see a lot of other people that day too, but I honestly have no plan as of yet and so whatever happens, happens. And I love it. Also, we've been collecting art supplies for a while now to donate to the Child Life department of the hospital and Lanie is super thrilled to get to hand those off to our very favorite librarian, Laurie. After that, Rachel and Lanie and I are planning on going to Ronald McDonald for dinner tomorrow night and hang out with all of our amazing friends there (that place is literally the best. Like for real. Everyone thinks so). Tuesday Rachel works all day and Lanie has all of her millions of doctor appointments. These should be interesting. I'm anxious to hear about her pancreas, and plan for transplant with that. And in hearing about how THEY think that she's doing, because, I mean, she's sure blowing me out of the water with how amazing things are going!

- But in the same breath I am in a serious mourning period. And something in me struggles with the rejoicing aspect of the sweet and beautiful one year anniversary without sincerely and deeply acknowledging the other one year anniversary of tomorrow. The one where a sweet and beautiful life was lost. And you guys, I don't know if it's my own heart playing tricks on me, or my crazy woman emotions or the dare I say 'shame' of rejoicing when I feel like I should also be mourning, or whatever it is inside me, but the battle that is happening is real and that's for certain. God however, is lovingly reminding me through all of this that I have the incredible opportunity to pray specifically for a family that I hope to one day meet. And hug for, like an hour. And cry with. And also rejoice with. Luke, Jackson, Lanie and I are all writing letters to them again to let them know how much we love them. I've sat down to write this letter at least 7 times now and every single time I fall apart. No words can fully express the gratitude and love that overflows in my heart.

- Also! The plain and simple idea that has been reminded to me time and time again...everything we have or get to do or be a part of is a gift. EVERY. SINGLE. THING. It has been incredibly hard for me to not feel the need to pay things back, or even pay things forward, I guess. Whether it's financial help, or trips, or food, or gas, or support from the awesome people in our lives...or just anything. I couldn't pay it back even if I wanted to! No possible way, you guys. And in the same way, God has been teaching me about gratitude. And not gratitude like, 'wow, I found $20 on the ground outside of the grocery store tonight!' (Which actually did happen to me and let me tell ya...I was thankful!), but gratitude that can thank God because of who He is. Period. I read this awesome book by Steven Furtick called 'Crash the Chatterbox' (everyone go out and read this book. It's awesome. And while you're at it read the book 'Seven' by Jen Hatmaker and 'A million Miles in a Thousand Years' by Donald Miller...who doesn't want summer reading material?!?) And in one of the last chapters he said 'gratitude reinterprets the situations in our lives, beginning with the baseline acknowledgement that we don't deserve any of what we've been given'. SO TRUE! And so anti-cultural right? Right. I wish I could just copy and paste the rest of the chapter here because it goes on and on about this, but I won't. This post is getting long as it is, and I kinda need to wrap this all up somehow...

- And lastly, oh man, you guys...I'm excited. Looking back over this last year has lit a fire inside me. I'm so excited about what God is doing. I'm excited about what he's doing in Iowa City. And in my friends' lives. And my families. And in the different people I have met because of this. One of the pastors of our church in Iowa City was preaching last week on Easter and he said that he would rather be in a crappy situation with God than on a beautiful island without Him (I'm paraphrasing of course) and it's so true! I couldn't agree more. Life with God really is an adventure. A constant abiding in who He is. And it is incredible. And exciting. And there is no place I would rather be...

I can't wait to update you guys on the next few days. It's gonna be a bit of a ride, I think.

Seriously...you guys are amazing. Thank you for listening to me and loving on my family

May 2, 2014 8:49am

Hi guys!! So obviously in the whirlwind of Minneapolis I forgot to let you guys know how things went!!

Things really were somewhat nonstop while were in the cities this time but in such a GOOD way!

- Monday I got to Minneapolis and picked up Rachel (ahhhhhh so much hugging!) and we drove over to meet a couple of our sweet nurse sisters! I mean, how better to celebrate?!

- Because we know such fantastic people, the nurses already had a chocolate chip cookie cake made to celebrate her 1 year transplant anniversary. And of course, I cried a little...pish posh. I MOSTLY held myself together. It was so good to catch up and hang out. We LOVE those girls (and when I say love, I mean, Lanie told them she would rather go to the hospital

- AND BE INPATIENT - and hang out with them then be anywhere else. This child is mad...

- after we left the nurses, we headed straight over to the Ronald McDonald House to see our sweet Saudi friends who have been there close to two years. TWO years! Can you imagine?!? They thought that they would be here six months or so and two years later they are going home. They are the sweetest, most generous people in the galaxy. I want them to be part of my immediate family, but I'm not really sure how that works. I kid...but not really.

- Rachel's sister Leah (who I absolutely ADORE, met us at Ron Mcdon also, which is so great because it ended up being the only time I could see her. I'm pretty sure she and Jackson are the same people and I love that!

- you guys, we are so blessed with people who love us well. Because I wasn't ready to tell Rachel bye, I told her to come spend the night with me at the family's house I was staying at (the Wild's...and how great of a name is that?!? They are such an incredible gift!) And of course, she did. Which was awesome. I feel like this says something about me (I invite people to things and never assume anything other than the more the merrier) and about Rachel (she agrees with me) and about the Wild's (they are the most hospitable and gracious people ever...and I'm sure believe the more the merrier as well. Or just a really amazing job at playing along).

- Tuesday morning, the Wild's and Rachel all left for work and Lanie and I headed to the hospital. First we stopped at the library to drop off the art supplies for the hospital...giving is so contagious. It ALWAYS makes me want to give more. God is so incredible to put that piece of Himself in us!!

- After the library, we headed over to all the appointments. These were actually so good! I mean, we are literally only a year out of transplant and Lanie is rockin it! Her scar is barely seen. Her liver and kidney function is on point and she's been inpatient free since January. I honestly didn't think it could go any better! The doctors mostly agree. The biggest surprise to me was that even though she's grown about 4 inches since transplant (btw that's more than she grew from the time she was 3 to 7...so yeah, that's a lot for her little self) her kidney doc feels like she really needs to be growing more. The plan is to wait and see what her fabulous little body does until July and then look at next steps, which could be going back to taking the growth hormone shots...blech

- otherwise, everything looks great, because, well, the sick are healed and the dead are raised at the power of HIS great name! (Also, Veritas church...please quit singing this song. Yep, I cry. EVERY. SINGLE. TIME. And it's expensive to buy makeup that stays on through that. Cut it out

- because Tuesday appointments went way longer than I thought I missed seeing lots of people that I had wanted to get a chance to see. I guess that's how things work, but still I was a little disappointed. We did make one last stop before heading home, though, to see a family that I honestly just adore and their enormous dog that Lanie would steal if she could figure out to get him into our car. I have a smallish car. It isn't gonna happen.

Oh man, you guys, writing this update just reminds me (even more than the healing part of transplant, which is INCREDIBLE to say the least) that the people in my life are the biggest gifts I could ask for. The families, the friends, the strangers even, and all of you guys...it's unbelievable! And it's overwhelming to know all of you and how great you are because I realize what an incredible gift relationships are to me. Thank you. Every single one of you!

You truly have been not only a blessing but also an inspiration and a picture of love and compassion. Wow...

Thank you

Chapter 38: Summertime

June 19, 2014

Hi everyone! So it's the middle of June, right? Wow! Summer is like, in full swing or something. And we are loving every second of it.

We have been back to Minneapolis since Lanie's appointments at the end of April for her 1 year check up (Woop!). I cannot even believe it. The whole year before transplant we spent at least a week in the hospital every single month. EVERY MONTH! But now we're like "oh we are livin the life and saving the gas and playing in the sun (using more sunscreen than I've ever seen in my life of course) and doing all things summer".

When I think about what happened last summer, it feels like a thousand years ago. But also a little bit like yesterday. Funny how that works.

And life today is funny, and confusing, and sweet, and lonely at times, and busy, and somewhat creative. Here's a little glimpse into how...

- school's out for the summer! So this is fun, right?? Let me tell you, I'm not a mom who is creative or crafty or who plans educational and fun things everyday for her kids' summer vacation. I wish I was. Really I do. But alas, I feel productive if my kids have more highs in their days than lows and if we get them to bed by 10:00. This spring, in my pre-summer excitement, I actually enlisted the kids' help and made a summer bucket list...in permanent marker. Oh my goodness. What have I done? If we get a third of the 50 something things done, I will see my entire summer spent with my children as a massive success.

- I learned to make coffee. I mean, it honestly tastes like crap most of the time, but coffee is coffee. And I'm trying to be more self sufficient so I'm gonna go ahead and give myself a win in this category.

- We went to Hawaii for Lanie's Make-A-Wish. I want to tell you guys every single thing about this but every single time I sit down to write about it I am literally speechless or wordless or whatever it is that happens when you want to write and there are no words. That's what happens. The only thing I keep saying to people is that God is so incredibly good and I don't understand his gifts or the amazing things that we have been able to do this last year but I know that I know that I know that we don't deserve it and we may never receive another gift and God will STILL be just as good. I truly believe that looking over our whole last year, the thing that I KNOW the most about is how incredible God's goodness is and how our circumstances can be devastating or incredible and His goodness remains the same.

- I just got back this last week from moving some of my sweetest friends to Texas. My heart broke. Mostly because I love them so much and it's hard to imagine doing day to day things without them or their kids there. Those guys are my family and it's hard let family do things that don't involve me. That doesn't sound selfish at all right? I've never been more thankful for Skype, FaceTime, Snapchat, and every other form of social media right now. The other MUCH smaller, but still significant piece of my heart break comes from the fact that I moved them to College Station, Texas. This feels wrong on so many levels. The colors maroon and white give me hives when they are added to the irritating thumbs up sign (I know how dumb it is to love the Texas Longhorns as much as I do, but there is something in my DNA that loves Texas orange and Austin and college football and all things University of Texas. I can't change it and it's silly to ask me to). I just feel like there is a whole big world out there and these friends could be anywhere and God had them move to BCS. I JUST CAN'T! Hook em!

- Jackson and Luke leave for China on July 17th and will be there for a few weeks. Lanie isn't able to go yet - no green light from the doctors yet - and is struggling a little with that. I am so incredibly excited for the boys to get to go and love on kids and have the same amazing experience I did 2 years ago, and am trying to hold back the teeny bit jealous side of me that wants to complain and whine because Lanie and I won't be able to take part. The boys going together is so good. It's actually the BEST. And I hope Jackson is fine with me asking him 500 thousand questions about everything.

- While Jackson and Luke are gone, Lanie and I are heading to Texas for a week and then back to Iowa for a wedding and then to Minneapolis the very next day for lots and lots of appointments and loving on Minneapolis friends and places. Summer is gonna fly right on by at this rate.

- I'm in the midst of making a ton of decisions about this next fall. Should I go back to work full time counseling? Or part time? Or stay home and do what I have been doing this last year, which is hanging out with girls and doing some very part time counseling and being a wife and a mom and a traveler and a professional dinner maker. I feel like Lanie's looming eyelet transplant (pancreas) is always on my mind and I just don't know what is good. Or even more so...what is best. This summer will hopefully give me some clarity on that.

- Other than those things we are just living life here in Iowa City. We are waking up and having coffee and hanging out with so many amazing people and playing in the water and in the sun and at the parks. We are making new things to eat and jumping on the trampoline. We laugh and talk and catch up and stay up later than we should sometimes.

And it is so incredibly good.

July 25, 2014

Hi everyone!! We head to Minneapolis this weekend for doctors appointments and play time with some of our favs! I am so excited! I know, know, know that God has done amazing things in Lanie's body and I am SO PUMPED to hear the doctors give glory to God (even if they use medical jargon!).

Can't wait to update you guys!

Chapter 39: It's mostly about God being so incredible and everything

August 4, 2014

I will try and limit my use of exclamation points, but I make no promises.

Minneapolis is incredible...3 seasons out of the year. Every single time we go, we fall more and more in love. If you are from there, you clearly understand this. My friend, Jenny came with me this trip, which is awesome for at least 3 reasons.

First, Lanie loves to show off her favorite spots in the city. If you are ever visiting the city, here a just a few things for you to do: The Dowling Studio in the Guthrie (I'm not kidding about this one. I think if I were ever going on a date in Minneapolis, this room would somehow be involved). Gold Medal Park. Izzy's ice cream (homemade ice cream daily and dairy free amazingness in gluten free cones, y'all!! Need I say more?!?). The Stone Arch Bridge. Minnehaha Falls. One of the lakes (just pick one. There all pretty awesome. We usually somehow end up at Calhoun or Harriet). Pizza Luce. Nomads. And the amazing park off Riverside.

Second, I didn't have to go to appointments alone! This doesn't really need a lot more explanation, right. Together is better.

And lastly, because Lanie is feeling SO GOOD she has more energy than I know what to do with. It takes roughly 2 to 10 adults to keep up with her. All hands on deck.

I know that there are amazing people everywhere. I really do. But you guys haven't met my Iowa city and Minneapolis people. I have no clue how so many generous and loving people can live in one place. It blows my mind. Nurses. Doctors. Friends. Parents. Kids. Every time I go, I ask God to make me more like the people I spend my time with while I'm there.

AND NOW FOR THE MEDICAL PART

Before going into these appointments we prayed for some VERY specific things:

1. That Lanie would grow. Last year before transplant, Lanie was pretty consistently in a size 4. She had maybe grown about a fourth of an inch to a half an inch a year. Maybe. After transplant, she still struggled some with growing. I mean...that kidney took a long while before deciding that it liked its new home. In September she started to grow. By the time April came around and we went to Minneapolis for her 1 year appointments, she had grown around 3 inches. UNHEARD OF! Unfortunately, she still wasn't on the charts and the doctors were still a little concerned. In April, the doctors told us if Lanie hadn't grown enough to touch the bottom graph line, they would probably consider starting her on growth hormones again. No. There is nothing I like about giving her shots. She's a champ and allows me to do them but even the fact that she's used to things of that sort makes me frustrated. I poured out my heart to God. I asked for her to be on the line, even though it felt like a selfish request. You guys...she had to go straight up on the chart to even get close to the line and she had 3 months to do it. BUT GUESS WHAT?!? She grew another inch and a half in the last 3 months putting her EXACTLY ON THE BOTTOM GROWTH LINE!!! I had to buy her all new pants this year. And I have never had more fun doing it. Thanking God for His complete goodness. What's up size 7...I thought that I'd never actually meet you!

2. That God would show His healing power. I knew Alaina was doing better. I mean...for the love! She hasn't been hospitalized since January! No Cholangititis. No high blood pressures. No pancreatitis episodes. And no high fevers. I mean, c'mon! Her liver doctor was impressed to say the least. Also. Why is it nearly impossible to get a doctor to show excitement? This isn't a rhetorical question. I just really don't know. So I decided to ask about the pancreas...I felt ready for a solid answer. It'd been a good morning so far, after all. And get this! The doctor looked me straight in the eye and said they don't usually do intense operations on healthy kids and then she sort of smiled. *tears* Excuse me. Did you say a HEALTHY kid?!? The doctors have said so many things in regards to Lanie. That she's unique. Hard. Complicated. Very sick. Struggling. A fighter. But never...NEVER...has she been referred to as a healthy kid. I'm pretty sure I almost passed out.

IF LANIE'S DOCTOR CALLING HER A HEALTHY KID IS NOT A SURE SIGN OF HEALING, THEN I HAVE NO CLUE WHAT IS!!

She will still need to have an MRI in 3 months to see what's going on in her pancreas, but I'm not even worried.

3. That the doctors would tell us of God's awesome and holy name even if they didn't know it. I prayed that God would be so glorified and that it would be out of the blue. Did you guys read #1 and 2?!? I'd say God answered. His name was so glorified. But you know what? He did more.

5 years ago we left Iowa City hospitals and headed to Minneapolis. Iowa City no longer knew what to do with the special needs that Lanie presented. Complicated, remember? We were referred to this amazing liver doctor in the Twin Cities. I cried the day we met her. I felt guilty for abandoning our Iowa City doctors. Luke and I had a heart to go overseas and this sweet liver doctor told us point blank, right after we met her that Lanie was very sick and that she had a long road ahead. And then she said something that I wasn't necessarily expecting..."I honestly don't think you guys will ever be able to take her overseas". I cried more. It was an incredibly difficult time. But honestly, I hadn't thought about it much anymore. I know that God can do anything. If He wanted us overseas, he would heal her. And we would go. And that was that.

YOU GUYS!

Our sweet and beautiful liver doctor, who we have now know for 5 years, sat on the edge of Lanie's bed and stared at me for what seemed like 10 minutes. Just at the point of awkward, she started talking. This is what she said..."You know, I have been thinking quite a bit lately about how when you guys first came to me, I told you that I never thought you would be able to go overseas with Lanie. I've always felt really bad about having to tell you that. I felt like I crushed your dreams and I know your heart loves stuff like that. Today I'm telling you that is no longer the case" (By this point my eyes were wide and teary, I kid you not). She went on, "I would start small with some shorter term trips and we would have to prepare her ahead of time with antibiotics and other things, but I just can't honestly see anything holding you back from living a life like you dreamt of". *silence*

GOD'S GLORY REIGN DOWN!! Never in my life. I didn't ask her about overseas. I honestly hadn't brought it up in 5 YEARS!

I'm not good enough with words to tell you guys about all the feels that we're taking place in that room. One thing was clear... God is sovereign. The doctors aren't in control. I'm certainly not in control (ask anyone) and Lanie is the most out of control of all of us (okay I'm kidding. But really) And PRAISE GOD that it works like that.

Getting to tell Luke about all of this after he got home from China was INCREDIBLE. You should have been in that car ride home from Chicago with me after picking him and Jackson up from the airport.

I was like "tell me a story of God's awesomeness" and he would. And then he was like tell me one. And I would. And on and on it went. For 4 freaking hours!!! Story after story of God's grace and love and holiness and justice and mercy.

You guys. God is so incredible. And it's not situational. It's really not. It's just who He is.

God did a lot of other things this week. He did things in Colorado and in China and in Thailand and Turkey and Minneapolis and Cambodia and Kirksville and San Francisco. He is present. And He is good.

Chapter 40: The Conclusion, but not really because life is still happening and all

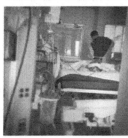

Today I am thankful for the direct healing hand of God and for people who come to sit by me and hug me when there are no words that exist. A year ago today was one of the scariest days of my life. But today. Today I sent Lanie out the door to school, but not before she did a couple cartwheels in the living room. And today she will laugh and play with her friends and her brother. And tonight I will take her to gymnastics where she will continue to amaze me with her strength and agility. And I will put her to bed and pray with her and kiss her forehead and probably cry a little. I can honestly say that I am overcome with thankfulness for every single second that God has blessed us with. It's sometimes funny to realize how God shows mercy on us. I believe that His mercy looks like allowing His children to go through hard things so that they learn to rely more on Him. And it looks like letting circumstances change us to look more like Him instead of changing our circumstances, even though He has the power to do so.

Highs would be nothing if we didn't understand the lows. God is good y'all. And He is sovereign.

Thank you...

To Luke: You pursued me when I didn't even know what that word meant. Thank you for loving me, challenging me, encouraging me, and for believing in a better story for us as a family. Thank you for the way that you lead our family: in truth and wisdom. You are one of the bravest people I know and I would literally follow you anywhere. And I love you and I like you.

To Jackson: Thank you for being so patient and gracious. Through every hospital stay, procedure, and drive to Minneapolis, you offered a joy and sweetness that couldn't be matched or contained. Thank you for taking amazing care of your dad when Lanie and I were gone for 5 months and for being so incredibly strong and loyal. You are such a stud. I love you to the moon and back.

To Lanie: You have taught me so much about strength and perseverance. And how to see circumstances from new eyes and a thankful heart. Thank you for allowing so many people into your life with excitement and enthusiasm. And thank you for helping me to see God apart from our situations. You're my strong and sassy little Lou. And I love you more every day.

To our parents: Thank you for teaching, loving, disciplining, and believing in us. Thank you for standing by our sides and watching our kids and teaching us how to be strong and brave. We love you incredible amounts.

To Tara, Steve, Adisu, Kian, Rae, and Gemene: Thank you for allowing me to be myself and for becoming a big part of my family. And thank you for challenging me in life and in love. Tara, you're my person and I can't remember a world without you.

To Rachel: You're a rockstar. Thank you for sitting with me day in and day out in Minneapolis. There is no one else in the world that exudes the joy and energy and life you bring with you everywhere you go. I would choose you again.

To Marcy: There is literally no one like you. You're heart bursts with love and generosity. Thank you for teaching me elegance and grace with a side of sass. Thank you for the laughs and road trips and encouragement and long and ridiculous runs. I love you friend.

To our siblings: Thank you for your love and support and for doing an amazing job being aunts and uncles to Jackson and Lanie. Thank you for driving all the way to Minneapolis and for the food calendar and for making sure that Jackson was taken care of and was loved on so well.

To Jenny and Tara and Erik and Mindy: for proofreading all of this over and over and over and for putting up with my impatience and need for approval. You guys are literally the best.

To all of the people who came and sat with us in the OR waiting room on transplant day. I have no clue what we would have done without your presence and love and encouragement.

To the Unit 5 nurses: Thank you for choosing to be a pediatric nurse to so many beautiful kiddos. Thank you for learning their stories and their parent's names and what they all love. You are nurses and counselors and professional colorers and game players, and stress reducers, and workout partners, and hug givers, and joy bringers and actual life savers. You go so far above and beyond any profession I have ever seen. You are the lifeblood of the hospital. My heart will always have a huge place that you occupy.

To Amplatz-The University of Minnesota Children's Hospital: Thank you for literally saving lives. And for specifically knowing the needs of every child in your care. There is no place better. Thank you specifically to Dr. Shwartzenberg, Dr. Najara, Dr. Chinakotla, Dr. Verghees, and the hundreds of other staff, residents, and physicians who work tirelessly to make sick kids well. You are all incredibles. That's not a typo…it's a plural use of a great word.

To our Iowa City community: Thank you for teaching me more about how life works when we do things together and for challenging me on giving in a way I didn't know possible. And thank you for caring for my family so well when I wasn't home to do it. You guys are the biggest blessing.

To Sumner: Thank you for being our family. Thank you for allowing two 24 year old kids a chance to grow up in a place so full of love and grace and humility. Thank you for showing us Jesus. My heart overflows with love for every single one of you.

To the Lynch Family: Thank you for caring for so much more than the American Dream. You are generous and beautiful and your kindness stretches over so many continents. Thank you for choosing Lanie and allowing us to become a part of your family.

To our Minneapolis friends: to the Brakefields and Trosens and Kipps and Zikans and Behrens and Wilds and Addinks and to Rachel and Leah. You guys. I can't even.

And to all of you who commented on Lanie's blog, donated to her benefits, texted me, called me, sent mail or gifts or coffee and came to visit: Thank you for being the actual hands and feet of Jesus. Thank you for caring about a family that you may not have known or heard of. And thank you for allowing me to share my raw and emotional heart with you. You are a huge part of my story. I pray that God allows me to meet more of you and hug you in person.

To Jesus: For saving me and speaking truth daily to me about who You are and what You have accomplished. Thank you for setting me free. I will love you every minute of every day and seek to walk in obedience to the story that you ask me to walk. There's no place I would rather be.

About The Author:

I'm a Texan girl in an Iowa City world. And by God's grace I am loving every second of it.

A few things that I adore: Being married to my very best friend. My two crazy, silly, strong children. The outdoors. Hammocks. Running. Having real-life conversations with people (I don't understand politics and I don't care about weather). Jesus (His love continues to stretch me). Sunsets and Sunrises. Organic Discipleship. BBQ. Anything having to do with coffee, tea, or mixed drinks. Grace and second chances. And I guess that I also really like writing now.

If you would like to keep following along, you can find me at:

http://transplantedjoy.blogspot.com/

ali.hettinger@facebook.com

Living Thru Lanie: facebook page

alberteingayle@yahoo.com

Instagram: alberteingayle

Twitter: ali Hettinger

Oh social media...why are you everywhere??

22727709R00153

Made in the USA
San Bernardino, CA
19 July 2015